THE ANVIL
Rings

D1564065

ERIC LYONS, M.MIN.

VOLUME 2

APOLOGETICS PRESS

Apologetics Press, Inc.

230 Landmark Drive
Montgomery, Alabama 36117-2752

© Copyright 2005

ISBN: 0-932859-67-4

Printed in China

Library of Congress Cataloging-in-Publication

Eric Lyons, 1975 -
  The Anvil Rings: Answers to Alleged Bible Discrepancies / Eric Lyons—
Volume 2
  Includes bibliographic references and subject, Scripture, and name indices.

ISBN 0-932859-67-4

1. Apologetics and polemics. 2. Christian Theology. I. Title

213—dc21   2005923515

DEDICATION

To my parents, Cliff and Marty Lyons. Thank you for bringing me up "in the nurture and admonition of the Lord." Thank you for teaching me that the Lord and His church are more important than anything else in this world. Your efforts during the 1970s in New Zealand, during the 1990s and 2000s in Russia, and your many years of working with the Lord's church stateside, have impressed upon my mind that you love the Lord more than me. Thank you for putting Terry, Andy, and me second place in your life, and not first. I look forward to eternity when we can forevermore enjoy the blessings of heaven together.

THE ANVIL

Last eve I passed beside a blacksmith's door,

And heard the anvil ring the vesper chime;

Then looking, I saw upon the floor,

Old hammers, worn with beating years of time.

"How many anvils have you had," said I,

"To wear and batter all these hammers so?"

"Just one," said he, and then with twinkling eye;

"The anvil wears the hammers out, ye know."

And so, thought I, the anvil of God's Word,

For ages skeptic blows have beat upon;

Yet though the noise of falling blows was heard

The anvil is unharmed...the hammers gone.

John Clifford (1836-1923)

TABLE OF CONTENTS

FOREWORD

Scarcely a day passes that those of us at Apologetics Press are not questioned about the trustworthiness of the Bible. We receive phone calls from parents and grandparents regarding difficult Bible passages that they are attempting to explain to their children or grandchildren. We receive letters on a regular basis from prisoners who, while being incarcerated, spend days on end critically pondering whether or not the Bible really is a special, inspired revelation from Almighty God. We receive e-mails from college students whose faith is being tested seriously for the first time in their young lives. As they begin to see the need to develop their own faith, being out from under their parents' watchful eye for more than eight months out of the year, they struggle with the most basic tenets of Christianity: Does God really exist, or is He just a figment of our imagination? Is the Bible the product of God, or is it the result of man's intellect? Was Jesus really the Son of God? How do we know that Christ is "the way" (John 14:6), rather than Confucius, Buddha, or Muhammad?

One of the more disturbing messages we have received at our offices since the inception of our work was the result of a phone call from an elder of a church in the heart of the "Bible belt." The gentlemen informed us that a fellow leader in the church, a man more than sixty years old (whose father and grandfather also had served as spiritual shepherds years earlier), and a man who had worn the name of Christ for nearly half a century, suddenly had given up his long-held belief in the trustworthiness of the Bible. In a letter that this defunct elder and his wife wrote to the church, explaining their recent departure from the faith, they indicated that many things in the Bible troubled them. In earlier years, their beliefs basically went unchallenged. What few things that had given them minor trouble were tossed aside without much investigation. Now, all of that had changed. Although they professed a desire to believe in the reliability of the Bible, they no longer could overlook what they felt were inconsistencies in Scripture.

Aside from the fact that such a recantation of faith by a leader in the Lord's church has the potential to spark immense turmoil within a congregation, another disturbing thought is why this elder and his wife waited so long to investigate the Bible's claims of inspiration. Why did they fail to inquire about the Bible's reliability when they were in their late teens or early twenties?

The fact is, questioning one's faith earlier in life, and taking the time and effort to find answers to those questions, is a good (and necessary) thing if a person wants to have a fortified faith. Too often, young people grow up in Christian homes without ever developing their **own** faith in God, the Bible, and Jesus. Too often, young people leave for college without the tools to combat the infidels, atheists, and skeptics who inundate their classrooms. What will happen when they come face to face with statements they never previously have pondered? What will happen when they are asked to defend their belief in a book written more than 1,900 years ago?

Admittedly, every question that we face later in life cannot be foreseen and answered by parents. But we can commit ourselves to equipping saints (especially the young, but also the older ones) with the tools that they will need to fight the "good fight of faith" (1 Timothy 6:12). Volumes one and two of *The Anvil Rings* were written in order to assist Christians in their fight against skepticism, and to help non-Christians see how logical it is to believe in an inspired, inerrant Bible. Whether you are a plumber or a preacher, a biochemist or a bricklayer, a student or a secretary, when questions are raised regarding an alleged contradiction between two or more passages of Scripture, it is my earnest hope that *The Anvil Rings* can assist you in your search for, and defense of, the Truth.

Eric Lyons
February 22, 2005

Chapter 1

BIBLICAL INERRANCY

When a person begins reading the Bible, it will not take long until he or she comes across statements such as "God said…," "thus says the Lord," or these are "the words of the Lord…." These kinds of statements appear hundreds of times in both the Old and New Testaments. The Decalogue begins with the phrase: "And God spoke all these words…" (Exodus 20:1). Thirty-three times in the book of Leviticus we read the words, "the Lord spoke to Moses" (4:1; 5:14; etc.). In Psalm 119 alone, the Scriptures are exalted as the Word of God some 175 times. In the New Testament, the apostle Paul claimed that his message was not received from man, rather "it came through the revelation of Jesus Christ" (Galatians 1:12). Similarly, as he wrote to the church at Thessalonica, he claimed that his message was "by the word of the Lord" (1 Thessalonians 4:15). Truly, the writers of both the Old and New Testaments placed great emphasis on the declaration that their message was of divine origin—that they spoke, not by the will of man, but "by the Holy Spirit" (2 Peter 1:21).

DEFINING INSPIRATION

Not only does the Bible claim to be inspired, it also describes and defines what it means by inspiration. In 2 Timothy 3:16, Paul claimed that "all scripture is given by inspiration of God." The Greek term underlying the word "inspiration" (*theopneustos*) means "God-breathed." Thus, Paul affirmed that Scripture is the product of the breath of God. God actually breathed out the Scriptures. The Bible is **God's** words–not man's. Three verses later (in 2 Timothy 4:2), Paul declared: "Therefore...preach the word...." Why? Because it is **God's** Word. Just as surely as God's breath brought the Universe into existence (Psalm 33:6), so the Bible declares itself to be the result of God's out-breathing.

In 2 Peter 1:16-21, Peter alluded to the momentous occasion of Christ's transfiguration when God literally spoke from heaven directly to Peter, James, and John. God had orally boomed forth His insistence that Jesus is His beloved Son, and that human beings are commanded to hear Him (Matthew 17:5). Peter then declared: "And so we have the prophetic word confirmed,...knowing this first, that no prophecy of the Scripture is of any private interpretation." Peter was saying that the Scriptures provided to us by the prophets are just as certain and just as authoritative as the voice of God that spoke on the mount of transfiguration.

He further explained that the prophetic word (the Scriptures) was not of "any private interpretation"; thus, the Scriptures did not originate on their own, or in the minds of those who wrote them. Scripture did not come from "the will of man." It is not the result of human research or human investigation into the nature of things. Scripture is not the product of its writers' own thinking. On the contrary, "holy men of God spoke as they were moved by the Holy Spirit" (2 Peter 1:21). The word "moved" in the original language means "borne" or "brought." Peter stated that the Holy Spirit, in essence, "picked up" the writers (the prophets) and brought them to the goal of His choosing. Thus, the Scriptures, though written by means of human instrumentality, were so superintended by God that the resulting writings are truly God's.

This is the same Peter who, while awaiting the coming of the Spirit in Acts 2 on Pentecost, stood up among fellow disciples and declared, "Men and brethren, this Scripture had to be fulfilled, which the Holy Spirit spoke before by the mouth of David concerning Judas," and then he quoted from the Psalms (Acts 1:16ff). Peter believed that the Holy Spirit governed what David wrote, and the result of that writing is designated "Scripture."

This is the same Peter who, in 1 Peter 1:10-12, explained: (1) that the Old Testament inspired spokesmen did not always understand all the information given by God through them; (2) it was the Spirit of Christ that was operating upon them; (3) this same inspired information was being presented in Peter's day by the apostles; and (4) the same Holy Spirit was directing their utterances. That means inspired men had their own minds engaged as they produced inspired material, but the product was God's, since they did not always grasp the significance of their productions.

This is the same Peter who, in 2 Peter 3:15-16, referred to "our beloved brother Paul" as having "written to you." He then noted: "as also in all his epistles, speaking in them of these things; in which are some things hard to be understood, which untaught and unstable people twist to their own destruction, as they do also the rest of the Scriptures." Notice that Peter made clear that: (1) Paul wrote epistles; (2) those epistles are classified with "the rest of Scriptures"—so Paul's letters are Scripture every bit as much as the Old Testament and other New Testament writings; and (3) these writings are authoritative and divine, since Peter said to twist them is to invite "destruction"—an obvious reference to God's disfavor and the spiritual harm that results from disobeying God's words.

The Bible unquestionably claims for itself the status of "inspiration"—having been breathed by the Almighty Himself. That inspiration entails such superintendence by God that even the words have come under His influence. King David once stated: "The Spirit of the Lord spoke by me, and His word was on my tongue" (2 Samuel 23:2). Observe that David did not say God's "thoughts" or "concepts" were on his tongue, but that Jehovah's **Word** was on his tongue. In 1 Corinthians chapter 2, the apostle Paul declared that the things of God were revealed to men by God's Spirit. Then, concerning the divine messages, he said, "which things we speak, not in **words** which man's wisdom teacheth, but which the Spirit teacheth; combining spiritual things with spiritual words" (1 Corinthians 2:13, ASV, emp. added; cf. John 17:8). The words of divine revelation are Spirit-directed words, not words of mere human wisdom. This is **verbal** inspiration. This does not mean that the writers merely took "dictation." Rather, the Bible indicates that God adapted His inspiring activity to the individual temperament, vocabulary, and stylistic idiosyncrasies of each writer.

BIBLICAL INERRANCY
AND ITS ENEMIES

One question that a seemingly growing number of people in recent times have asked is whether or not **every** word of Scripture is inspired truth. Infidels, atheists, and skeptics have long ridiculed the idea of biblical inerrancy. That is, they do not believe the Bible (whether in its original or current state) to be free from error or untruths. [NOTE: The word "errant" comes from the Latin infinitive *errare*, meaning "to wander," while the prefix *in* negates the word. Thus, to purport biblical inerrancy is to affirm that the Scriptures adhere to the truth, rather than departing, or "wandering" from it (see Preus, 1984, pp. 91-93; Packer, 1958, p. 95).] To unbelievers, the Bible simply is another fallible book written by imperfect men. These critics point to countless passages in Scripture as contradicting either other passages of Scripture or some "known" historical, geographical, or scientific truth. Unfortunately, because they frequently occupy prominent positions in public schools, universities, businesses, and in the media, Bible critics have become much more powerful and influential in recent times. More and more skeptics can be heard throughout the world on radio, on television, on the Internet, and in classrooms. In their book, *Surveying the Religious Landscape: Trends in U.S. Beliefs*, George Gallup Jr. and D. Michael Lindsay addressed the shift in the attitudes of Americans toward the Bible when they wrote:

> More Americans are moving toward an interpretation of the Bible as a book of fables, history, and moral precepts.... Attempts at demythologizing the Bible that have been ongoing in the academy for years seem to be moving more and more from the classroom to the pews.... As recently as 1963, two persons in three viewed the Bible as the actual word of God, to be taken literally, word for word. Today, only one person in three still holds to that interpretation (1999, p. 36).

Certainly, for years skeptics have been hard at work in their attempts to undermine one of the foundational pillars of the Christian's faith–the Bible being the inerrant, inspired Word of God. As damaging as their doctrine is, however, perhaps a more damaging message of biblical errancy can be heard from a number of people who **claim** to be Christians.

Since the rise of liberal "scholarship" in the eighteenth century, ruthless attacks have been levied on the integrity of the Bible from within Christendom. The Mosaic authorship of the Pentateuch, the historicity of the book of Jonah, and even the miracles of Christ are only a sampling of the Bible topics that liberal scholars have attacked relentlessly over the past three centuries. Names such as Karl Graf, Julius Wellhausen, and Rudolf Bultmann are frequently cited in scholastic settings where the integrity of the Bible is challenged. In the late twentieth century, George Marsden, in his book titled *Re-*

forming Fundamentalism (1987), documented how one of the
most popular theological seminaries in America (Fuller Seminary) had dropped its commitment to the inerrancy of Scripture as early as the 1960s. Sadly, this trend has had a snowball
effect throughout America so that increasingly more schools
of theology, even ones of a much more conservative background than Fuller Theological Seminary, are rejecting the
belief that the Bible is accurate in all that it teaches.

In 2002, the ACU Press published a book titled *God's Holy
Fire* written by three professors from the Graduate School of
Theology at Abilene Christian University. Taking issue with
the usefulness and appropriateness of the term "inerrancy,"
Kenneth Cukrowski, Mark Hamilton, and James Thompson
asked if "inerrancy even applies to minor narrative details"
(p. 40)? According to these men, "[I]n numerous instances in
the Bible, one finds apparent inconsistencies in the narratives" (p. 40). Examples they gave included: (1) the raising of
Jairus' daughter; (2) Jesus' cursing of the fig tree; (3) the cleansing of the temple; and (4) Matthew's quotation of Jeremiah in
27:9. Following these alleged internal inconsistencies, they
then stated: "Sometimes the narrative does not correspond
to the historical record" (p. 40). Although Cukrowski, Hamilton, and Thompson admitted that "more information might
actually resolve many of these difficulties" (p. 41), they later
stated: "Because the Bible has come to us through human beings, our view of the divine origin of Scripture is not a matter
of mathematical certainty, but ultimately an affirmation of
faith" (p. 45). Finally, these men described, not skeptics, but
"well-meaning Christians" who hold to Scripture as being the
truthful Word of God in **all** that it says, as those who "in their
attempts to provide absolute certainty,…have created a crisis of faith," because they are "always feeling a responsibility
to provide an answer for every potential discrepancy" (p. 44).
According to these writers, Christians merely "**assume** that
God ensured the precise accuracy of the original versions"
(p. 42, emp. added).

Perhaps the most perplexing stance by alleged Bible believers regarding the inerrancy of Scripture comes from a very popular book frequently used by Christian apologists when defending biblical inerrancy. *Hard Sayings of the Bible* is a compilation of articles by four fairly well-known Bible scholars–Walter Kaiser, Peter Davids, Manfred Brauch, and F.F. Bruce–who are supposed to help Bible readers find answers to difficult questions without compromising the biblical text. It is very troubling, therefore, to see how one of the writers explained a passage of Scripture in 1 Corinthians 10. In answering how Paul concluded that 23,000 Israelites fell in the Old Testament as a result of their sexual immorality (1 Corinthians 10:8), rather than 24,000, which Moses mentioned in Numbers 25:9 as the number that died, Peter Davids wrote:

> It is possible that Paul, citing the Old Testament from memory as he wrote to the Corinthians, referred to the incident in Numbers 25:9, but **his mind slipped** a chapter later in picking up the number.... We cannot rule out the possibility that there was some reference to 23 or 23,000 in his local environment as he was writing and that caused **a slip in his mind**.

> Paul was not attempting to instruct people on Old Testament history and certainly not on the details of Old Testament history.

> Thus here we have a case in which **Paul apparently makes a slip of the mind** for some reason (unless he has special revelation he does not inform us about), but the mental error does not affect the teaching. How often have we heard preachers with written Bibles before them make similar errors of details that in no way affected their message? If we notice it (and few usually do), we (hopefully) simply smile and focus on the real point being made. As noted above, Paul probably did not have a written Bible to check (although at times he apparently had access to scrolls of

the Old Testament), but in the full swing of dictation
**he cited an example from memory and got a de-
tail wrong** (1996, pp. 598-599, parenthetical comments in orig., emp. added).

Supposedly, Paul just made a mistake. He messed up, just
like when a preacher today mistakenly misquotes a passage
of Scripture. According to the repetitive testimony of Davids,
Paul merely had "a slip of the mind" (thereby experiencing
what some today might call a "senior moment"), and our reaction (as well as the skeptics') should be to "simply smile
and focus on the real point being made."

Unbelievable! Walter Kaiser, Peter Davids, Manfred Brauch,
and F.F. Bruce pen an 800-page book in an attempt to answer
numerous alleged Bible contradictions and to defend the integrity of the Bible, and yet Davids has the audacity to say
that the apostle Paul "cited an example from memory and
got a detail wrong." Why in the world did Davids spend so
much time (and space) answering various questions that skeptics frequently raise, and then decide that the man who penned
almost half of the New Testament books made mistakes in his
writings?! He has concluded exactly what the infidels teach—
Bible writers made mistakes. Furthermore, if Paul made one
mistake in his writings, he easily could have blundered elsewhere. And if Paul made mistakes in other writings, how can
we say that Peter, John, Isaiah, and others did not "slip up"
occasionally? In fact, why not just explain **all** alleged discrepancies as the result of a momentary slip of the writer's mind?

The fact is, if Paul, or any of these men, made mistakes in
their writings, then they were not inspired by God (cf. 2 Timothy 3:16-17; 2 Peter 1:20-21), because God does not make
mistakes (cf. Titus 1:2; Psalm 139:1-6). And if the Scriptures
were not "given by inspiration of God," then the Bible is not
from God. And if the Bible is not from God, then the skeptic
is right. **But the skeptic is not right!** First Corinthians 10:8

can be explained logically without assuming Paul's writings are inaccurate. The answer lies in the fact that Paul stated that 23,000 fell **"in one day,"** while in Numbers 25:9 (the probable "sister" passage to 1 Corinthians 10:8) Moses wrote that the **total number** of those who died in the plague was 24,000. Moses never said how long it took for the 24,000 to die, but only stated that this was the number "who died in the plague." Thus, the record in 1 Corinthians simply supplies us with more knowledge about what occurred in Numbers 25—23,000 of the 24,000 who died in the plague died **"in one day."**

Sadly, Peter Davids totally dismisses the numerous places where Paul claims his writings are from God. When Paul wrote to the churches of Galatia, he told them that his teachings came to him "through revelation of Jesus Christ" (1:12). In his first letter to the Thessalonian Christians, he claimed the words he wrote were "by the word of the Lord" (4:15). To the church at Ephesus, Paul wrote that God's message was "revealed by the Spirit to His holy apostles and prophets" (3:5). And in the same epistle where Davids claims that Paul "made a slip of the mind," Paul said, "the things which I write to you are the commandments of the Lord" (1 Corinthians 14:37). Paul did not invent facts about Old Testament stories. Neither did he have to rely on his own fallible memory to recall particular numbers or names. His writings were inspired Scripture (2 Peter 3:16). The Holy Spirit revealed the Truth to him— **all** of it (cf. John 14:26; John 16:13). Just like the writers of the Old Testament, Paul was fully inspired by the Holy Spirit (cf. 2 Samuel 23:2; Acts 1:16; 2 Peter 1:20-21; 3:15-16; 2 Timothy 3:16-17).

WHAT DID JESUS AND THE BIBLE WRITERS "ASSUME" ABOUT SCRIPTURE?

What liberal theologians do not tell their readers is that the Bible itself provides compelling evidence about the nature of its inspiration. Perhaps of most significance is the fact that neither Jesus nor any Bible writer **ever** called a single passage of Scripture into question. Jesus and the writers of Scripture believed in the truthfulness and historical reliability of even the most disputed parts of the Old Testament. Notice a few examples.

- While speaking to the Pharisees in the region of Judea beyond the Jordan, Jesus confirmed His belief in the real existence of an original couple created during the Creation week (Matthew 19:4; cf. Genesis 2:24).
- In writing to the church at Corinth, Paul affirmed his belief in Adam as the first human (1 Corinthians 15:45). Then, in his first letter to Timothy, he attested to the fact that Eve was created after Adam (2:13; cf. Genesis 2:7,21-25).
- Paul regarded the serpent's deception of Eve as a historical event (2 Corinthians 11:3; 1 Timothy 2:13-14; cf. Genesis 3).
- Both Jesus and the apostle Peter believed that Noah was a real person and that the global Flood was a historical event (Matthew 24:37-39; 2 Peter 2:5; 3:6; cf. Genesis 6-8).
- Jesus and Peter also affirmed their belief in the historicity of Lot, and the destruction of Sodom (Luke 17:28-32; 2 Peter 2:6-7; cf. Genesis 19).
- Paul attested to the Israelites' crossing of the Red Sea, and affirmed his belief in them drinking water from a rock (1 Corinthians 10:1-4; cf. Hebrews 11:29; cf. Exodus 14), while Jesus confirmed His belief in the miraculous healing of the Israelites who fixed their eyes on the bronze snake set up by Moses in the desert (John 3:14; cf. Numbers 21:4-9).
- Finally, unlike many people today, including some of those who **claim** to believe the Bible to be the inspired Word of God, Jesus regarded the record of Jonah's three days and nights in the belly of a great fish as a historical event (Matthew 12:39-40).

Truly, numerous other examples like these exist that demonstrate the trustworthiness of Scripture. The Old Testament writers who came after Moses expressed **total trust** in the Pentateuch, as well as in each others' writings. Furthermore, Jesus and the New Testament writers **always** viewed statements by each other and the Old Testament writers as being truthful, regardless of the subject matter.

Although today it is not at all unusual for one religious writer to take issue with another, even when they share the same religious views or are members of the same religious group, **Bible writers never criticized each other**–even when one might expect them to do so. For example, Paul rebuked Peter publicly for his dissimulation (Galatians 2:11ff.). Yet Peter never avenged himself by denigrating Paul's writings. In fact, as noted earlier, Peter stated that Paul's writings were as authoritative as "the other Scriptures" (2 Peter 3:15-16). Additionally, in defending the right of elders to receive remuneration from the church treasury for their work, Paul quoted Deuteronomy 25:4 and Luke 10:7, classifying them both as "Scripture" (1 Timothy 5:18). It is clear that the Bible writers **always** considered each others' works to be truthful. How can anyone who claims to be a Christian hold to the viewpoint that the Scriptures contain legitimate errors? Jesus and the Bible writers **always** "assumed" that God ensured the precise accuracy of the original versions (cf. Cukrowski, et al., 2002, p. 42, emp. added). Why should we do any different?

INERRANCY TO THE "T"

Jesus endorsed the entirety of the Old Testament at least a dozen times, using such designations as: the Scriptures (John 5:39); the Law (John 10:34); the Law and the Prophets (Matthew 5:17); the Law, the Prophets, and the Psalms (Luke 24:44); or Moses and the Prophets (Luke 16:29). In addition, the Son of God quoted, cited from, or alluded to incidents in at least eighteen different Old Testament books. But to what degree did Christ believe in inspiration? The following references document beyond doubt that the Lord affirmed **verbal** inspiration down to the very letters of Scripture. In Matthew 5:17-18, Christ exclaimed:

> Do not think that I came to destroy the Law or the Prophets. I did not come to destroy but to fulfill. For assuredly, I say to you, till heaven and earth pass away, one jot or one tittle will by no means pass from the law till all is fulfilled.

The "jot" (*yod*) was the smallest Hebrew letter, and the "tittle" was the tiny stroke on certain Hebrew letters. It is equivalent to saying that even the dotting of "i"s and crossing of "t"s will stand. When Jesus employed these specific terms as examples, He affirmed the minutest accuracy for the Old Testament.

In John 10:34-35, Jesus involved Himself in an interchange with some Jews who accused Him of blasphemy. He repelled the charge by quoting Psalm 82:6, referring to the passage as "law." Jesus could refer to a Psalm as "law" in the sense that the Psalms are part of Scripture. Jesus was thus ascribing legal authority to the entire corpus of Scripture. He did the same thing in John 15:25. Likewise, the apostle Paul quoted from Psalms, Isaiah, and Genesis and referred to each as "the Law" (1 Corinthians 14:21; Romans 3:19; Galatians 4:21). After Jesus quoted from the Psalm and called it "law," He added, "and the Scripture cannot be broken." What an incredible declaration! Notice that He was equating "law" with "Scripture"—using the terms as synonyms. When He declared that "law," or "Scripture," "cannot be broken," He was making the point that **it is impossible for Scripture to be annulled, for its authority to be denied, or its truth to be withstood** (see Warfield, 1970, pp. 138-140). "It cannot be emptied of its force by being shown to be erroneous" (Morris, 1995, p. 468).

Jesus quoted a relatively obscure passage of the Old Testament and declared it to be authoritative, because "the Scripture cannot be broken." His Jewish listeners understood this fact. If they were of the mindset that many liberals are today, they might have brushed aside this passage saying that the psalmist made a mistake, or that this section of Scripture contained errors. They might have responded by asking Jesus, "How do you know this portion of Scripture is true, if others are not true?" Notice, however, that this was not their response. Both Jesus and His audience understood that the psalm from which He quoted was true **because it is a part of Scripture**. Truly, Jesus considered every part of Scripture, even its most "casual" phrases, to be the authoritative Word of God.

Once, when Jesus challenged the Pharisees to clarify the identity of the Messiah (Matthew 22:41-45), He focused on David's use of the single term "Lord" in Psalm 110:1. He questioned the Pharisees saying, "If David then calls Him 'Lord,' how is He his Son?" (Matthew 22:45). Jesus' whole point depends on verbal inspiration.

After Jesus' resurrection, Luke recorded how Jesus appeared to two men on the road to Emmaus who were saddened and somewhat perplexed by the recent crucifixion of the one Whom they were hoping "was going to redeem Israel" (Luke 24:21). With their eyes being restrained, "so that they did not know Him" (24:16), they rehearsed to Jesus what had transpired over the past few days regarding His death and the empty tomb. The text indicates that Jesus then rebuked these two men, saying, "O foolish ones, and slow of heart to believe in **all** that the prophets have spoken! Ought not the Christ to have suffered these things and to enter into His glory?" (24:25-26, emp. added). Notice that Jesus did not chastise them for being slow to believe in **some** of what the prophets spoke, but for neglecting to believe in **all** that they said about the Christ. For this reason, Jesus began "at Moses and all the Prophets," and "expounded to them in all the Scriptures the things concerning Himself" (24:27).

No wonder Jesus would rebuke His religious challengers with such phrases as: "Have you not read even this Scripture?" (Mark 12:10; cf. Matthew 21:42); or "You do err, not knowing the Scriptures" (Matthew 22:29); or "if you had known what this means..." (Matthew 12:7); or "Go and learn what this means..." (Mark 9:13). The underlying thought in such statements is that **God's truth is found in Scripture, and if you are ignorant of the Scriptures, you are susceptible to error**.

PRECISE PROOF THAT
INSPIRATION IMPLIES INERRANCY

In the midst of His discussion with the Sadducees about their denial of the resurrection of the dead (Matthew 22:23-33), Jesus referred to Exodus 3:6 wherein God said to Moses: "I am the God of Abraham, and the God of Isaac, and the God of Jacob." When God spoke these words, Abraham had been dead almost 400 years, yet He still said, "I am the God of Abraham." As Jesus correctly pointed out to the Sadducees, "God is not the God of the dead, but of the living" (Matthew 22:32). Thus, Abraham, Isaac, and Jacob must have been living. The only way they could be living was if their spirits continued to survive the death of their bodies. That kind of conscious existence implies a future resurrection of the body— the very point Christ was pressing. Of interest, however, is the fact that His entire argument rested on the **tense** of the verb! [NOTE: The claim that Jesus made arguments based even on the tense of verbs is true. Nevertheless, this statement needs clarification. Hebrew actually has no past, present, or future tense. Rather, action is regarded as being either completed or uncompleted, and so verbs occur in the Hebrew as perfect or imperfect. No verb occurs in God's statement in Exodus 3:6. Consequently, tense is implied rather than expressed. In this case, the Hebrew grammar would allow any tense of the verb "to be." Jesus, however, clarified the ambiguity inherent in the passage by affirming what God had in mind. Matthew (22:32) preserves Jesus' use of the Greek **present tense** (*ego eimi*), which is also used in the Greek translation of the Old Testament in Exodus 3:6.]

Similarly, on another occasion while being tested by a group of Jews regarding whether or not He had really seen their "father" Abraham, Jesus responded by saying, "Most assuredly, I say to you, before Abraham was, I **am**" (John 8:58, emp. added). As when God wanted Moses to impress upon Egypt His eternal nature, calling Himself, **"I am who I am"** (Exodus 3:14), Jesus sought to impress upon the Jews His eternality. Jesus is not a "was" or a "will be"—He **is**…"from everlasting to everlasting" (Psalm 90:2). Once again, He based His entire argument on the **tense** of the verb.

The same kind of reliance on a single word was expressed by Paul (as he referred to Genesis 22:18) in Galatians 3:16: "Now to Abraham and his Seed were the promises made. He does not say, 'And to seeds,' as of many, but as of one, 'And to your **Seed**,' who is Christ" (emp. added). The force of his argument rested on the number of the noun (singular, as opposed to plural).

In light of the fact that Jesus and the Bible writers viewed the words of Scripture as being inspired (and thus truthful)—even down to the very tense of a verb and number of a noun—so should all Christians. Truly, as the psalmist of long ago wrote: "The **sum** of thy word is truth; and **every one** of thy righteous ordinances endureth for ever" (Psalm 119:160, ASV, emp. added). Or, as it is translated in the NKJV: "The **entirety** of Your word is truth" (emp. added). It is all true, and it is all from God. It is accurate in all of its parts. The **whole** of the Bible is of divine origin, and therefore is reliable and trustworthy. Yes, God used human beings to write the Bible, and in so doing, allowed them to leave their mark upon it (e.g., type of language used, fears expressed, prayers offered, etc.).

But, they wrote without making any of the mistakes that human writers are prone to make under normal circumstances. God made certain that the words produced by the human writers He inspired were free from the errors and mistakes characteristic of uninspired writers. Truly, hundreds of Bible passages encourage God's people to trust the Scriptures completely, but no text encourages any doubt or even slight mistrust in Scripture. To rely on the inerrancy of every historical detail affirmed in Scripture is to follow the teaching and practice of the biblical authors themselves.

WHEN THE SCRIPTURES SPEAK, GOD SPEAKS

Time and again, Jesus and the Bible writers affirmed that **God is the author of Scripture**. Notice in Matthew 19:4-6 how Jesus assigned the words of Genesis 2:24 to God as the Author. He asked the Pharisees who came testing him, "Have you not read that **He** who made them at the beginning 'made them male and female,' and **said**, 'For this reason a man shall leave his father and mother and be joined to his wife, and the two shall become one flesh?' " (emp. added). Interestingly, in Genesis 2:24, no indication is given that God was the speaker. Rather, the words are simply a narrational comment written by the human author Moses. When Jesus attributed the words to God, He made clear that **all** of Scripture is authored by God (cf. 2 Timothy 3:16). Paul, writing to the Christians in Corinth, treated the matter in the same way (1 Corinthians 6:16).

On numerous occasions in Scripture, God is said to say certain things that are, in their original setting, merely the words of Scripture. For example, Hebrews 3:7 reads: "Wherefore, even as the Holy Spirit says...," and then Psalm 95:7 is quoted. In Acts 4:25, God is said to have spoken by the Holy Spirit through the mouth of David the words of Psalm 2:1. In Acts 13:34, God is represented as having stated the words of Isaiah 55:3 and Psalm 16:10. In each of these cases, the words attributed to God are not specifically His words in their original setting, but merely the words of Scripture itself. The writers of the New Testament sometimes referred to the Scriptures as if they were God (cf. Romans 9:17; Galatians 3:8), and they sometimes referred to God as if He were Scripture. The Bible thus presents itself as the very words of God.

In Hebrews 1:5-13, the writer quoted from Psalm 2:7, 2 Samuel 7:14, Deuteronomy 32:43, Psalm 104:4, Psalm 45:6-7, Psalm 102:25-27, and Psalm 110:1. The Hebrews writer attributed each of these passages to God as the speaker. Yet in their original setting in the Old Testament, sometimes God is the speaker, while sometimes He is not the speaker, and is, in fact, being spoken to or spoken about. Why would the writer of Hebrews indiscriminately assign all of these passages to God? Because they all have in common the fact that they are the words of Scripture and, as such, are the words of God. Even the words of Satan recorded in Matthew 4 are the words of God! That is, God reported those words to us as being what Satan actually said. Thus, every word of the Bible is the Word of God! And, as Jesus prayed on the night of His betrayal, God's "word is truth" (John 17:17).

GOD CANNOT LIE

From beginning to end, the Bible reveals that the infinite, eternal Being Who created everything and everyone that exists in the Universe, other than Himself, is truthful. His "Spirit is truth" (1 John 5:6), His "words are true" (2 Samuel 7:28), His "law is truth" (Psalm 119:14), His "commandments are truth" (Psalm 119:151), His "judgments...are true" (Psalm 19:9), and His "works are truth" (Daniel 4:37). He literally embodies truth. When the Son of God was on Earth, He claimed to be truth (John 14:6). There is nothing false about God. When Paul wrote to Titus, he described God as the One "who cannot lie" (1:2). Similarly, the writer of Hebrews declared that "it is impossible for God to lie" (6:18).

If God is perfect, and the Bible is the Word of God (which it claims to be, as the previous sections demonstrate), then it follows that the Bible (in its original form) must be perfect. The Scriptures cannot err if they are "borne" of God. Try as one might, logically, one cannot have it both ways. The Bible is either from God (and thus flawless in its original autographs), or it contains mistakes, and is not from the God of truth. There is no middle ground.

Some argue: "But the Bible was written down by humans. And 'to err is human.' Thus, the Bible could not have been perfect from the beginning." Consider the fallacy of such reasoning. If a person concludes that all humans err, regardless of the circumstances, then Jesus must have sinned. (1) Jesus was a human being (Galatians 4:4). (2) Human beings sin (Isaiah 53:6). (3) Therefore, Jesus sinned. But most any Bible student knows that Jesus did not sin. The New Testament declares that He was "pure" and "righteous" (1 John 3:3; 2:1), "Who committed no sin, nor was deceit found in His mouth" (1 Peter 2:22). He was "a lamb without blemish and without spot" (1 Peter 1:19), "Who knew no sin" (2 Corinthians 5:21). Since we know that Jesus did not sin, something must be wrong with the above argument. But what is it?

> The mistake is to assume that Jesus is like any other human. Sure, mere human beings sin. But, Jesus was not a **mere** human being. He was a perfect human being. Indeed, Jesus was not only human, but He was also God. Likewise, the Bible is not a mere human book. It is also the Word of God. Like Jesus, it is both divine and human. And just as Jesus was human but did not sin, even so the Bible is a human book but does not err. Both God's living Word (Christ) and His written Word (Scripture) are human but do not err. They are divine and cannot err. There can no more be an error in God's written Word than there was a sin in God's living Word. God cannot err, period (Geisler and Howe, 1992, pp. 14-15, emp. in orig.).

Admittedly, it is normal to make blunders. (In fact, this book is likely to have one or more mistakes in it.) But, the conditions under which the Bible writers wrote was anything but normal. They were **moved** and **guided** into all truth by God's Spirit (John 16:13; 2 Peter 1:21).

THE RATIONALITY OF INERRANCY

Sadly, it is not uncommon to hear liberal theologians, and those sympathetic with them, suggest that the "spiritual" sections of Scripture are inspired, but that all other portions dealing with matters of history, geography, astronomy, medicine, and the like, are not. This concept, known as the doctrine of "partial inspiration," is faulty for at least three reasons. First, there are no statements in Scripture that lead a person to believe this manner of interpreting the Bible is acceptable. Conversely, as already indicated, both Jesus and the Bible writers **always** operated on the basis that the **entirety** of God's Word is true (Psalm 119:160), not partially true.

Second, were it the case that only the "spiritual" sections of the Bible are inerrant, everyone who reads the text would have the personal responsibility of wading through the biblical documents to decide which matters are "spiritual" (thus, inspired) and which are not (thus, uninspired). Such an interpretation of Scripture, however, makes a mockery of biblical authority.

> The Bible can be authoritative if, and only if, it is truly and verifiably the Word of God. That his word has been passed through men does not negate its authority so long as he has so controlled them as to guard them from all error. If his control over the biblical writers was not total, we can never be sure where the writer was accurate (thus believable) and where he was mistaken (thus worthy of rejection). In such a case, the Bible would be authoritative only when we declared it to be so. Then the circle has come

full, and man is authoritative over the Bible rather
than submitted to its direction (Shelly, 1990, p. 152,
parenthetical comments in orig.).

If Christians abandon the doctrine of biblical inerrancy, then
having a standard of truth by which all humans are to live
their lives would be impossible. Like the son who obeys his
father insofar as he agrees with his father's rules, a Christian
would have his own standard of authority because the Bible
would be authoritative only when he or she judged it to be a
reliable guide. Simply put, Scripture cannot be demonstrated to be divinely authoritative if the Bible (in its original autographs) contained factual errors.

Finally, if a Christian believes that the Bible is fallible, then
one is forced to conclude that on some occasions, God "breathed" truth, while on others He "breathed" error (cf. 2 Timothy
3:16). If all of Scripture is indicated as being from God–even
narrational comments and statements from unbelievers–then
an attack upon the trustworthiness of **any** passage is an attack
upon Almighty God. **If God can inspire a man to write
theological and doctrinal truth, He can simultaneously
inspire the same man to write with historical and scientific precision.** If the Bible is not reliable and trustworthy in
its allusion to peripheral matters, how can it be relied upon to
be truthful and accurate in more central matters? Is an omnipotent God incapable of preserving human writers from
making false statements in their recording of His words? It
will not do to point out that the Bible was not intended to be a
textbook of science or history. If, in the process of pressing
His spiritual agenda, God alluded to geography, cosmology,
or medicine, God did not lie. Nor would He allow an inspired
person to speak falsely.

The question must be asked: If God cannot handle correctly "trivial" matters (such as geographical directions, or
the name of an individual), why would anyone think that they

could trust Him with something as critically important as the safety of their immortal soul, and expect Him to handle it in a more appropriate fashion? Or, looking at this matter from another angle, consider the question Jesus asked Nicodemus: "If I have told you earthly things and you do not believe, how will you believe if I tell you heavenly things" (John 3:12)? Implied in this statement is the fact that had Jesus told Nicodemus earthly things, they would have been true. The same reasoning follows with the Bible. Because it is God's Word, it would be correct in whatever matters it addresses. Furthermore, if the Bible is not truthful in physical matters, then it cannot be trusted when it addresses spiritual matters. Truly, the concept of partial inspiration impugns the integrity and nature of God, conflicts with the evidences for inspiration, and should be rejected as heresy.

People rightly believe that an actual discrepancy within the Bible would discredit the authenticity of Scripture for the simple reason that those people have been created by God to function rationally! They recognize that truth, by definition, must be consistent with itself. The very nature of truth is such that it contains no contradictions or errors. If God is capable of communicating His truth to human beings, it is unthinkable and logically implausible that He could not or would not do so with complete consistency and certainty. Infallibility without inerrancy cannot be sustained without logical contradiction.

How sad that the attempt to compromise the integrity of the sacred text is unnecessary in view of the fact that no charge of discrepancy against the Bible has ever been sustained. As you will read throughout the remaining nine chapters of this book, plausible explanations exist if we will study and apply ourselves to an honest, thorough evaluation of the available evidence. Indeed, God has provided sufficient evidence for the honest person to arrive at the truth and to come to know His will (John 6:45; 7:17; 8:32).

Chapter 2

ALLEGED CONTRADICTIONS REGARDING GOD'S ATTRIBUTES

DOES GOD REALLY KNOW EVERYTHING?
Psalm 44:21; 139:1-8; 1 John 3:20; Genesis 18:21

Numerous passages of Scripture clearly teach that God is omniscient. The psalmist declared that God "knows the secrets of the heart" (44:21), that His eyes "are in every place" (15:3), and that "His understanding is infinite" (147:5). Of Jehovah, the psalmist also wrote:

> O Lord, You have searched me and known me. You know my sitting down and my rising up; You understand my thought afar off. You comprehend my path and my lying down, and are acquainted with all my ways. For there is not a word on my tongue, but behold, O Lord, You know it altogether.... Such knowledge is too wonderful for me; it is high, I cannot at-

tain it. Where can I go from Your Spirit? Or where
can I flee from Your presence? If I ascend into heav-
en, You are there; if I make my bed in hell, behold,
You are there (139:1-4,6-8).

The New Testament reemphasizes this truth, saying, "**God**
is greater than our heart, and **knows all things**" (1 John 3:
20, emp. added). Not only does He know the past and the
present, but the future as well (Acts 15:18; cf. Isaiah 46:10).
There is nothing outside of the awareness of God.

If God knows (and sees) everything, some have questioned
why certain statements exist in Scripture that seem to indicate otherwise. Why was it that God questioned Cain regarding the whereabouts of his brother Abel if He already knew
where he was (Genesis 4:6)? Why did the Lord and two of
His angels ask Abraham about the location of his wife if He is
omniscient (Genesis 18:9)? And, if God knows all and sees
all, why did He say to Abraham concerning Sodom and Gomorrah: "I will go down now and see whether they have done
altogether according to the outcry against it that has come to
Me; and **if not, I will know**" (Genesis 18:21, emp. added; cf.
Genesis 22:12)? If God is omniscient, why would He need to
"go" somewhere to "see whether" a certain people were wicked
or not? Does God really know everything?

First, when critics claim that the questions God asked Cain
or Sarah (or Satan–cf. Job 1:7; 2:2) suggest that God's knowledge is limited, they are assuming that all questions are asked
solely for the purpose of obtaining information. Common
sense should tell us, however, that questions often are asked
for other reasons. Are we to assume that God was ignorant of
Adam's whereabouts when He asked him, "Where are you?"
(Genesis 3:9). At the beginning of God's first speech to Job,
God asked the patriarch, "Where were you when I laid the
foundations of the earth?" (38:4). Are we to believe that God
did not know where Job was when He created the world? Cer-

tainly not! What father, having seen his son dent a car door, has not asked him, "Who did that?" Obviously, the father did not ask the question to obtain information, but to see if the son would admit to something the father knew all along. On occasion, Jesus used questions for the same purpose. When He questioned the Pharisees' disciples and the Herodians regarding whose inscription was on a particular coin, it clearly was not because He did not know (Matthew 22:15-22). Likewise, when Jesus asked the multitude that thronged Him, "Who touched Me?" (Luke 8:45), it was not because the woman who touched Him was hidden from Him (Luke 8:47). Jesus knew the woman was made well by touching His garment before she ever confessed to touching Him (Mark 5:32). Thus, His question was intended to bring attention to her great faith and His great power (Mark 5:34). Truly, in no way are the questions God asks mankind an indication of Him being less than divine.

But what about Jehovah's statement to Abraham recorded in Genesis 18:21? Did He not know the state of Sodom and Gomorrah prior to His messengers' visit (Genesis 18:22; 19: 1-29)? Did He have to "learn" whether the inhabitants of these two cities were as evil as some had said? The Bible's usage of phrases such as "I will know" (18:21) or "now I know" (22:12) in reference to God, actually are for the benefit of man. Throughout the Bible, human actions (such as learning) frequently are attributed to God for the purpose of helping us better understand His infinity. When Jehovah "came down to see the city and the tower" built at Babel (Genesis 11:5), it was not for the purpose of gaining knowledge. Anthropomorphic expressions such as these are not meant to suggest that God is not fully aware of everything. Rather, as in the case of Babel, such wording was used to show that He was "officially and judicially taking the situation under direct observation and consideration, it having become so flagrant that there was danger (as in the days of Noah) that the truth of

God's revelation might be completely obliterated if it were allowed to continue" (Morris, 1976, p. 272). Almighty God visited Sodom and Gomorrah likely "for appearance' sake, that men might know directly that God had actually seen the full situation before He acted in judgment" (p. 342). As Jamieson, Fausset, and Brown noted in their commentary on Genesis: "These cities were to be made ensamples to all future ages of God's severity, and therefore ample proof given that the judgment was neither rash nor excessive (Ezek 18:23; Jer 18:7)" [1997].

Similar to how God instructs man to pray and make "known" to Him our petitions for our benefit (Philippians 4:6), even though He actually already knows our prayers and needs before they are voiced (Matthew 6:8), **for our profit** the all-knowing God sometimes is spoken of in accommodative language as acquiring knowledge.

CAN GOD DO ANYTHING?
Genesis 17:1; Titus 1:2

Both Christians and atheists generally have assumed that if the God depicted in the Bible exists, He can do **anything**— since He is represented as being all-powerful (cf. Genesis 17:1). However, this assumption is incorrect. The Bible does not claim that the omnipotence of God implies that He can do anything and everything. In reality, "omnipotence" does not, and cannot, apply to that which does not lend itself to power. Skeptics and atheists have posed queries that they feel nullify the notion of omnipotence, thereby demonstrating the non-existence of God. For example, "Can God create a boulder so large that He, Himself, cannot lift it?"

Separate and apart from the fact that God is not, Himself, physical, and that He created the entire physical Universe, though He is metaphysical and transcendent of the Universe, the question is a conceptual absurdity. It's like asking, "Can God create a round square or a four-sided triangle?" No, He cannot—but not for the reasons implied by the atheist (i.e., that He does not exist or that He is not omnipotent). Rather, it is because the question is, itself, self-contradictory and incoherent. It is nonsensical terminology. Rather than saying God **cannot** do such things, it would be more in harmony with the truth to say simply that such things **cannot be done at all**! God is infinite in power, but power meaningfully relates only to what can be done, to what is **possible** of accomplishment—not to what is impossible! It is absurd to speak of any power (even infinite power) being able to do what simply **cannot** be done. Logical absurdities do not lend themselves to being accomplished, and so, are not subject to power, not even to infinite power (see Warren, 1972, pp. 27ff.).

To suggest that God is deficient or limited in power if He cannot create a rock so large that He cannot lift it, is to imply that He could do so if He simply had more power. But this is false. To propose that God could create a rock that He, Himself, cannot lift, create a four-sided triangle, make a ball that is at the same time both white all over and black all over, create a ninety-year-old teenager, or make a car that is larger on the inside that it is on the outside, is to affirm logical contradictions and absurdities. Such propositions do not really say anything at all. Though one can imagine logical absurdities that cannot be accomplished, they do not constitute a telling blow against the view that God is infinite in power.

So, no, the concept of "omnipotence" does not mean that there are no limits to what an omnipotent being can do. In fact, the Bible pinpoints specific things that God **cannot** do. While God can do whatever is **possible** to be done, in reality, He will do only what is in harmony with His nature. For example, the Bible states unequivocally that God cannot lie (Numbers 23:19; Titus 1:2; Hebrews 6:18). He is a Being whose very essence entails truthfulness. Falsehood is completely out of harmony with His divine nature. Another impossibility pertaining to God's power is the fact that He shows no par-

tiality or favoritism (Deuteronomy 10:17; Romans 2:11). He
is "open and above board"–evenhanded–with all His creatures. He can be counted on to interact with human beings as
He said He would. His treatment of us centers on our own
self-chosen behavior–not on our ethnicity or skin color (Acts
10:34-35; 1 Samuel 16:7).

A third instance that qualifies the meaning of "omnipotent" is seen in God's unwillingness to forgive the individual
who will not repent and forsake his or her sin (Joshua 24:19;
Proverbs 28:13; Matthew 6:15; 18:35; Luke 13:3,5). As great
and as magnificent as the mercy and forgiveness of God are,
it is out of harmony with His nature to bestow forgiveness
upon the person who does not seek that forgiveness by meeting the pre-conditions of remission (Romans 1:16; 2:8; 2 Thessalonians 1:8; 1 Peter 4:17). It is imperative that every human
being recognizes the need to understand His will, and to conform one's behavior to that will. It is imperative that every individual avoid placing self in the precarious position of being
in need of **that which God cannot (and will not) do**.

DOES GOD NEED REST?

Isaiah 40:28; Genesis 2:2

As previously noted, many passages of Scripture describe
God as omnipotent, or all-powerful. In Genesis 17:1, God described Himself to Abraham by saying, "I am Almighty God."
Abraham's son, Isaac, in blessing his son Jacob, said: "May
God Almighty bless you…." The omnipotent nature of God
can be seen throughout the Bible. The psalmist wrote: "Great
is our Lord, and mighty in power; His understanding is infinite" (Psalm 147:5). From such verses, we get the idea that
God can do anything that can be accomplished with power
(i.e., anything that is in harmony with His nature). We also
get the idea that God's power never runs out, and that He
does not get tired. As Isaiah wrote: "Have you not known?

Have you not heard? The everlasting God, the Lord, the Creator of the ends of the earth, **neither faints nor is weary**" (40:28, emp. added).

But if God does not get tired, why does the Genesis account of creation say that "on the seventh day God ended His work, which He had done, and He **rested** on the seventh day from all His work which He had done" (Genesis 2:2, emp. added)? What does the Bible mean when it says that God "rested"? Were the rigors of creating the Universe so difficult for God that He needed a break? Did His creative power need to be rejuvenated? And, does this "resting" not militate against the idea that God does not "faint nor is weary?" The answers to these questions are really very simple.

When we hear the English verb "rest," most of us immediately think of being tired or needing to recuperate drained energy, but the Hebrew word translated "rest" in Genesis 2:2 does not always carry that same idea. In fact, the first two definitions given for this Hebrew word (*shābat* or *shābath*) are to "cease, desist." The *Enhanced Strong's Lexicon* documents that, of the 71 times it is used, 47 of those times it is simply translated "cease," and only 11 of those times is it translated "rest" ("Shabath," 1995). The *Theological Wordbook of the Old Testament* states: "The translation 'to cease, desist' can be illustrated in the following verses: 'Day and night shall not cease' (Genesis 8:22)...." (Harris, et al., 1980, 2:902).

A brief look at the original word translated "rest" or "rested" shows that God did not get tired, nor did He need a day to convalesce or build up His strength. He simply **stopped creating** the Universe. He finished in six days and stopped on the seventh day in order to set a pattern for a seven-day week (cf. Exodus 20:8-11). God does not need to rest or relax, because He "neither faints nor is weary." In dealing with questions like this one, sometimes a brief look at the original language can easily solve the "problem."

DID GOD TEMPT ABRAHAM?
Genesis 22:1; James 1:13

We serve an upright and just God "...who will not allow you to be tempted beyond what you are able, but with the temptation will also make the way of escape, that you may be able to bear it" (1 Corinthians 10:13). Also, "[l]et no one say when he is tempted, 'I am tempted by God'; for God cannot be tempted by evil, **nor does He Himself tempt anyone**..." (James 1:13, emp. added). But how, some skeptics have asked, can James be correct if Genesis 22:1 says that God tempted Abraham into sacrificing Isaac? The passage reads:

> And it came to pass after these things, that God did **tempt** Abraham, and said unto him, Abraham: and he said, Behold, here I am (KJV).

> And it came to pass after these things, that God did **prove** Abraham, and said unto him, Abraham. And he said, Here am I (ASV).

> After these things God **tested** Abraham, and said to him, "Abraham!" And he said, "Here am I" (RSV).

> Now it came to pass after these things that God **tested** Abraham, and said to him, "Abraham!" And he said, "Here I am" (NKJV).

> Now it came about after these things, that God **tested** Abraham, and said to him, "Abraham!" And he said, "Here I am" (NASV).

> Some time later God **tested** Abraham. He said to him, "Abraham!" "Here I am," he replied (NIV).

Of the six common translations listed, only the King James Version says that God "tempted" Abraham. The Hebrew word *nissâ*, which the King James renders as "tempt," is defined as "test" in both the *Theological Lexicon of the Old Testament* (Botterweck, et al., 1998, 9:443-455) and the *Theological Dictionary of*

the Old Testament (Jenni and Westerman, 1997, 2:741-742). The
American Standard Version, which many consider the most
literal translation of the Bible available, and the New King
James Version, do not render *nissâ* as "tempt." In fact, four of
the five other translations listed use "test" for *nissâ*, which fits
with both the context of the verse and the Hebrew word used.
And, as Wayne Jackson stated:

> For instance, one meaning of tempt is "a solicitation
> to sin, an enticement to evil." It is an action designed
> to entrap a victim, hence, to bring about his fall. A
> holy God (cf. Isaiah 6:3 and Revelation 7:14) never
> could be guilty of such a base activity, and this is the
> thrust of James' description of this matter in the pas-
> sage cited above (1987, p. 14).

The case of God tempting Abraham is no more than a mis-
translation by the seventeenth-century translators of the King
James Version.

So why did God command Abraham to sacrifice Isaac?
The simple reason is given in the verse itself: **God was testing Abraham's obedience**. Isaac was the only son of Abraham and Sarah, and the heir to God's promise of a great nation (Genesis 12:1-3), so what better way for God to test Abraham's loyalty to Him than by asking Abraham to give up what
was perhaps his greatest possession (cf. Hebrews 11:17-19)?
And God, by keeping Abraham from completing the sacrifice, obviously never intended for Isaac to be slaughtered at
the hands of his father (cf. Jeremiah 7:31; 32:35), but merely
sought to prove Abraham's faith.

DID GOD INCITE DAVID
TO NUMBER ISRAEL?
2 Samuel 24:1; 1 Chronicles 21:1

Census-taking under the Law of Moses was not inherently
evil. In fact, God actually commanded Moses to number the

Israelite soldiers on two different occasions—once in the second year after deliverance from Egyptian bondage, and again about forty years later near the end of Israel's wanderings in the desert (Numbers 1:1-3,19; 26:2-4). Even though the book of Numbers describes many of their experiences while wandering through a barren land, the book takes its name (first assigned by the translators of the Septuagint) from these two numberings of the Israelites. Indeed, the taking of a census was a legitimate practice under the old law (cf. Exodus 30:11-16). Sometimes, however, one's motives can turn lawful actions into sinful deeds (cf. Matthew 6:1-18). Such was the case with King David when he decided to number the Israelites in the latter part of his reign. God had not commanded a census to be taken, nor did David instigate it for some noble cause. Instead, the Bible implies that David's intentions (and thus his actions) were dishonorable, foolish, and sinful (cf. 2 Samuel 24:3,10ff.).

For many Bible readers, the parallel accounts that describe David's numbering of Israel (found in 2 Samuel 24 and 1 Chronicles 21) pose a serious problem. "Why does 2 Samuel 24:1 state that **God** 'moved' David against Israel, while 1 Chronicles 21:1 says that it was **Satan** who 'stood up against Israel, and moved David to number Israel' "? Can both passages be right, or is this a contradiction?

The Hebrew verb *wayyaset*, translated "moved" (NKJV) or "incited" (NASV), is identical in both passages. God and Satan's actions are described using the same word. The difference lies with the sense in which the word is used: Satan incited (or tempted—cf. 1 Thessalonians 3:5) David more directly, while God is spoken of as having incited David because He **allowed** such temptation to take place. The Hebrews often used active verbs to express "not the doing of the thing, but the **permission** of the thing which the agent is said to do" (Bullinger, 1898, p. 823, emp. in orig.). Throughout the Bible, God's allowance of something to take place often is described by the sacred writers as having been done **by the Lord**.

The book of Exodus records how "God hardened Pharaoh's heart" (Exodus 7:3,13; 9:12; 10:1; et al.), but it was not the case that God directly forced Pharaoh to reject His will. Rather, God hardened his heart in the sense that God provided the circumstances and the occasion for Pharaoh to reject His will. God sent Moses to place His demands before Pharaoh, even accompanying His Word with miracles to confirm the divine origin of the message (cf. Mark 16:20). Pharaoh made up his own mind to resist God's demands. God merely provided the occasion for Pharaoh to demonstrate his unyielding attitude. If God had not sent Moses, Pharaoh would not have been faced with the dilemma of whether or not to release the Israelites. So God was certainly the initiator of the circumstances that led to Pharaoh's sin, but He was not the author (or direct cause) of Pharaoh's defiance (see Butt and Miller, 2003).

Another instance where this idiomatic language can be found is in the book of Job. In fact, the situation regarding God and Satan inciting David to number Israel probably more closely parallels the first two chapters of Job than any other passage of Scripture. Satan went into the presence of God on two different occasions in Job 1-2. The first time, he charged that righteous Job only served God because of the blessings God showered upon him (1:9-11). God thus permitted Satan to afflict Job with suffering, telling Satan, "Behold, all that he has is in your power; only do not lay a hand on his person" (1:12). After Satan used both humans and natural agency to destroy Job's wealth and all of his children (1:13-19), Satan returned to the Lord's presence. Notice the exchange of words between God and Satan (in view of the Hebrew idiomatic thought: what God **permits**, He is said to **do**).

> Then the Lord said to Satan, "Have you considered
> My servant Job, that there is none like him on the
> earth, a blameless and upright man, one who fears
> God and shuns evil? And still he holds fast to his in-
> tegrity, although **you incited Me against him**, to
> destroy him without cause." So Satan answered the
> Lord and said, "Skin for skin! Yes, all that a man has
> he will give for his life. But stretch out **Your hand**
> now, and touch his bone and his flesh, and he will
> surely curse You to Your face!" And the Lord said to
> Satan, "Behold, he is in **your hand**, but spare his
> life." So Satan went out from the presence of the Lord,
> and struck Job with painful boils from the sole of his
> foot to the crown of his head (Job 2:3-7, emp. added).

Even though God knew that Satan was the direct cause for
Job's suffering (recorded in chapter one), He told Satan: "You
incited Me against him, to destroy him without cause" (2:3,
emp. added). As a result of Job's abstaining from sin during
this time of suffering, Satan then proposed a new challenge
to God, saying, "But stretch out Your hand now, and touch
his bone and his flesh, and he will surely curse You to Your
face" (vs. 4). In essence, God said, "Okay. I will," but He did
not do it **directly**. He merely allowed **Satan** to do it: "Behold, he [Job] is in your hand, but spare his life" (vs. 6). So
Satan "struck Job with painful boils from the sole of his foot
to the crown of his head" (vs. 7). The dialog between God
and Satan in Job chapter 2 leaves no doubt that **what God
permits** to take place often is described by sacred writers as
having been **done by God**. The inspired author of Job even
reiterated this point forty chapters later, when he wrote:
"Then all his [Job's] brothers, all his sisters, and all those
who had been his acquaintances before, came to him and
ate food with him in his house; and they consoled him and
comforted him **for all the adversity that the Lord had
brought upon him**" (42:11, emp. added).

In his commentary on 2 Samuel, Burton Coffman made mention that the same principle still is operative in the Christian dispensation.

> Paul pointed out that people who do not love the truth but have pleasure in unrighteousness are actually incited by God to believe a falsehood that they might be condemned (2 Thessalonians 2:9-12). "Therefore God sends upon them a strong delusion to make them believe what is false, so that all may be condemned, etc." (1992, p. 329).

Those discussed in 2 Thessalonians 2 made a decision to reject the truth of God's Word (cf. vs. 10), and believe a lie. God sends a delusion, in the sense that He controls the world's drama.

The problem of how a loving God (1 John 4:8) can send a "strong delusion" (2 Thessalonians 2:11), harden someone's heart (Exodus 9:12), or incite someone to sin (as in the case of David numbering Israel–2 Samuel 24:1), can be compared to God's work in nature. In one sense, a person could speak of God killing someone who jumps from a 100-story building to his death, because it was God Who set in motion the law of gravity (but He did not force the person over the edge). Some inspired writers wrote from this viewpoint, which was customary in their culture.

Similar to how Pharaoh hardened his heart because God gave him occasion to do such, and similar to how Job suffered because God allowed Satan to strike Job with calamity, God allowed Satan to incite David to sin (1 Chronicles 21:1). Israel suffered as a direct result of Satan's workings in the life of King David–workings that God allowed. Thus, both God and Satan legitimately could be said to have incited the king– but in different ways (and for different reasons).

LOVE IS NOT JEALOUS, SO WHY IS GOD?

1 John 4:8; 1 Corinthians 13:4; Exodus 20:5

The argument goes something like this: (1) 1 John 4:8 indicates that "God is love;" (2) 1 Corinthians 13:4 says that "love is not jealous" (NASV); and yet (3) Exodus 20:5, along with several other passages, reveals that God is "a jealous God." "How," the skeptic asks, "can God be jealous when several verses say God is love and 1 Cor. says love is not jealous?" (McKinsey, 1992). Simply put, if love is not jealous, and God is love, then God logically cannot be called jealous. Or conversely, if love is not jealous, and God is jealous, then God cannot be considered loving. Right? How can these verses be anything but contradictory?

The term "jealousy" most often carries a negative connotation in twenty-first-century America. We pity the man who is jealous of his coworker's success. We frown upon families who react to a neighbor's newly found fortune by being overcome with jealousy. And we are perturbed to hear of a jealous husband who distrusts his wife, and questions every possible wrong action that she might make, even going so far as demanding that she never leave the house without him. Add to these feelings about jealousy what various New Testament passages have to say on the subject, and one can understand why some might sincerely question why God is described at times as "jealous." The apostle Paul admonished the Christians in Rome to "behave properly," and put off "strife and **jealousy**" (Romans 13:13, NASV). To the church at Corinth, Paul expressed concern that when he came to their city he might find them involved in such sinful things as gossip, strife, and **jealousy** (2 Corinthians 12:20). And, as noted above, he explicitly told them that "**love is not jealous**" (1 Corinthians 13:4). James also wrote about the sinfulness of jealousy, saying that where it exists "there is disorder and every evil thing" (3:16; cf. Acts 7:9). One religious writer described such jealousy as "an infantile resentment springing from unmortified covetousness, which expresses itself in envy, malice, and meanness of action" (Packer, 1973, p. 189). It seems, more often than not, that both the New Testament and the "moral code" of modern society speak of "jealousy" in a negative light.

The truth is, however, sometimes jealously can be spoken of in a good sense. The word "jealous" is translated in the Old Testament from the Hebrew word *qin'ah*, and in the New Testament from the Greek word *zelos*. The root idea behind both words is that of "warmth" or "heat" (Forrester, 1996). The Hebrew word for jealousy carries with it the idea of "redness of the face that accompanies strong emotion" (Feinberg, 1942, p. 429)–whether right or wrong. Depending upon the usage of the word, it can be used to represent both a good and an evil passion. Three times in 1 Corinthians, Paul used this word in a good sense to encourage his brethren to "earnestly desire (*zeeloúte*)" spiritual gifts (12:31; 14:1,39). He obviously was not commanding the Corinthians to sin, but to do something that was good and worthwhile. Later, when writing to the church at Corinth, the apostle Paul was even more direct in showing how there was such a thing as "godly jealousy." He stated:

> **I am jealous for you with godly jealousy.** For I have betrothed you to one husband, that I may present you as a chaste virgin to Christ. But I fear, lest somehow, as the serpent deceived Eve by his craftiness, so your minds may be corrupted from the simplicity that is in Christ. For if he who comes preaches another Jesus whom we have not preached, or if you receive a different spirit which you have not received, or a different gospel which you have not accepted– you may well put up with it (2 Corinthians 11:2-4, emp. added).

Paul's burning desire was for the church at Corinth to abide in the love of God. As a friend of the bridegroom (Christ),

Paul used some of the strongest language possible to encourage the "bride" of Christ at Corinth to be pure and faithful.

In a similar way, Jehovah expressed His love for Israel in the Old Testament by proclaiming to be "a jealous God" (Exodus 20:5; Deuteronomy 4:24). He was not **envious** of the Israelites' accomplishments or possessions, but was communicating His strong **love** for them with anthropomorphic language. The Scriptures depict a spiritual marriage between Jehovah and His people. Sadly, during the period of the divided kingdom, both Israel and Judah were guilty of "playing the harlot" (Jeremiah 3:6-10). God called Israel's idolatrous practice "adultery," and for this reason He had "put her away and given her a certificate of divorce" (3:8). This is not the "lunatic fury of a rejected or supplanted suitor," but a "zeal to protect a love-relationship" (Packer, 1973, p. 189). Jehovah felt and did for Israel "as **the most affectionate husband** could do for his spouse, and **was jealous** for their fidelity, because he willed their invariable happiness" (Clarke, 1996, emp. added). Song of Solomon 8:6 is further proof that love and jealousy are not always opposed to each other. To her beloved, the Shulamite said: "Put me like a seal over your heart, like a seal on your arm. **For love is as strong as death, jealousy is as severe as Sheol**; its flashes are flashes of fire, the very flame of the Lord" (NASV). In this passage, love and jealousy actually are paralleled to convey the same basic meaning (see Tanner, 1997, p. 158)–that (aside from one's love for God) marital love is "the strongest, most unyielding and invincible force in human experience" (*NIV Study Bible*, 1985, p. 1012). In this sense, being a jealous husband or wife is a **good** thing. As one commentator noted, married persons "who felt no jealousy at the intrusion of a lover or an adulterer into their home would surely be lacking in moral perception; for the exclusiveness of marriage is the essence of marriage" (Tasker, 1967, p. 106).

Truly, love has a jealous side. There is a sense in which one legitimately can be jealous for what rightfully belongs to him (see Numbers 25). Such is especially true in the marriage relationship. Israel was God's chosen people (Deuteronomy 7: 6). He had begun to set them apart as a special nation by blessing their "father" Abraham (Genesis 12:1ff.; 17:1-27). He blessed the Israelites with much numerical growth while living in Egypt (Exodus 1:7,12,19; Deuteronomy 26:5; cf. Genesis 15:5; 46: 3). He delivered them from Egyptian bondage (Exodus 3-12). And, among other things, He gave them written revelation, which, if obeyed, would bring them spiritually closer to Him, and even would make them physically superior to other nations, in that they would be spared from various diseases (see Exodus 15:26). Like a bird that watches over her eggs and young with jealousy, preventing other birds from entering her nest, God watched over the Israelites with "righteous" jealousy, unwilling to tolerate the presence of false gods among his people (see Exodus 20:3-6; Joshua 24:14-16,19-20). Such "godly jealousy" (cf. 2 Corinthians 11:2) was not what Paul had in mind in 1 Corinthians 13:4.

SUFFERING AND AN ALL-LOVING GOD
1 John 4:8

All one has to do is walk through the halls of the nearest hospital or mental institution to see people of all ages suffering from various diseases and illnesses. Suffering is everywhere, and thus such questions as the following inevitably arise. "If there is a God, why am I afflicted with this illness?" "If there is a God, why was my son not allowed to see his sixteenth birthday?" "If there is a God, why are my parents afflicted with Alzheimer's disease?" These and hundreds of similar questions have echoed from the human heart for millennia. They are as old as the first tear, and as recent as the latest newscast.

For many people, the existence of pain and suffering serves as a great obstacle to belief in God. Skeptics and infidels, both past and present, have held that the existence of evil is an embarrassment for those who believe in God. How do theists reconcile the presence of suffering with the existence of an omnipotent and all-loving God? Some have argued that illness and other kinds of suffering are illusionary, and spring from a false belief. Others have maintained that no explanation is necessary, because mere mortals should not have to justify the ways of God to men. But most Christians acknowledge that suffering is real, and that it is a "problem" that deserves careful attention.

Even though man cannot explain in specific detail every instance of human suffering, contrary to what many believe, there are several logical reasons why people experience mental and physical pain. One of the foremost reasons is rooted in the fact that God is love (1 John 4:8), and His love allows freedom of choice. God did not create men and women as robots to serve Him slavishly without any kind of free moral agency on their part (cf. Genesis 2:16-17; Joshua 24:15; Matthew 7:13-14). God does not control His creation as a puppeteer controls a doll. God has, as an expression of His love, granted mankind free will, and that free will enables human beings to make their own choices.

Man frequently brings suffering upon himself because of the wrong decisions he makes. The apostle Peter wrote: "But let none of you suffer as a murderer, a thief, an evildoer, or as a busybody in other people's matters..." (1 Peter 4:15). When people suffer the consequences of their own wrong choices, they have no one to blame but themselves. If a person makes the decision to kill someone, he will suffer the consequences of making a wrong choice. He may be put in prison, or perhaps even be killed himself. If a fornicator is found to have a sexually transmitted disease, again, it is because he made the wrong decision to have intercourse with someone who was infected. Thus, oftentimes man's suffering results from a misuse of his own freedom.

Man also suffers because of the personal wrong choices of others. If God allows one person freedom of choice, He must allow **everyone** that freedom to be consistent in His love for the world. God is no respecter of persons (cf. Acts 10:34; Romans 2:11). In the Bible, we read where Uriah the Hittite suffered because of David's sins (2 Samuel 11). Uriah ultimately was killed because of David's attempt to cover up the wrong decisions he had made. Today, families may suffer because a father is thrown in jail for drunk driving. In that case, he is the cause of the family's suffering. If a man smokes all of his life, and then eventually dies at an early age because of lung cancer, he and his family suffer because of his decision to smoke. God cannot be blamed for man's personal wrong choices; nor can He be blamed for the wrong decisions that others have made.

Closely related to the first two reasons man suffers today is a third reason—the personal wrong choices of former generations. Who is to blame for millions starving in India today? A partial answer would be—some of their ancestors. Years ago, people began teaching that it was wrong to eat cows because they might be eating an ancestor. The doctrine of reincarnation has deprived millions of people throughout the world of good health. Is God to be blamed when people will not eat the beef that could give them nourishment? Many of the decisions of former generations have caused much pain and suffering for those in the world today.

Much is said about reaping from the wrong choices of others, but people often forget that when one man does well, oftentimes profit is felt by many. People living in the twenty-first century have a multitude of advantages because of the work of former generations. Human beings are living longer because of various medical discoveries. Advances in technology allow man to have conveniences that previously were only imagined. Thus, just as man suffers because of the sins of former generations, he also reaps the benefits of their good labors. If man truly is free, it must be possible for him to both suffer the consequences, and reap the benefits, of his own decisions, as well as those of others.

Another reason man suffers today is because there are those who ignore law and order. God created a world ruled by natural laws established at the Creation. These laws were implemented for man's own good, but if these laws are challenged, then man will suffer the consequences. If a man steps off the roof of a twenty-story building, gravity will pull him to the pavement beneath. If a boy steps in front of a moving freight train, since two objects cannot occupy the same space at the same time, the train will strike the child and likely kill him. Why? Because he has (knowingly or unknowingly) gone against the natural order of this world. The natural laws that God created allow man to produce fire. But the same laws that enable him to cook his food also allow him to destroy entire forests. Laws that make it possible to have things **constructive** to human life also introduce the possibility that things **destructive** to human life may occur. How can it be otherwise? A car is matter in motion, and takes us where we wish to go. But if someone steps in front of that car, the same natural laws that operated to our benefit will similarly operate to our detriment. The same laws that govern gravity, matter in motion, or similar phenomena also govern weather patterns, water movement, and other geological/meteorological conditions. **All** of nature is regulated by these laws—not just the parts that we find convenient. If God suspended natural laws every time His creatures were in a dangerous situation, chaos would corrupt the cosmos, arguing more for a world of **atheism** than a world of **theism**!

Everyone (believer and unbeliever alike) must recognize the natural laws God established or else suffer the consequences. In Luke 13:2-5, Jesus told the story of eighteen men who perished when the tower of Siloam collapsed. Had these men perished because of their sin? No, they were no worse sinners than their peers. They died because a natural law was in force. Fortunately, natural laws work continually so that we can understand and benefit from them. We are not left to sort out some kind of haphazard system that works one day but not the next.

Furthermore, as much as the unbeliever hates to admit it, there **are** times when suffering actually is **beneficial**. Think of the man whose chest begins to throb as he enters the throes of a heart attack. Think of the woman whose side begins to ache at the onset of acute appendicitis. Is it not true that pain often sends us to the doctor for prevention or cure? Is it not true also that, at times, suffering helps humankind develop the traits that people treasure the most? Bravery, heroism, altruistic love, self-sacrifice—all flourish in less-than-perfect environments, do they not? Yet people who exhibit such traits are cherished and honored as having gone "above and beyond the call of duty." Was this not the very point Christ was making when He said: "Greater love has no one than this, than to lay down one's life for his friends" (John 15:13)?

Finally, no one can suggest—justifiably—that suffering per se is contrary to the existence or goodness of God in light of the series of events that transpired at Calvary almost two thousand years ago. The fact that **even Jesus, as the Son of God,** was subjected to evil, pain, and suffering (Hebrews 5:8; 1 Peter 2:21ff.) proves that God loves and cares for His creation. He is not the unloving, angry, vengeful God depicted by atheism and infidelity. Rather, "when we were enemies we were reconciled to God through the death of His Son, much more, having been reconciled, we shall be saved by His life" (Romans 5:10). God could have abandoned us to our own sinful devices but instead, "God demonstrates His own love toward us, in that while we were still sinners, Christ died for us" (Romans 5:8; cf. 1 John 4:9-10).

Chapter 3

ANSWERING ATTACKS UPON THE DISPOSITION AND DEITY OF CHRIST

WAS JESUS A REAL PERSON?

Before answering direct attacks upon the disposition and deity of Christ, it first must be stressed that Jesus was indeed a real person. It seems that a growing number of people in the world today actually think that Jesus is nothing more than a fantasy figure that various secret societies created 2,000 years ago. Allegedly, His name belongs in the same fictional writings that contain such fairy-tale characters as Peter Pan, Hercules, and Snow White and the seven dwarfs. Gerald Massey, in his book, *Gnostic and Historic Christianity*, has "informed" us that "[w]hether considered as the God made human, or as man made divine, this character [Jesus–EL] never existed as a person" (1985, p. 22). Skeptics like Massey, Acharya (1999), Brian Flemming (director of the movie *The Beast*), and many others believe that Christians have been deceived into thinking that there really was a man named Jesus, when, in fact, He never lived.

How do those who believe in the historicity of Jesus Christ respond to such allegations? Can we really **know** that there was a sinless, miracle-working, death-defying man named Jesus who lived upon the Earth approximately 2,000 years ago, or have we accepted His existence blindly?

Even though the New Testament, which enjoys far more historical documentation than any other volume ever known, proves beyond the shadow of a doubt that Jesus actually lived, it is by no means the only historical evidence available. Around the year A.D. 94, a Jewish historian by the name of Josephus mentioned Jesus' name twice in his book, *Antiquities of the Jews*. In section 18 of that work, Josephus wrote: "And there arose about this time **Jesus**, a wise man, if indeed we should call him a man; for he was a doer of marvelous deeds, a teacher of men who receive the truth with pleasure" (emp. added). Then, in section 20, Josephus documented how a man named Ananus brought before the Sanhedrin "a man named James, **the brother of Jesus who was called the Christ**, and certain others" (emp. added). [NOTE: Certain historians regard Josephus' comments about Jesus as being a "Christian interpolation." There is, however, no evidence from textual criticism that would warrant such an opinion (see Bruce, 1953, p. 110). In fact, every extant Greek manuscript contains the disputed portions. The passage also exists in both Hebrew and Arabic versions. And although the Arabic version is slightly different, it still exhibits knowledge of the disputed sections (see Chapman, 1981, p. 29; Habermas, 1996, pp. 193-196).]

About 20 years later, Tacitus, a Roman historian, wrote a book surveying the history of Rome. In it he described how Nero (the Roman emperor) "punished with every refinement the notoriously depraved Christians (as they were popularly called)." He went on to write that "their originator, **Christ**, had been executed in Tiberius' reign by the governor of Judea, Pontius Pilatus" (*Annals* 15:44, emp. added). Even though Tacitus, Josephus, and other historians from the first and second centuries A.D. were not followers of Christ, they did have **something** to say about Him. They verified that Jesus was a **real** person—Who was so famous that He even attracted the attention of the Roman emperor himself!

Another obvious reason to believe that Jesus was a real person is because our entire dating method is based upon His existence. The letters "B.C." stand for "before Christ," and the letters "A.D." (standing for *Anno Domini*) mean "in the year of the Lord." So when a history teacher speaks of Alexander the Great ruling much of the world in 330 B.C., he or she is admitting that Alexander lived about 330 years before Jesus was born.

Even though this is only a sampling of the evidence relating to the man known as Jesus, it is enough to prove that He was a real person, and not just some imaginary character. We do not accept His existence blindly—it is a historical fact!

IN WHAT WAY WAS GOD GREATER THAN JESUS?
John 10:30; 14:28; Mark 13:32

According to the apostle John, "in the beginning was the Word, and the Word was with God, and **the Word was God**.... And the Word became flesh and dwelt among us, and we beheld His glory, the glory as of the only begotten of the Father, full of grace and truth" (John 1:1,14, emp. added). Unquestionably, this Word (God), Whom John claims became flesh, was Jesus Christ (1:17). This same apostle recorded other statements in his account of the Gospel that convey the same basic truth. He wrote how, on one occasion, Jesus told a group of hostile Jews, "I and My Father are one" (10:30). Later, he recorded how Jesus responded to Philip's request to see God by saying, "He who has seen Me has seen the Father" (14:9). He even told about how Jesus accepted worship from a blind man whom He had healed (9:38; cf. Matthew 8:2). And, since

only God is to be worshipped (Matthew 4:10), the implication is that Jesus believed He was God (cf. John 1:29,41,49;
20:28; Mark 14:62).

Some, however, see an inconsistency with these statements
when they are placed alongside John 14:28, in which Jesus
declared: "My Father is greater than I" (John 14:28). Allegedly, this verse (among others—cf. 1 Corinthians 11:3; Mark
13:32; Colossians 3:1) proves that Jesus and the Bible writers
were contradictory in their portrayal of Jesus' divine nature.
Jesus could not be **one with God** and **lesser than God** at
the same time, could He? What is the proper way to understand John 14:28?

Statements found in passages like John 14:28 (indicating
that Jesus was lesser than God), or in Mark 13:32 (where Jesus
made the comment that even He did not know on what day
the Second Coming would be), must be understood in light
of what the apostle Paul wrote to the church at Philippi concerning Jesus' self-limitation during His time on Earth. Christ,

> being in the form of God, did not consider it rob-
> bery to be equal with God, but **made Himself of no
> reputation [He "emptied Himself"**—NASV], tak-
> ing the form of a bondservant, and coming in the
> likeness of men. And being found in appearance as
> a man, **He humbled Himself** and became obedient
> to the point of death, even the death of the cross (Phi-
> lippians 2:6-8, emp. added).

While on Earth, and in the flesh, Jesus was **voluntarily** in a
subordinate position to the Father. Christ "emptied Himself" (Philippians 2:7; He "made **Himself** nothing"—NIV).
Unlike Adam and Eve, who made an attempt to seize equality with God (Genesis 3:5), Jesus, the last Adam (1 Corinthians 15:47), humbled Himself, and obediently accepted the
role of a servant. Jesus' earthly limitations (cf. Mark 13:32),
however, were not the consequence of a less-than-God **na-**

ture; rather, they were the result of a **self-imposed submission** reflecting the exercise of His sovereign will. While on Earth, Jesus assumed a position of complete subjection to the Father, and exercised His divine attributes only at the Father's bidding (cf. John 8:26,28-29) [*Wycliffe*, 1985]. As A.H. Strong similarly commented many years ago, Jesus "resigned not the possession, nor yet entirely the use, but rather the independent exercise, of the divine attributes" (1907, p. 703).

Admittedly, understanding Jesus as being 100% God and 100% human is not an easy concept to grasp. When Jesus came to Earth, He added humanity to His divinity (He was "made in the likeness of men"). For the first time ever, He was subject to such things as hunger, thirst, growth (both physical and mental), pain, disease, and temptation (cf. Hebrews 4:15; Luke 2:52). At the same time Jesus added humanity to His divinity, however, He put Himself in a subordinate position to the Father in terms of role function (1 Corinthians 11:3). In short, when Jesus affirmed, "The Father is greater than I" (John 14:28), He was not denying His divine nature; rather, He was asserting that He had subjected Himself voluntarily to the Father's will.

WAS JESUS TRUSTWORTHY?
John 5:31; 8:14

When Christ spoke to a group of hostile Jews in Jerusalem regarding God the Father, and His own equality with Him (John 5:17-30; cf. 10:30), He defended His deity by pointing to several witnesses, including John the Baptizer, the Father in heaven, and the Scriptures (5:33-47). One statement that has confused some Bible readers concerning Jesus' defense of His deity is found in John 5:31. Jesus began this part of His discourse by saying, "If I bear witness of Myself, **My witness is not true**" (emp. added). According to many Bible critics, this declaration blatantly contradicts the following statement He made on another occasion when speaking to the Pharisees. He said: "Even if I bear witness of Myself, **My witness is true**" (John 8:14, emp. added). How could He say that His witness was both true, and not true, without being contradictory?

Consider the following illustration. An innocent man on trial for murder is judged to be guilty by the jury, even after proclaiming his innocence. (Someone had framed the defendant for the murder, and all the evidence the jury heard pointed to the defendant as the offender.) When leaving the court house, if the man who was wrongly convicted is asked by a reporter, "Are you guilty?," and he responds by saying, "If the court says I'm guilty, I'm guilty," has the man lied? Even though the statements, "I am guilty," and "I am not guilty," are totally different, they may not be contradictory, depending on the time and sense in which they are spoken. After the trial, the wrongly accused defendant simply repeated the jury's verdict. He said, "I am guilty," and meant, "The court has found me guilty."

When Jesus conceded to the Jews the fact that His witness was "not true," He was not confessing to being a liar. Rather, Jesus was reacting to a well-known law of His day. In Greek, Roman, and Jewish law, the testimony of a witness could not be received in his own case (Robertson, 1997). "Witness to anyone must always be borne by someone else" (Morris, 1995, p. 287). The Law of Moses stated: "One witness shall not rise against a man concerning any iniquity or any sin that he commits; by the mouth of two or three witnesses the matter shall be established" (Deuteronomy 19:15; cf. Matthew 18:15-17). The Pharisees understood this law well, as is evident by their statement to Jesus: "You bear witness of Yourself; Your witness is not true" (John 8:13). In John 5:31, "Jesus points to the impossibility of anyone's being accepted on the basis of his own word.... He is asserting that if of himself he were to bear witness to himself, that would make it untrue" in a court of law (Morris, p. 287). If Jesus had no evidence in a trial regarding His deity other than His own testimony about Himself, His testimony would be inconclusive and inadmissible. Jesus understood that His audience had a right to expect more evidence than just His word. Similar to the above illustration where an innocent man accepts the guilty verdict of the jury as final, Jesus said, "My witness is not true," and meant that, in accordance with the law, His own testimony apart from other witnesses would be considered invalid (or insufficient to establish truth).

But why is it that Jesus said to the Pharisees at a later time that His "witness **is** true" (John 8:14)? The difference is that, in this instance, Jesus was stressing the fact that **His words** were true. Even if in a court of law two witnesses are required for a fact to be established (a law Jesus enunciated in verse 17), that law does not take away the fact that Jesus was telling the truth, just as it did not take away the fact that the wrongly accused man mentioned above was telling the truth during his trial. Jesus declared His testimony to be true for the simple reason that His testimony revealed the true facts regarding Himself (Lenski, 1961b, p. 599). He then followed this pronouncement of truth with the fact that there was another witness–the Father in heaven Who sent Him to Earth (8:16-18). Thus, in actuality, His testimony was true in two senses: (1) it was true because it was indeed factual; and (2) it was valid because it was corroborated by a second unimpeachable witness–the Father.

God the Father (John 8:18; 5:37-38), along with John the Baptizer (John 5:33), the miraculous signs of Jesus (5:36), the Scriptures (5:39), and specifically the writings of Moses (5:46), all authenticated the true statements Jesus made regarding His deity. Sadly, many of His listeners rejected the evidence then, just as people reject it today.

HOW RUDE!?

John 2:4; Ephesians 6:2

Imagine your mother asking you to do something for a neighbor, and you responding to her by saying, "**Woman**, what does that have to do with me?" If your mother is anything like mine, she probably would have given you "the look" (among other things) as she pondered how her son could be so rude. Responding to a mother's (or any woman's) request in twenty-first-century America with the refrain, "Woman...," sounds impolite and offensive. Furthermore, a Christian, who is commanded to "honor" his "father and mother" (Ephesians 6:2), would be out of line in most situations when using such an expression while talking directly to his mother.

In light of the ill-mannered use of the word "woman" in certain contexts today, some question how Jesus could have spoken to His mother 2,000 years ago using this term without breaking the commandment to "[h]onor your father and your mother" (Exodus 20:12; cf. Matthew 15:4; Matthew 5:17-20). When Jesus, His disciples, and His mother were at the wedding in Cana of Galilee where there was a depletion of wine, Mary said to Jesus, "They have no wine" (John 2:3). Jesus then responded to his mother, saying, "Woman, what does your concern have to do with Me? My hour has not yet come" (John 2:4). Notice what one skeptic has written regarding what Jesus said in this verse.

> In Matt. 15:4 he [Jesus–EL] told people to "Honor thy father and thy mother"; yet, he was one of the first to ignore his own maxim by saying to his mother in John 4:24, "Woman, what have I to do with thee?" (McKinsey, 1995, p. 44).

> Imagine someone talking to his own mother in such a disrespectful manner and addressing her by such an impersonal noun as 'woman.' Talk about an insolent offspring! (1995, p. 134).

> Jesus needs to practice some parental respect... (2000, p. 251).
>
> Apparently Jesus' love escaped him (n.d., "Jesus...").
>
> Why was Jesus disrespectful of his mother? In John 2:4, Jesus uses the same words with his mother that demons use when they meet Jesus. Surely the son of God knew that Mary had the blessing of the Father, didn't he, (and she was the mother of God—Ed.) not to mention the fact that the son of God would never be rude? (n.d., "Problems...", parenthetical comment in orig.).

As one can see, Mr. McKinsey is adamant that Jesus erred. He used such words to describe Jesus as disrespectful, insolent, unloving, and rude. Is he correct?

As with most Bible critics, Mr. McKinsey is guilty of judging Jesus' words by what is common in twenty-first-century English vernacular, rather than putting Jesus' comments in its proper first-century setting. It was not rude or inappropriate for a man in the first century to speak to a lady by saying, "Woman (*gunai*)...." This "was a highly respectful and affectionate mode of address" (Vincent, 1997) "with no idea of censure" (Robertson, 1932, p. 34). The New International Version correctly captures the meaning of this word in John 2:4: "'**Dear woman**, why do you involve me?' " (NIV, emp. added). Jesus used this word when complimenting the Syrophoenician woman's great faith (Matthew 15:28), when affectionately addressing Mary Magdalene after His resurrection (John 20:15), and when speaking to His disconsolate mother one last time from the cross (John 19:26). Paul used this same word when addressing Christian women (1 Corinthians 7:16). As Adam Clarke noted: "[C]ertainly no kind of disrespect is intended, but, on the contrary, complaisance, affability, tenderness, and concern, and in this sense it is used in the best Greek writers" (1996).

As to why Jesus used the term "woman" (*gunai*) instead of "mother" (*meetros*) when speaking to Mary (which even in first-century Hebrew and Greek cultures was an unusual way to address one's mother), Leon Morris noted that Jesus most likely was indicating

> that there is a new relationship between them as he enters his public ministry…. Evidently Mary thought of the intimate relations of the home at Nazareth as persisting. But Jesus in his public ministry was not only or primarily the son of Mary, but "the Son of Man" who was to bring the realities of heaven to people on earth (1:51). A new relationship was established (1995, p. 159).

R.C.H. Lenski added: "[W]hile Mary will forever remain his [Jesus'–EL] mother, in his calling Jesus knows no mother or earthly relative, he is their Lord and Savior as well as of all men. The common earthly relation is swallowed up in the divine" (1961b, p. 189). It seems best to conclude that Jesus was simply "informing" His mother in a loving manner that as He began performing miracles for the purpose of proving His deity and the divine origin of His message (see Miller, 2003a, pp. 17-23), His relationship to His mother was about to change.

Finally, the point also must be stressed that honoring fathers and mothers does not mean that a son or daughter never can correct his or her parents. Correction and honor are no more opposites than correction and love. One of the greatest ways parents disclose their love to their children is by correcting them when they make mistakes (Hebrews 12:6-9; Revelation 3:19). Similarly, one of the ways in which a mature son might honor his parents is by taking them aside when they have erred, and lovingly pointing out their mistake or oversight in a certain matter. Think how much more honorable this action would be than to take no action and allow them to continue in a path of error without informing them of such. We must keep in mind that even though Mary was a great woman "who found favor with God" (Luke 1:30), she was not perfect (cf. Romans 3:10,23). She was not God, nor the "mother of God" (viz., she did not originate Jesus or bring Him into existence). But, she was the one chosen to carry the Son of God in her womb. Who better to correct any misunderstanding she may have had than this Son?

DID JESUS CONDONE LAW-BREAKING?
Matthew 12:1-8

The Pharisees certainly did not think that the Son of God was beyond reproach. Following Jesus' feeding of the four thousand, they came "testing" Him, asking Him to show them a sign from heaven (Matthew 16:1). Later in the book of Matthew (19:3ff.), the writer recorded how "the Pharisees also came to Him, **testing Him**, and saying to Him, 'Is it lawful for a man to divorce his wife for just any reason?' " It was their aim on this occasion, as on numerous other occasions, to entangle Jesus in His teachings by asking Him a potentially entrapping question—one that, if answered in a way that the Pharisees had anticipated, might bring upon Jesus the wrath of Herod Antipas (cf. Matthew 14:1-12; Mark 6:14-29) and/or some of His fellow Jews (e.g., the school of Hillel, or the school of Shammai). A third time the Pharisees sought to "entangle Him in His talk" (Matthew 22:15) as they asked, "Is it lawful to pay taxes to Caesar, or not?" (22:17). The jealous and hypocritical Pharisees were so relentless in their efforts to destroy the Lord's influence, that on one occasion they even accused Jesus' disciples of breaking the law as they "went through the grainfields on the Sabbath...were hungry, and began to pluck heads of grain and to eat" (Matthew 12:1ff.). [NOTE: "Their knowledge of so trifling an incident shows how minutely they observed all his deeds" (Coffman, 1984, p. 165). The micro-

scopic scrutiny under which Jesus lived, likely was even more
relentless than what some "stars" experience today. In one
sense, the Pharisees could be considered the "paparazzi" of
Jesus' day.] Allegedly, what the disciples were doing on this
particular Sabbath was considered "work," which the Law of
Moses forbade (Matthew 12:2; cf. Exodus 20:9-10; 34:21).

Jesus responded to the criticism of the Pharisees by giving
the truth of the matter, and at the same time revealing the
Pharisees' hypocrisy. As was somewhat customary for Jesus
when being tested by His enemies (cf. Matthew 12:11-12; 15:
3; 21:24-25; etc.), He responded to the Pharisees' accusation
with two questions. First, He asked: "Have you not read what
David did when he was hungry, he and those who were with
him: how he entered the house of God and ate the showbread
which was not lawful for him to eat, nor for those who were
with him, but only for the priests?" (12:3-4). Jesus reminded
the Pharisees of an event in the life of David (recorded in 1
Samuel 21:1ff.), where he and others, while fleeing from king
Saul, ate of the showbread, which divine law restricted to the
priests (Leviticus 24:5-9). Some commentators have unjusti-
fiably concluded that Jesus was implying innocence on the
part of David (and that God's laws are subservient to human
needs–cf. Zerr, 1952, 5:41; Dummelow, 1937, p. 666), and
thus He was defending His disciples "lawless" actions with
the same reasoning. Actually, however, just the opposite is
true. Jesus explicitly stated that what David did was wrong
("not lawful"–12:4), and that what His disciples did was right–
they were "guiltless" (12:7). Furthermore, as J.W. McGarvey
observed: "If Christians may violate law when its observance
would involve hardship or suffering, then there is an end to
suffering for the name of Christ, and an end even of self-de-
nial" (1875, p. 104). The disciples were not permitted by Jesus
to break the law on this occasion (or any other) just because it
was inconvenient (cf. Matthew 5:17-19). The Pharisees simply were wrong in their accusations. The only "law" Jesus'

disciples broke was the pharisaical interpretation of the law
(which seems to have been more sacred to the Pharisees than
the law itself). In response to such hyper-legalism, Burton
Coffman forcefully stated:

> In the Pharisees' view, the disciples were guilty of
> threshing wheat! **Such pedantry, nit-picking, and
> magnification of trifles would also have made
> them guilty of irrigating land, if they had chanced
> to knock off a few drops of dew while passing
> through the fields!** The Pharisees were out to "get"
> Jesus; and any charge was better than none (1984, p.
> 165, emp. added).

Jesus used the instruction of 1 Samuel 21 to cause the Pharisees to recognize their insincerity, and to justify His disciples. David, a man about whom the Jews ever boasted, blatantly violated God's law by eating the showbread, and yet
the Pharisees justified him. On the other hand, Jesus' disciples merely plucked some grain on the Sabbath while walking through a field—an act that the law did not forbid—yet the
Pharisees condemned them. Had the Pharisees not approved
of David's conduct, they could have responded by saying,
"You judge yourself. You're all sinners." Their reaction to Jesus' question—silence—was that of hypocrites who had been
exposed.

Jesus then asked a second question, saying, "Have you not
read in the law that on the Sabbath the priests in the temple
profane the Sabbath, and are blameless?" (Matthew 12:5).
Here, Jesus wanted the Pharisees to acknowledge that even
the law itself condoned **some** work on the Sabbath day. Although the Pharisees acted as if **all** work was banned on this
day, it was actually the busiest day of the week for priests.

> They baked and changed the showbread; they per-
> formed sabbatical sacrifices (Num. xxviii. 9), and
> two lambs were killed on the sabbath in addition to

the daily sacrifice. This involved the killing, skin-
ning, and cleaning of the animals, and the building
of the fire to consume the sacrifice. They also trimmed
the gold lamps, burned incense, and performed various other duties (McGarvey, n.d., pp. 211-212).

One of those "other duties" would have been to circumcise young baby boys when the child's eighth day fell on a
Sabbath (Leviticus 12:3; John 7:22-23). The purpose of Jesus
citing these "profane" priestly works was to prove that the
Sabbath prohibition was not unconditional. [NOTE: Jesus
used the term "profane," not because there was a real dese-
cration of the temple by the priests as they worked, but "to
express what was true according to the mistaken notions of
the Pharisees as to manual works performed on the Sabbath"
(Bullinger, 1898, p. 676).] The truth is, the Sabbath law "did
not forbid work absolutely, but labor for worldly gain. Activity in the work of God was both allowed and commanded"
(McGarvey, n.d., p. 212). Coffman thus concluded: "Just as
the priests served the temple on the Sabbath day and were
guiltless, his [Jesus'–EL] disciples might also serve Christ, the
Greater Temple, without incurring guilt" (p. 167). Just as the
priests who served God in the temple on the Sabbath were
totally within the law, so likewise were Jesus' disciples as they
served the "Lord of the Sabbath" (Matthew 12:8), Whose ho-
liness was greater than that of the temple (12:6).

WAS JESUS IGNORANT OF
THE OLD TESTAMENT?
John 3:13; 2 Kings 2:11; Genesis 5:24

When Jesus spoke to Nicodemus regarding the need to be
"born again" (John 3:1-8), He also sought to impress upon
the mind of this ruler of the Jews that His words were from
above. Jesus spoke of spiritual things that no man knew (Matthew 13:35; cf. 7:28-29; Luke 2:47). One of the reasons Jesus

gave for being able to expound on such spiritual truths is found in John 3:13. Here, the apostle John recorded that Jesus said to Nicodemus, "No one has ascended to heaven but He who came down from heaven, that is, the Son of Man" (John 3: 13). According to the skeptic, this statement by Jesus is severely flawed. Since the Old Testament reveals that Elijah escaped physical death and "went up by a whirlwind **into heaven**" (2 Kings 2:11; cf. Genesis 5:24; Hebrews 11:5), allegedly Jesus could not truthfully tell Nicodemus, "No one has ascended to heaven." Is the skeptic right?

For Jesus' statement to contradict what the Bible says about Elijah, one first must presuppose that Jesus was referring to the exact same place to which Elijah ascended. For a contradiction to exist between two Bible passages, one must prove that the one doing the speaking (or writing) is referring to the same person, place, or thing (see Jevons, 1928, p. 118). Can the skeptic be certain that the "heaven" to which Jesus referred, is the same one into which the body of Elijah ascended? The words "heaven" or "heavens" appear in our English Bibles about 700 times. And yet, in many of the passages where "heaven(s)" is found, the inspired writers were not discussing the spiritual heaven with which we most often associate the word. For example, in Genesis 1 and 2, the Hebrew word for heaven appears 15 times in 14 verses. Yet in every instance, the word is referring to something besides the spiritual heaven where God dwells. The word "heaven(s)" (Hebrew *shamayim*, Greek *ouranos*) is used by Bible writers in three different ways. It is used to refer to the atmospheric heavens in which the airplanes fly, the birds soar, and the clouds gather (Genesis 1: 20; Jeremiah 4:25; Matthew 6:26, ASV). "Heaven(s)" also is used in the Bible when referring to the firmament where we find the Sun, Moon, and stars–the sidereal heavens, or outer space (Genesis 1:14-15; Psalm 19:4,6; Isaiah 13:10). The third "heaven" frequently mentioned in Scripture is the spiritual heaven in which Jehovah dwells (Psalm 2:4; Hebrews 9:24), and where, one day, the faithful will live forevermore (Revelation 21:18-23; John 14:1-3). The context of John 3 clearly indicates that Jesus is referring to the spiritual heavens wherein God dwells (cf. John 3:27). The passage in 2 Kings 2:11, however, is not as clear. The writer of 2 Kings easily could have meant that the body of Elijah miraculously ascended up high into the air, never to be seen by anyone on Earth again. Nowhere does the text indicate that he left Earth at that moment to dwell in God's presence. He definitely went somewhere, but we have no evidence that he was transferred to the actual throne room of God Almighty.

The Bible indicates that when God's faithful servants leave this Earth, their spirits are taken to dwell in a place referred to as paradise (or "the bosom of Abraham"–Luke 16:19-31). Recall when Jesus was fastened to the cross, and told the penitent thief, "Today, you will be with Me in Paradise" (Luke 23: 43). The word paradise is of Persian derivation, and means a "garden" or "park." Where was it that Jesus and the thief went? Neither of them went to heaven to be with God the Father on that very day, for in John 20:17 after His resurrection, Jesus reassured Mary that **He had not yet ascended to the Father**. So where did Jesus and the thief go after dying on the cross? Peter gave the answer to that question in his sermon in Acts 2 when he quoted Psalm 16. Acts 2:27 states that God would not abandon Christ's soul in **hades**, nor allow Christ to undergo decay. So while Christ's body was placed in a tomb for three days, Christ's spirit went to hades. [NOTE: The word hades occurs ten times in the New Testament, and always refers to the unseen realm of the dead–the receptacle of disembodied spirits where all people who die await the Lord's return and judgment. One part of hades, where Jesus and the thief went, is known as paradise. For additional reading on the subject of hades, see Thompson, 2001, pp. 69ff.] Peter argued that David, who penned Psalm 16, was not referring to himself, since David's body was still in the tomb (Acts 2:29), and his spirit was still in the hadean realm (Acts 2:34). Acts 2 indicates that a faithful servant of God does not go directly to

be with God the Father when he dies; rather, he goes to a
holding place in hades known as paradise–the same place
where Abraham went after he died (Luke 16:22ff.), and the
same place where the spirit of Elijah went after he was caught
up from the Earth. In short, the Bible does not teach that Elijah left Earth to begin immediately dwelling in the presence
of the Father (where Jesus was before His incarnation–John
1:1). Thus, technically he did not ascend to the "place" whence
Jesus came.

For the sake of argument, consider for a moment that the
skeptic is right, and that Elijah's spirit did not go to paradise,
but was taken to dwell in the very presence of God. Could Jesus still have made the statement He did, and yet not be inaccurate? I believe so. Notice again the response to Nicodemus'
question, "How can these things be?" Jesus said: "If I have
told you earthly things and you do not believe, how will you
believe if I tell you heavenly things? **No one has ascended
to heaven** but He who came down from heaven, that is, the
Son of Man" (John 3:12-13, emp. added). It may be that Jesus
meant nothing more than that no one has ever gone up to
heaven "by his own act" or "on his own terms" (see Bullinger,
1898, pp. 281-282). Elijah and Enoch had been **taken** by God,
which is different than freely ascending up into heaven with
one's own ability. Furthermore, Jesus' words, "No one has ascended to heaven," also could have meant that no one has
ever gone up into heaven to then return and speak firsthand
about what he saw, and to spread the same saving message
that Jesus preached. Jesus was emphasizing to Nicodemus
how no one on Earth at that time was revealing such spiritual
truths as Christ was, because no one ever had ascended to
heaven only to return and talk about what he had seen and
learned. Such seems to have been the main point Jesus was
making in John 3:13. No one on Earth had seen what Jesus
had seen, and thus could not teach what He taught.

Truly, the skeptic's accusation that Jesus either lied or was mistaken regarding his comment to Nicodemus about no one having ascended to heaven is unsubstantiated. Perhaps the word heaven used in 2 Kings 2:11 was not meant to convey the idea of the spiritual heavens in which God dwells. Or, considering the Bible's teaching on departed spirits of the righteous being in a holding place known as paradise, and not in the actual presence of Almighty God, Jesus could have meant that no person has ever ascended to the throne room of God from which He came. Furthermore, it also is interesting to note that Nicodemus, being "a man of the Pharisees" (John 3:1), and thus one who would have been very well acquainted with the details of the Old Testament, did not respond to Jesus by saying, "Wait a minute, Rabbi. What about Elijah and Enoch? Isn't it written in the law and prophets that they ascended to heaven?" Surely, had Jesus contradicted something in the law and the prophets, it would have been brought to His attention, especially by a Pharisee. Yet, the apostle John never records such a statement.

Admittedly, at first glance, it might appear as if the statements, "Elijah went up by a whirlwind into heaven" (2 Kings 2:11), and, "No man has ascended to heaven" (John 3:13), are contradictory. However, when a person considers all of the possible solutions to the alleged problem, he must admit that such a conclusion is unjustified.

DID CHRIST DENY
MORAL PERFECTION?
Mark 10:18

Near the end of Jesus' earthly ministry, a wealthy young ruler (whose name remains anonymous) came running to Jesus with an urgent question. When he finally reached Him, the young man humbly knelt before the Christ and asked, "Good Teacher, what shall I do that I may inherit eternal life?"

(Mark 10:17). Before Jesus answered the gentleman's question, He first responded by saying, "Why do you call Me good? No one is good but One, that is, God" (Mark 10:18). Jesus then proceeded to answer the rich man's question by instructing him to keep the commandments of God.

What did Jesus mean when he stated that "no one is good but One, that is, God"? Was the Lord's question intended to teach that no one else but God ought to be called "good"? Was His question ("Why do you call me good?") asked because He did not believe He was good in the sense of God being good? Skeptics charge that Jesus was denying moral perfection–that He was not really God in the flesh like so many had claimed (cf. Matthew 16:16; John 20:28; etc.). What is the truth of the matter?

First of all, Jesus was not teaching that we can never describe others by using the adjective "good." If so, then this contradicts not only other statements by Jesus, but also the rest of Scripture. The psalmist stated that the man who "deals graciously and lends" is "a good man" (Psalm 112:5). The wise man said that one who "leaves an inheritance to his children's children" is "a good man" (Proverbs 13:22). In his history of the early church, Luke recorded that "Barnabas was a good man" (Acts 11:24). Even Jesus stated previous to His encounter with the rich young ruler that "a good man out of the good treasure of his heart, brings forth good things" (Matthew 12:35). Thus, when Jesus spoke to the wealthy ruler He was not using "good" in the sense of a **man** being "good." Rather, He was using it in the sense of **God** being "**supremely good**." The kind of goodness to which He was referring belonged only to God.

We understand that Jesus did **not** mean that we must expunge the word "good" from all conversations unless we are describing God. But was Christ implying that He was not God or that He was not morally perfect? No. Jesus indicated on several other occasions that He was deity (cf. Mark 14:62;

John 9:36-38; 10:10; etc.), and so His statements recorded in
Mark 10:17-22 (as well as Matthew 19:16-22 and Luke 18:18-
23) certainly were not meant to discredit His Godhood. Furthermore, the Bible reveals that Jesus never sinned—i.e., He
was morally perfect. He "was in all points tempted as we are,
yet without sin" (Hebrews 4:15). Jesus "committed no sin,
nor was deceit found in His mouth" (1 Peter 2:22). In His
conversation with the rich ruler, Jesus did not intend to deny
divinity, but instead was actually asserting that He was God
(and thus morally perfect). Jesus simply wanted this young
man to appreciate the significance of the title he had employed,
and to realize to Whom he was speaking. In short, Christ's
words could be paraphrased thusly: "Do you know the meaning of this word you apply to me and which you use so freely?
There is none good save God; if you apply that term to me,
and you understand what you mean, you affirm that I am
God" (Foster, 1971, p. 1022.).

Yes, truly Jesus is the Son of God. He claimed it (John 10:
30). His works testified to it (John 20:30-31). His friends confessed it (John 20:28). And many of His enemies eventually
admitted it (Matthew 27:4,54; Acts 6:7).

WAS JESUS A HYPOCRITE?
Matthew 5:22; 23:16-17

A man who instructs a person to refrain from doing something he deems inappropriate, but then proceeds to do the
very thing he forbade the other person to do, is considered a
hypocrite. A preacher who teaches about the sinfulness of
drunkenness (cf. Galatians 5:21), but then is seen a short while
later stumbling down the street, intoxicated with alcohol, could
be accused of being guilty of hypocrisy. Some have accused
Jesus of such insincere teaching. Allegedly, in the very sermon in which He condemned the Pharisees for their unrighteousness (Matthew 5:20), Jesus revealed His own sinfulness
by way of condemning those who used a word He sometimes

uttered. Based upon His forbiddance of the use of the word "fool" in Matthew 5:22, and His use of this word elsewhere, skeptics have asserted that Jesus (Who the Bible claims "committed no sin, nor was deceit found in His mouth"–1 Peter 2: 22; cf. 2 Corinthians 5:21), was guilty of hypocrisy (see Morgan, 2003b; Wells, 2001). In Matthew 5:21-22, Jesus stated:

> You have heard that it was said to those of old, "You shall not murder, and whoever murders will be in danger of the judgment." But I say to you that whoever is angry with his brother without a cause shall be in danger of the judgment. And whoever says to his brother, "Raca!" shall be in danger of the council. But **whoever says, "You fool!" shall be in danger of hell fire** (Matthew 5:21-22, emp. added).

Whereas in this passage Jesus warned against the use of the word "fool," in other passages Jesus openly used this term to describe various people. Near the end of the Sermon on the Mount, Jesus likened the person who heard His teachings, but did not follow them, to **"a foolish man** who built his house on the sand" (Matthew 7:26). When teaching about the need to be prepared for His second coming, Jesus compared those who were not ready for His return to **five foolish virgins** (Matthew 25:1-12). Then, while Jesus was condemning the Pharisees for their inconsistency in matters of religion, He stated: "Woe to you, blind guides, who say, 'Whoever swears by the temple, it is nothing; but whoever swears by the gold of the temple, he is obliged to perform it.' **Fools and blind!** For which is greater, the gold or the temple that sanctifies the gold?" (Matthew 23:16-17; cf. 23:18-19). The question that some ask in response to these alleged hypocritical statements is, "How could Jesus condemn the use of the word 'fool' in Matthew 5:22, but then proceed to use this word Himself on other occasions?"

First, for Jesus' statement in Matthew 5:22 to contradict His actions recorded in other passages, the skeptic must prove that the term "fool," as used in 5:22, is the same word used elsewhere. The Greek word "Raca," used earlier in Matthew 5:22, is a transliteration of the Aramaic term whose precise meaning is disputed. [Most likely, it means "an empty one who acts as a numskull" (Lenski, 1961a, p. 219; cf. also Robertson, 1930, p. 44).] The exact meaning of the term "fool" (Greek *mōre*) in this context also is debated. "Most scholars take it, as the ancient Syrian versions did, to mean **you fool**" (Bauer, et al., 1957, p. 533, emp. in orig.). Although some assume that *mōre* is the vocative of the Greek *moros*, in all likelihood,

> just as "Raca" is a non-Greek word, so is the word *mōre* that Jesus used here. If so, then it is a word which to a Jewish ear meant "rebel (against God)" or "apostate"; it was the word which Moses in exasperation used to the disaffected Israelites in the wilderness of Zin… (Numbers 20:10). For these rash words, uttered under intense provocation, Moses was excluded from the Promised Land (Kaiser, et al., 1996, p. 359).

Thus, it is quite possible that *mōre* (translated "[Y]ou fool" in Matthew 5:22) is not the normal Greek *moros* (fool) that Jesus applied to the Pharisees on other occasions (Matthew 23:17,19), but represents the Hebrew *moreh* (cf. Numbers 20:10). [For this reason, translators of the American Standard Version added a marginal note to this word in Matthew 5:22: "Or, *Moreh*, a Hebrew expression of condemnation."] Obviously, if two different words are under consideration, Jesus logically could not be considered a hypocrite.

Second, it must be remembered that Jesus' comments in Matthew 5:22 were made within a context where He was condemning unrighteous anger (5:21-26). Whereas the Pharisees condemned murder, but overlooked the evil emotions and attitudes that sometimes led to the shedding of innocent blood, Jesus condemned both the actions and the thoughts. Instead

of dealing with only "peripheral" problems, Jesus went to the
heart of the matter. As someone Who "knew what was in man"
(John 2:25), Jesus was more than qualified to pronounce judgment upon the hypocritical Pharisees (cf. John 12:48). Like
the unrighteousness that characterized the Pharisees' charitable deeds (Matthew 6:1-4), prayers (6:5-15), fasting (6:16-18),
and judgments (7:1-5), Jesus also condemned their unrighteous anger. [NOTE: Jesus did not condemn **all** anger (cf. Ephesians 4:26; John 2:13-17), only **unrighteous** anger.] It was in
this context that Jesus warned against the use of the word "fool."
Jesus was not prohibiting a person from calling people "fools"
if it was done in an appropriate manner (cf. Psalm 14:1), but
He was forbidding it when done in the spirit of malicious con-
tempt. He "warned against using the word fool as a form of
abuse" that indicated "hatred in one's heart toward others"
("Fool," 1986; cf. Matthew 5:43-48). As in many other situations, it seems that the attitude, rather than actual words, is
the focus of the prohibition.

While this verse, when taken in its context, is seen to be
consistent with Jesus' words and actions recorded elsewhere
in the gospel accounts, His prohibition regarding the **manner** of a word's usage should not be overlooked in the apologist's effort to defend biblical inerrancy. We may call an atheist a "fool" for not acknowledging God's existence (Psalm 14:
1), but to do so in a hateful, malicious manner is sinful. Remember, the Christian is called to "give a defense to everyone" in a spirit of "meekness and fear" (1 Peter 3:15).

WHAT'S SO IMPORTANT ABOUT
JESUS' RESURRECTION?
1 Corinthians 15:12-19

After the widow's son of Zarephath died, Elijah prayed to
God, "and the soul of the child came back to him, and he re-
vived" (1 Kings 17:22). A few years later, the prophet Elisha

raised the dead son of a Shunammite (2 Kings 4:32-35). Then, after Elisha's death, a dead man, in the process of being buried in the tomb of Elisha, was restored to life after touching Elisha's bones (2 Kings 13:20-21). When Jesus was on Earth, He raised the daughter of Jairus from the dead (Mark 8:21-24,35-43), as well as the widow of Nain's son (Luke 7:11-16), and Lazarus, whose body had been buried for four days (John 11:1-45). After Jesus' death and resurrection, Matthew recorded how "the graves were opened; and many bodies of the saints who had fallen asleep were raised; and coming out of the graves after His resurrection, they went into the holy city and appeared to many" (27:52-53). Then later, during the early years of the church, Peter raised Tabitha from the dead (Acts 9:36-43), while Paul raised the young man Eutychus, who had died after falling out of a three-story window (Acts 20:7-12). All of these people died, and later rose to live again. Although some of the individuals arose very shortly after death, Lazarus and (most likely) the saints who were raised after the resurrection of Jesus, were entombed longer than was Jesus. In view of all of these resurrections, some have asked, "What is so important about Jesus' resurrection?" If others in the past have died to live again, what makes His resurrection so special? Why is the resurrection of Jesus more significant than any other?

First, similar to how the miracles of Jesus were performed in order to set Him apart as the Son of God and the promised Messiah, even though all others who worked miracles during Bible times were not God in the flesh, the resurrection of Jesus is more significant than any other resurrection simply because the inspired apostles and prophets said that it was. Many people throughout the Bible worked miracles in order to confirm their divine message (cf. Mark 16:20; Hebrews 2:1-4), but only Jesus did them as proof of His divine **nature**. Once, during the Feast of Dedication in Jerusalem, a group of

Jews surrounded Jesus and asked, "If You are the Christ, tell us plainly" (John 10:24)? Jesus responded to them saying, "I told you, and you do not believe. The works that I do in My Father's name, they bear witness of Me.... I and My Father are one" (John 10:25,30). These Jews understood that Jesus claimed to be the Son of God in the flesh (cf. 10:33,36), and Jesus wanted them to understand that this truth could be known as a result of the miracles that He worked, which testified of His deity (cf. John 20:30-31). Why? **Because He said they did** (10:25,35-38; cf. John 5:36). The miracles that Jesus performed bore witness of the fact that He was from the Father (John 5:36), **because He said He was from the Father**. A miracle in and of itself did not mean the person who worked it was deity. Moses, Elijah, Elisha, Peter, Paul, and a host of others worked miracles, with some even raising people from the dead, but not for the purpose of proving they were God in the flesh. The apostles and prophets of the New Testament worked miracles to confirm their message that Jesus was the Son of God, not to prove that they were God (cf. Acts 14:8-18). Jesus, on the other hand, performed miracles to bear witness that He was the Son of God, just as He claimed to be (cf. John 9:35-38).

Likewise, one reason that Jesus' miraculous resurrection is more significant than the resurrections of Lazarus, Tabitha, Eutychus, or anyone else who was raised from the dead, is simply because the inspired apostles and prophets in the early church said that it was more important. Like the miracles He worked during His earthly ministry that testified of His deity, His resurrection also bore witness of His divine nature. There is no record of anyone alleging that Lazarus was God's Son based upon his resurrection, nor did the early church claim divinity for Eutychus or Tabitha because they died and came back to life. None of the above-mentioned individuals who were resurrected ever claimed that their resurrection was proof of deity, nor did any inspired prophet or apostle. On the other

hand, Jesus was "declared to be the Son of God with power...
by the resurrection from the dead" (Romans 1:4). His resurrection was different because of Who He was–the Son of God.
Just as the miracles He worked during His earthly ministry
testified of His divine message, and thus also of His divine
nature, so did His resurrection.

Second, the significance of Jesus' resurrection is seen in
the fact that He was the first to rise from the dead **never to
die again**. Since no one who has risen from the dead is still
living on Earth, and since there is no evidence in the Bible
that God ever took someone who had risen from the dead
into heaven without dying again, it is reasonable to conclude
that all who have ever arisen from the dead, died in later years.
Jesus, however, "having been raised from the dead, dies no
more. Death no longer has dominion over Him" (Romans 6:
9). Jesus said of Himself: "I am the First and the Last. I am He
who lives, and was dead, and behold, I am alive forevermore"
(Revelation 1:17-18). All others who previously were raised
at one time, died again, and are among those who "sleep"
and continue to wait for the bodily resurrection. Only Jesus
has truly conquered death. Only His bodily resurrection was
followed by eternal life, rather than another physical death.
Although it has been argued by skeptics that "it's the Resurrection, per se, that matters, not the fact that Jesus never died
again" (see McKinsey, 1983a, p. 1), Paul actually linked the
two together, saying, God "raised Him from the dead, **no
more to return to corruption**" (Acts 13:34, emp. added).
Furthermore, the writer of Hebrews argued for a better life
through Jesus on the basis of His termination of death. One
reason for the inadequacy of the old priesthood was because
"they were prevented by death." Jesus, however, because He
rose never to die again, "continues forever" in "an unchangeable priesthood," and lives to make intercession for His people (Hebrews 7:23-25).

A third reason why Jesus' resurrection stands out above all
others is because it alone was foretold in the Old Testament.
In his sermon on the Day of Pentecost, Peter affirmed that
God had raised Jesus from the dead because it was not possible for the grave to hold Him. As proof, he quoted Psalm 16:
8-11 in the following words:

> I foresaw the Lord always before my face, for He is at
> my right hand, that I may not be shaken. Therefore
> my heart rejoiced, and my tongue was glad; more-
> over my flesh also will rest in hope. For You will not
> leave my soul in Hades, nor will You allow Your Holy
> One to see corruption. You have made known to me
> the ways of life; You will make me full of joy in Your
> presence (Acts 2:25-28).

Peter then explained this quote from Psalms by saying:

> Men and brethren, let me speak freely to you of the
> patriarch David, that he is both dead and buried, and
> his tomb is with us to this day. Therefore, being a
> prophet, and knowing that God had sworn with an
> oath to him that of the fruit of his body, according to
> the flesh, He would raise up the Christ to sit on his
> throne, he, foreseeing this, spoke concerning the res-
> urrection of the Christ, that His soul was not left in
> Hades, nor did His flesh see corruption. This Jesus
> God has raised up, of which we are all witnesses (Acts
> 2:29-32).

The apostle Paul also believed that the psalmist bore witness to Christ, and spoke of His resurrection. In his address
at Antioch of Pisidia, he said:

> And we declare to you glad tidings—that promise
> which was made to the fathers. God has fulfilled this
> for us their children, in that He has raised up Jesus.
> As it is also written in the second Psalm: "You are
> My Son, today I have begotten You." And that He

raised Him from the dead, no more to return to corruption, He has spoken thus: "I will give you the sure mercies of David." Therefore He also says in another Psalm: "You will not allow Your Holy One to see corruption." For David, after he had served his own generation by the will of God, fell asleep, was buried with his fathers, and saw corruption; but He whom God raised up saw no corruption. Therefore let it be known to you, brethren, that through this Man is preached to you the forgiveness of sins; and by Him everyone who believes is justified from all things from which you could not be justified by the law of Moses (Acts 13:32-39).

Where is the prophecy for the resurrection of Jairus' daughter? When did the prophets ever foretell of Eutychus or Tabitha's resurrection? Such instances are not found within Scripture. No resurrected person other than Jesus had his or her resurrection foretold by an Old Testament prophet. This certainly makes Jesus' resurrection unique.

Fourth, the significance of Jesus' resurrection is seen in the fact that His resurrection was preceded by numerous instances in which He prophesied that He would defeat death, even foretelling the exact day on which it would occur. Jesus told some scribes and Pharisees on one occasion, "For as Jonah was three days and three nights in the belly of the great fish, **so will the Son of Man be three days and three nights in the heart of the earth**" (Matthew 12:40, emp. added). Matthew, Mark, and Luke all recorded how Jesus "began to show to His disciples that He must go to Jerusalem, and suffer many things from the elders and chief priests and scribes, and be killed, and **be raised the third day**" (Matthew 16:21, emp. added; cf. Mark 8:31-32; Luke 9:22). While Jesus and His disciples were in Galilee, Jesus reminded them, saying, "The Son of Man is about to be betrayed into the hands of men, and they will kill Him, and **the third day He will be raised** up" (Matthew 17:22-23, emp. added). Just before His triumphal entry into Jerusalem, Jesus again reminded His disciples, saying, "Behold, we are going up to Jerusalem, and the Son of Man will be betrayed to the chief priests and to the scribes; and they will condemn Him to death, and deliver Him to the Gentiles to mock and to scourge and to crucify. **And the third day He will rise again**" (Matthew 20:18-19, emp. added). Jesus' prophecies concerning His resurrection and the specific day on which it would occur were so widely known that, after Jesus' death, His enemies requested that Pilate place a guard at the tomb, saying, "Sir, we remember, while He was still alive, how that deceiver said, 'After three days I will rise.' Therefore command that the tomb be made secure **until the third day**..." (Matthew 27:63-64, emp. added). They knew exactly what Jesus had said He would do, and they did everything in their power to stop it.

Where are the prophecies from the widow's son of Zarephath? Had he prophesied of his resurrection prior to his death? Or what about the son of the Shunammite woman whom Elisha raised from the dead? Where are his personal prophecies? Truly, no one mentioned in the Bible who rose from the dead prophesied about his or her resurrection beforehand, other than Jesus. And certainly no one ever prophesied about the exact day on which he or she would arise from the dead, save Jesus. This prior knowledge and prophecy makes His resurrection a significant event. He overcame death, just as He predicted. He did **exactly** what he said He was going to do, on the **exact** day He said He was going to do it.

Finally, the uniqueness of Jesus' resurrection is seen in the fact that He is the only resurrected person ever to have lived and died without having committed one sin during His lifetime. He was "pure" and "righteous" (1 John 3:3; 2:1), "Who committed no sin, nor was deceit found in His mouth" (1 Peter 2:22). He was "a lamb without blemish and without spot"

(1 Peter 1:19), "Who knew no sin" (2 Corinthians 5:21). No one else who has risen from the dead ever lived a perfect life, and then died prior to his or her resurrection for the purpose of taking away the sins of the world (cf. John 1:29). Because Jesus lived a sinless life, died, and then overcame death in His resurrection, He alone has the honor of being called "the Lamb of God" and the "great High Priest" (Hebrews 4:14). "Christ was offered once to bear the sins of many," and because of His resurrection "those who eagerly wait for Him He will appear a second time, apart from sin, for salvation" (Hebrews 9:28).

Whether or not Eutychus, Tabitha, Lazarus, etc., rose from the grave, our relationship with God is not affected. Without Jesus' resurrection, however, there would be no "Prince and Savior, to give repentance to Israel and forgiveness of sins" (Acts 5:31). Without Jesus' resurrection, He would not be able to make intercession for us (Hebrews 7:25). Without Jesus' resurrection, we would have no assurance of His coming and subsequent judgment (Acts 17:31).

Most certainly, Jesus' resurrection is significant–more so than any other resurrection ever to have taken place. Only Jesus' resurrection was verbalized by inspired men as proof of His deity. Only Jesus rose never to die again. Only Jesus' resurrection was prophesied in the Old Testament. Only Jesus prophesied of the precise day in which He would arise from the grave, and then fulfilled that prediction. Only Jesus' resurrection was preceded by a perfect life–a life lived, given up, and restored in the resurrection for the purpose of becoming man's Prince, Savior, and Mediator.

Chapter 4

ALLEGED CONTRADICTIONS AND THE FLOOD

Name a Bible subject that has been scoffed at or ridiculed more than the account of Noah's Flood. Name a story that has been the brunt of more jokes, or has provided the unbeliever with more material with which to "poke fun" at the Bible, than Noah's ark. Likely it would be difficult to find any subject in our day and time that has received more derision, or been the subject of more mockery, than this story as recorded in Genesis 6-8.

The subject of the Great Flood, as presented in Genesis 6-8, is one of the most prominent stories in the Bible, with more attention given to it than even to Creation. Three of the first eleven chapters of Genesis are devoted to the record of the Flood, and there are numerous references to it within the pages of the New Testament. Yet the account of Noah, his ark, and the Great Flood has been ridiculed often by unbelievers. Even some religionists have joined in the fracas, suggesting that the Flood was little more than a local inundation, or that the record of the Flood is completely mythological in nature.

There can be no doubt that the Genesis record of a global, universal Flood has become the target of sustained, concentrated attacks–the goal of which is to discredit, in its entirety, that account. Unbelievers of all stripes delight in attempting to undermine the faith of the believer by showing the "ridiculous nature" of the story as recorded in the book of Genesis.

Before proceeding to answer some of the alleged problems with the Flood and Noah's involvement in it, let us first note that we are speaking of three chapters of the Bible that entail the overruling power of an Almighty God in many miraculous events. One also must keep in mind that we are dependent upon inspiration for exactly what **did** happen in the Flood. Critics of the Flood account have charged that, "If one wishes to retain a universal flood, it must be understood that a series of stupendous miracles is required. Further, one cannot beg off with pious statements that God can do anything" (Ramm, 1954, p. 165). Although a skeptic might consider any mention of the miraculous in connection with the Flood as a lame defense by a Bible believer, the simple truth is that God made it clear in Genesis 6-8 that He was in control–from the bringing of the animals to Noah (Genesis 6:19-20) to the shutting of the door of the ark (Genesis 7:16). It was a miraculous situation from beginning to end. And though skeptics would disagree, to deny the operation of supernatural forces in the launching and control of the Flood is tantamount to denying inspiration. "The simple fact of the matter is that one cannot have any kind of a Genesis Flood without acknowledging the presence of supernatural powers" (Whitcomb and Morris, 1961, p. 76).

The Genesis account makes it clear that God miraculously superintended the entire Flood process, and the Bible-believer who accepts verbal, plenary inspiration will not be the least bit embarrassed or ashamed to admit it. John Whitcomb, in his classic work, *The World That Perished*, listed at least six areas where supernaturalism was required in the Genesis Flood. Those areas are: (1) divinely revealed design of the ark; (2) gathering and care of the animals; (3) uplifting of oceanic waters from beneath; (4) release of waters from above; (5) formation of our present ocean basins; and (6) formation of our present continents and mountain ranges (1973, p. 19). There may be other areas where supernaturalism is present as well. One thing is for certain: **all** areas with which we have to deal in the account of the Flood cannot be accounted for by purely natural processes. However, we do not have to appeal to an "endless supplying of miracles to make a universal flood feasible" (Ramm, p. 167).

ADEQUATE ARK
OR DEFICIENT DINGHY?

According to Bible skeptics and liberal theologians, Noah's ark was not big enough or strong enough to accomplish its cargo-laden, year-long journey. J.H. Marks summarized such a position when he wrote: "The ark could never have weathered a storm such as Genesis describes, nor could it possibly have contained a pair of every existing species of animal and creeping thing, to say nothing of providing proper subsistence conditions for such a menagerie" (1962, 2:283). The truth is, the ark was more than adequate to accomplish its tasks.

God instructed Noah to make "the length of the ark three hundred cubits, the breadth of it fifty cubits, and the height of it thirty cubits" (Genesis 6:15). Using the **most conservative** estimate available for the length of the cubit (17.5 inches), Noah's ark would have been at least 437.5 feet long, 72.92 feet wide, and 43.75 feet high. (Generally, when the cubit is considered as being 18 inches long, the ark's dimensions are calculated to be 450 feet long, 75 feet wide, and 45 feet high.) In its three decks (Genesis 6:16), it had a total area of approximately 95,700 square feet—the equivalent of slightly more than twenty standard basketball courts. Its total volume would have been about 1,396,000 cubic feet. The gross tonnage (a meas-urement of cubic space rather than weight, one ton being equivalent to 100 cubic feet of usable storage space) was about 13,960 tons (Whitcomb and Morris, 1961, p. 10). This immense area was equivalent to the area of over 520 standard railroad boxcars–more than enough to contain the animals and cargo required for the trip.

In their scholarly book on the Noahic Flood, John Whit-comb and Henry Morris investigated the number of animals that would have been on the ark (using the highest possible estimates, and taxonomic figures provided by evolutionists), and showed that the biblical account **can** fit known scientific facts regarding these matters (1961, pp. 65-69). Their book, *The Genesis Flood*, was published in 1961. Thirty-five years later, John Woodmorappe expanded on their original work, and produced what is likely the most exhaustive, well-re-searched feasibility study ever put into print dealing specifi-cally with the ark's construction and contents (1996). His data-based conclusions established beyond any doubt that the ark could do what it was designed to do. Since God was the Cre-ator of all the animals, does it not make sense that He would know precisely how much room was needed on that boat?

Some will argue, however, that Noah could not possibly have taken animals from every one of the 2,000,000 to 5,000,000 species of animals (note, of course, that the majority of these species are tiny insects). But it is here that we need to re-member that the Genesis word "kind" (Hebrew *min*) is not the same as the biologists' "species" of today. Noah did not have to take two or seven of every **species** of animal. He had to take two (or seven) of every **kind**. That is to say, he did not have to take two German Shepherds, two Chihuahuas, two coyotes, or two dingoes. He simply had to take two of the dog "kind," not species. [Dogs, dingoes, coyotes, foxes, and wolves all can interbreed, and thus, are the same kind.]

HOW MANY ANIMALS OF EACH KIND
DID NOAH TAKE INTO THE ARK?
Genesis 6:19; 7:2-3

Ask most children who are somewhat familiar with the biblical account of the Flood how many animals of each kind Noah took into the ark, and the answer you likely will hear is, "Two!" These Bible students are familiar with the instructions recorded in Genesis 6:19 that God gave to Noah: "And of every living thing of all flesh you shall bring **two of every sort into the ark**, to keep them alive with you; they shall be male and female" (Genesis 6:19, emp. added; cf. 7:15). It seems that fewer people, however, are aware that God also instructed Noah, saying, "You shall take with you **seven** each of every clean animal, a male and his female; two each of animals that are unclean, a male and his female; also **seven** each of birds of the air, male and female, to keep the species alive on the face of all the earth" (Genesis 7:2-3, emp. added). According to Bible critics, these verses are contradictory. "Are clean beasts to enter by 2's or by 7's?" asked skeptic Dennis McKinsey (1983c, p. 1).

To answer McKinsey's question, the **clean** beasts and birds entered the ark "by sevens" (KJV), while the unclean animals went into the ark by twos. There is no contradiction here. Genesis 6:19 indicates that Noah was to take "two of every sort into the ark." Then, four verses later, God **supplemented** this original instruction, informing Noah in a more detailed manner to take more of the clean animals. It was necessary for Noah to take additional clean animals because, upon his departure from the ark after the Flood, he "built an altar to the Lord, and took of every clean animal and of every clean bird, and offered burnt offerings on the alter" (Genesis 8:20). If Noah had taken only two clean animals from which to choose when sacrificing to God after departing the ark, then he would have driven the various kinds of clean beasts and birds into extinction by sacrificing one of each pair. Thus, after God told Noah to take two of every kind of animal into the ark, He then instructed him to take extras of the clean animals. Similar to how Genesis chapter 2 supplements the first chapter of Genesis by giving a more detailed account of the Creation, the first portion of Genesis 7 merely supplements the end of the preceding chapter, "containing several particulars of a minute description which were not embraced in the general directions first given to Noah" (Jamieson, et al., 1997).

One translation difficulty that should not trouble a person's faith, but one of which a person might want to be aware, revolves around the actual number of clean animals taken into the ark. Through the years, serious Bible students have wondered whether this number was seven, or fourteen (Genesis 7:2). The Hebrew phrase *shibb'ah shibb'ah* is translated somewhat vaguely in both the King James and American Standard Versions. [According to the King James Version, clean animals were taken into the ark "by sevens" (Genesis 7:2). The America Standard Version says that the clean animals were taken "seven and seven."] Newer translations are worded more clearly, but there is general disagreement among them. The New King James and New International Versions both agree that Noah took **seven** of each clean animal into the ark, whereas the Revised Standard Version, the New English Bible, and the English Standard Version all translate *shibb'ah shibb'ah* to mean "seven pairs" of clean animals. Although it may be that "there can be no certainty on this point" (Willis, 1984, p. 171), some have been more decisive on the matter, believing real purpose and reason to the interpretation that there were only seven of every clean kind on the ark, rather than seven pairs. It is suggested that when Noah left the ark and offered a sacrifice to God "of every clean animal" (Genesis 8:20), three pairs were left for domestication by man so that he would have food, clothing, and possibly more animals to sacrifice in the immediate future. The pattern, as Matthew Henry noted, could be following that of the working week and Sabbath day, in that "God gives us six for one in earthly things, as in the days of the week," while the seventh is for devotion to God (n.d., p. 61). Admittedly, however, no concrete conclusion can be made in this particular matter.

Still, another allegation is brought up concerning Genesis 7:2. According to the skeptic, "Clean and unclean animals were not delineated until the eleventh chapter of Leviticus. The Mosaic law arose 600 years after the Flood. There were no Jews, Israelites, or clean/unclean animals in Noah's time" (McKinsey, 1983c, p. 1). Thus, regardless of how one answers the question concerning the number of animals on the ark, this second allegation still lingers in the minds of skeptics. Supposedly, instructions regarding clean and unclean animals were not given until hundreds of years after the Flood (see Leviticus 11 and Deuteronomy 14).

What skeptics refuse to see is that just because Moses made laws concerning clean and unclean animals at a much later time than the Flood, does not mean that such rules concerning animals could not have existed prior to Moses—yes, even prior to the Flood. As commentator John Willis noted: "A law or a truth does not have to have its origin with a certain individual or religion to be a vital part of that religion or to be distinctive in that religion" (p. 170). Jesus, for example, was not the first person to teach that man needed to love God with all of his heart (cf. Deuteronomy 6:5), or that man must love his neighbor (cf. Leviticus 19:18), **and** his enemies (cf. Proverbs 25:21-22). Yet these teachings were central to Christ's message (cf. Matthew 5:43-48; 22:34-40). In Genesis 17, God told Abraham to circumcise baby boys. Yet Moses wrote in the book of Leviticus, years after Abraham lived, saying, "If a woman has conceived, and borne a male child, then she shall be unclean seven days; as in the days of her customary impurity she shall be unclean. And **on the eighth day the flesh of his foreskin shall be circumcised**" (12:2-3, emp. added).

I have never heard a person allege that Moses believed he was writing a new law here. On the contrary, he knew very well what was expected from God concerning the matter of circumcision, even before he included this sort of instruction as part of Mosaic Law (read Exodus 4:24-26).

For skeptics to allege that differentiation between clean and unclean animals did not exist before the time of Moses is totally unsubstantiated. Humans had been sacrificing animals since the fall of man (cf. Genesis 3:21; 4:4). That God had given laws concerning animal sacrifices since the time of Cain and Abel is evident from the fact that the second son of Adam was able to offer an animal sacrifice "by faith" (Hebrews 11: 4; Genesis 4:4). Since "faith comes by hearing, and hearing by the word of God" (Romans 10:17), Abel must have received revelation from God on how to offer acceptable animal sacrifices. Such revelation easily could have dealt with which sacrificial animals were acceptable ("clean"), and which were unacceptable ("not clean"). Furthermore, more than 400 hundred years before Moses gave the Israelites laws differentiating clean and unclean animals, God made a covenant with Abraham concerning the land that his descendants eventually would possess (Genesis 15). Part of the "sign" that Abraham was given at that time involved the killing of a heifer, a female goat, a ram, a turtledove, and a pigeon (Genesis 15:9). "It just so happens" that all of these animals were later considered clean under the Law of Moses (cf. Leviticus 1:2,10,14).

Without doubt, the distinction between clean and unclean animals existed long before the Law of Moses was given. Although this distinction did not include all of the details and applications given by Moses (since prior to the Flood the distinction seems only to have applied to the matter of animals suitable for sacrifice, not for consumption—cf. Genesis 9:2-3), animal sacrifice to God **was practiced** during the Patriarchal Age, and it is apparent that the faithful were able to distinguish between the clean and unclean. Noah certainly knew of the difference.

THE GATHERING, STORAGE, AND CARE OF THE ANIMALS

Objections of every kind have been raised regarding the Genesis record of the Flood, but perhaps none has been so loudly echoed as those relating to the gathering, storage, and care of the animals once they were placed into the ark.

First, the objection has been raised that it would be impossible for creatures from different regions of the world to leave their respective homes and meet Noah in the Mesopotamian Valley. The unique creatures of Australia, for example, certainly could not have traveled to the ark, since Australia is separated by an ocean. And how could the polar bear survive a journey from his native land to the sultry plains of Mesopotamia? The variety of climates, the difficult geography, and other various items would seemingly make such journeys impossible. Some have viewed these "impossible journeys" as militating against the accuracy of the Flood account. Whitcomb and Morris, in commenting on such arguments, observed:

> An equally serious fault in this type of reasoning is that it begs the question of the extent and effects of the Deluge. It assumes, for example, that climatic zones were exactly the same before the Flood as they are now, that animals inhabited the same areas of the world as they do now, and that the geography and topography of the earth continued unchanged. But on the assumptions of a universal Deluge, all these conditions would have been profoundly altered. Arctic and desert zones may never have existed before the Flood; nor the great intercontinental barriers of high mountain ranges, impenetrable jungles, and open seas (as between Australia and Southeast Asia, and between Siberia and Alaska). On this basis, it is quite probable that animals were more widely distributed than now, with representatives of each cre-

ated kind of land animal living in that part of the earth
where Noah was building the Ark (1961, pp. 64-65).
[For more discussion on the antediluvian world, see
Thompson, 1999b, pp. 24-29.]

Rehwinkel has suggested that during the probationary period, "migration of these animals which God had intended to
save might have extended over several generations of animals" (1951, p. 75). Thus, when the ark was ready for its occupants, the animals were already in the nearby geographical regions. Furthermore, Genesis 6:19-20 makes it clear
that God caused the animals to "come unto Noah." Noah
did not have to "go after" all the various animals; they came
to him. The same "power" that brought the animals to Adam
to be named (Genesis 2:19) also brought them to Noah to be
saved from the Flood.

After acknowledging the gathering of the animals into the
ark by God's intervention, how do we explain the care of the
animals once in the ark? How could eight people possibly
feed and care for all the different animals on the ark? Bernard Ramm, as one such critic, complained: "The problem
of feeding and caring for them would be enormous. The task
of carrying away manure and bringing food would completely
overtax the few people in the ark." He further suggested that
the problem of "special diets and special conditions needed
for the animals overthrows the idea of a universal flood" (1954,
p. 167).

Ramm, however, apparently has missed some critical factors. First, if the animals could have been "prompted by divine instinct" (to use Ramm's own words) to come to the ark,
could they not also be cared for, once in the ark, by He Who
was responsible for that "divine instinct"? Second, Dr. Ramm
also seems to have overlooked an important Bible message.
In Genesis 8:1, it is stated quite clearly that God "remembered"
Noah and all the animals in the ark. The Hebrew word *zakar*,

translated "remembered," suggests God's continued watchful care over all the occupants of the ark. In the Scriptures, God's "remembering" always implies His movement toward the object(s) of His memory (cf. Genesis 19:29; Exodus 2:24; Luke 1:54-55, et al.). In fact, the primary meaning of *zakar*, according to Hebrew usage, is "granting requests, protecting, delivering," when God is the subject and humans are the object (Brown, Driver, Briggs, 1901, p. 270). The point is this: **God was with Noah and his family**. Those eight souls had received what basically amounted to a personal invitation from the Creator and Sustainer of the Universe to join Him on a year-long trip inside the ark.

Noah and his family were not left "on their own" to tackle this giant task. God was "with them" and "remembered them." The **how** of this process is not specifically stated in the inspired text. John Whitcomb has suggested that possibly God supernaturally imposed a year-long "hibernation process" on the animals, thereby minimizing the necessity of a great deal of food and care.

> What Biblical evidence do we find to support this significant concept? **First**, we must assume that God supernaturally controlled the bodily functions of these animals to bring them to the Ark in the first place, overcoming all of their natural instincts during that period of time. All alternative possibilities have been shown to be hopelessly inadequate. **Second**, there could have been no multiplication of animals (not even the rabbits) during the year of the Flood, for the Ark was built just large enough to carry two of each, and the animals entered the Ark two by two and a year later went out of the Ark two by two. Note that it was not until **after** Noah brought the creatures out of the Ark that God commanded them to "breed abundantly in the earth, and be fruitful, and multiply upon the earth" (8:17).... In the entire mat-

ter of gathering the animals to the Ark and caring for
them during the year of the Flood, the Book of Genesis is **consistently supernatural** in its presenta-
tion (1973, p. 32, emp. in orig.).

While it is impossible to assert dogmatically exactly what
God did in regard to gathering and caring for the animals
prior to, and during, their journey, it is clear that, to use the
words of Robert Jamieson, "They must have been prompted
by an overruling Divine direction, as it is impossible, on any
other principles, to account for their going in **pairs**" (1948,
p. 95, emp. in orig.). There was some divine "overruling" in
the storage, feeding, and care of the animals, to be sure. How
much, the Bible does not say. However, as Rehwinkel has
observed:

> [I]f we are willing to accept the possibility of the mi-
> raculous, some such solution is at least conceivable.
> The Flood as a whole was a stupendous, miraculous
> interference with the laws governing the entire uni-
> verse; a temporary suspension of the laws governing
> the routine and habits of a select group of animals for
> one year is but an insignificant detail in comparison.
> The Biblical account of the Flood is so brief, and our
> knowledge of the world before the Flood, and partic-
> ularly of the ark, is so limited that here, as elsewhere,
> many questions must remain unanswered (1951, p.
> 76).

How the animals became so widely distributed over the
Earth, once they disembarked from the ark after the Flood, is
not explained in the Genesis account. Whitcomb and Morris
have made some very viable suggestions in *The Genesis Flood*
(1961, pp. 79-86). Migrations may well have taken place by
land bridges, by air, or even by direct supernatural intervention of God Himself. Other possibilities exist. For example,
perhaps after the Flood those animals which came off the ark

lived in or around the mountains of Ararat, and there they were able to "breed abundantly in the earth, and multiply upon the earth" (Genesis 8:17). Their **descendants** then migrated slowly, generation after generation, until the Earth was once again filled with animal life. Critics often are heard to ask questions like, "How did the unique animals like marsupials get back to Australia, for example?" There is a significant assumption in that question, however. Who can **prove** that the marsupials were in Australia **before** the Flood in the first place? After the Flood, marsupials may have migrated to Australia across land connections or narrow waterways. Furthermore, God, having created specially equipped creatures, may have directed them to settle in Australia. If God can arrange for all the animals to go to Noah (Genesis 6:20), then He very well could assist and direct them in their migration from Ararat once they left the ark (Genesis 8:17).

Some points we do know; some we do not. We do know that a certain number of every "kind" of air-breathing animal went into the ark; representatives of each "kind" came off the ark; those that came off the ark bred and multiplied, filling the Earth once more with animal life. Exactly how they migrated (or were distributed) to various parts of the Earth, how long that took, or why some animals later became extinct, we may not be able to distinguish conclusively. These are simply questions that will have to remain unanswered—but they do not discredit the biblical text.

WERE SEA CREATURES ON THE ARK?
Genesis 6:19

One question concerning the Flood and Noah's ark that frequently is asked has to do with whether or not Noah was required to take water-living creatures into the ark during the Flood. Genesis 6:19 reads: "And of every living thing of **all flesh** you shall bring two of every sort into the ark, to keep them alive with you; they shall be male and female" (emp. added). The phrase "all flesh" has been interpreted on occasion to mean that God commanded Noah to take even water-living creatures on board the ark. Dennis McKinsey asked in his journal, *Biblical Errancy*, "How did water creatures such as whales, porpoises, sea snakes, dolphins, and so forth enter the ark?" (1983b, p. 2). Undoubtedly, McKinsey and others ask such questions because of the use of the phrase "all flesh" in Genesis 6:19. But what exactly is the meaning—in the context—of the phrase "all flesh"?

The text that follows in Genesis 6:20 goes on to explain verse 19, saying, "Of the birds after their kind, and of the cattle after their kind, of every creeping thing of the ground after its kind, two of every sort shall come unto thee, to keep them alive." God therefore limited "all flesh" by specifying three categories: (1) birds (or fowl); (2) cattle; and (3) creeping things. In her book, *Science in the Bible*, Jean S. Morton presented an excellent treatise on how the Bible classifies animals, and the differences between biblical classification schemes and modern-day classification schemes. "Animals," she wrote, "are classified in Scripture according to simple characteristics that give quick recognition. For example, animals are classified as creeping, crawling, flying, and so forth" (1978, p. 154). Biblical commentator Adam Clarke noted that God's command to Noah in Genesis 6:19-20 was that "a male and female of all kinds of animals that could not live in the waters [were] to be brought into the ark" (n.d., 1:68). Furthermore, Genesis 7:21-22 records: "All flesh died that moved upon the earth, both birds, and cattle, and beasts, and every creeping thing that creepeth upon the earth, and every man: all in whose nostrils was the breath of the spirit of life, **of all that was on the dry land, died**" (emp. added).

The English word for birds (or fowl) is the translation of the Hebrew *'owph*, which means flying creatures, fowl, or birds.

Therefore, the first classification clearly is referring to those creatures that fly. Water-living creatures, by definition, would be omitted from this group.

The word "cattle" (King James/American Standard versions) is a generic term that can refer to domesticated (or wild) land animals or beasts. The Hebrew term (*behemah*) is used 188 times in the Old Testament. In the KJV, it is translated as beast 136 times, and as cattle 52 times, depending on the specific context (Young, 1974). Neither of these two terms is descriptive of water-living creatures; therefore, water-living creatures clearly may be omitted from the second category as well.

The final classification, "creeping things" (Hebrew *remes*), refers to reptiles, insects, and other small creatures (Strong, 1996). Davidson, in his *Analytical Hebrew and Chaldee Lexicon*, defined *remes* as "a reptile; that which moves on the earth; ...any land animal, in opposition to fowls" (1970, p. 685). *Remes* is used in a variety of ways in the Bible. In Genesis 9:3, it refers to the realm of living, moving creatures—in contrast to plants. In not a single instance in which the word *remes* is used is a **specific** creature described. T.C. Mitchell of the British Museum of Natural History noted that *remes* "is unlikely to correspond exactly to any modern scientific category, referring rather to all creatures which appear to the observer to move close to the ground" (1974, p. 274). *The New Brown-Driver-Briggs-Gesenius Hebrew and English Lexicon* suggests that the word *remes* conveys the idea of anything that has the motion of creeping, crawling, etc. (Brown, et al., 1979, pp. 942-943). H.C. Leupold, in his *Exposition of Genesis*, defined *remes* as:

> ...from the root meaning "to move about lightly" or to "glide about." "Creepers" almost covers the term, however, "creeping things" is too narrow, for it does not seem to allow for bigger creatures like reptiles. "Reptiles" again is too narrow, for it does not allow for the smaller types of life. Everything, therefore,

large or small, that moves upon the earth or close to
the earth, having but short legs, may be said to be included (1942, 1:83-84).

Remes, used in reference to land creatures, is different from
the Hebrew *sherets*, which apparently includes a broader spec-
trum of creatures. In Leviticus 11:20, for example, *sherets* is
used to describe certain animals. The word describes "teem-
ing, swarming, creeping things" (see Harris, et al., 1980, 1:
957). The word *remes* is used to describe the movement of
those animals under the category of *sherets*. So, God said: "Let
there be moving creatures [*sherets*]," and He created creatures
that moved by creeping (*remes*). *Remes* (a noun) includes reptiles and most insects (*sherets*) because they *remes* (a verb). As
it is employed in Genesis 6:20, the term *remes* clearly excludes
water-living creatures.

Furthermore, the terms used in Genesis 6:20 must be interpreted in light of their use in previous verses. In Genesis 1:
26, for example, the terms are used **in contrast** to other animal groups that specifically **include** fish: "And God said, 'Let
us make man in our image, after our likeness: and let them
have dominion over the **fish** [*dagah*] of the sea, and over the
birds [*'owph*] of the heavens, and over the **cattle** [*behemah*],
and over all the earth, and over every **creeping thing** [*remes*]
that creepeth upon the earth' " (emp. added). The same three
terms are used in Genesis 6:7, where God pledged to destroy
"man, and beast [*behemah*], and creeping things [*remes*], and
birds [*'owph*] of the heavens." With the exception of man, the
other three categories in Genesis 6:7 match those used in 6:
20 where God told Noah which creatures were to be taken on
board the ark. God never pledged to destroy fish in the first
place. Water-living creatures were not among the categories
of living creatures that God told Noah to take into the ark.

The question sometimes is asked as to how fresh-water fish
could survive in the salty seawater that covered the Earth dur-

ing the Flood. Obviously, fresh-water deposits would have been contaminated with salt water as the flood waters covered "every high mountain over the whole earth" (Genesis 7: 19-20). One of the problems here, of course, is that we cannot speak with certainty regarding the salinity of the oceans before the Flood. Nor do we know very much about the predecessors of many present-day fresh-water fish. Thus, any suggestion that fresh-water fish could not have survived in a post-Flood world assumes three things not in evidence: (1) that the salinity of the oceans and seas in Noah's day was the same as the salinity of those today; (2) that fresh-water fish cannot live in diluted salt water; and (3) that the ability of water-living creatures in Noah's day to survive in saline environments was the same as that of creatures found in today's oceans and seas.

The first assumption—that the salinity of the oceans and seas of Noah's day has remained constant—does not agree with the available scientific evidence. Based on a study of various factors of the past and present, some scientists believe that the salinity of the oceans may have been one-half of what they are currently (see, for example, Austin and Humphreys, 1990, 2:27, and Walter Lammerts as quoted in Whitcomb and Morris, 1961, p. 70). There is no reason that the fresh-water fish of Noah's day could not have survived, provided the salinity of the waters was less than it is today. Leonard Brand has noted: "[W]e would expect changes in the chemistry of seas and lakes—from mixing fresh and salt water.... Each species of aquatic organism would have its own physiological tolerance for these changes" (1997, p. 283). In addition, as Brand commented regarding the fresh/salt-water mixture that would have ensued during and immediately after the Flood: "[T]he less dense fresh water may not mix quickly with the salt water and it stays on top long enough to provide a temporary refuge for fresh-water organisms. Perhaps, too, many animals have a greater potential for adaptation to changing water conditions than we have recognized" (1997, p. 301-302).

The second assumption–that fresh-water fish cannot live in diluted salt water–is now known to be false, as Whitcomb and Morris pointed out as long ago as 1961 in their classic text, *The Genesis Flood* (p. 387, footnote).

The third assumption–that the ability of water-living creatures in Noah's day to survive in saline environments was the same as that of creatures found in today's oceans and seas– similarly is known to be incorrect. Many fresh-water fish have relatives that once lived in saline environments (see Batten and Sarfati, 2000). Furthermore, even today there are fish (e.g., large-mouth bass) that thrive in brackish waters such as those where the Mississippi River dumps its fresh water into the salt water of the Gulf of Mexico. Thus, in the end, the skeptics' claim that Noah's ark likely included giant fish tanks is wrong.

THE "WINDOW" OF THE ARK
Genesis 6:16

After informing Noah about an upcoming worldwide flood, and commanding him to build a massive boat of gopher wood (approximately 450 feet long, 75 feet wide, and 45 feet high), God instructed His faithful servant, saying, "You shall make **a window** for the ark, and you shall finish it to a cubit from above" (Genesis 6:16, emp. added; NOTE: A cubit is approximately 18 inches). Upon reading about this window in Noah's ark, many people have contemplated its usefulness (or lack thereof). Since, historically, windows have served two basic purposes (that of lighting and ventilation), inquiring minds want to know what good one window 18 inches square would be on an ark with a capacity of about 1,400,000 cubic feet full of animals. Dennis McKinsey, the one-time editor of the journal *Biblical Errancy* (touted as "the only national periodical focusing on biblical errors"), once asked: "How could so many creatures breathe with only one small opening which was closed for at least 190 days? [sic]" (1983b, p. 1). Other skeptics also have ridiculed the idea that sufficient ventilation for the whole ark could have come through this one window (see Wells, 2001). In fact, anyone even slightly familiar with animal-house ventilation needs are somewhat taken aback by the apparent lack of airflow allowed by the ark's design. Unless God miraculously ventilated the ark, one little window on a three-story boat, the length of which was a football-field-and-a-half long, simply would not do.

Questions regarding the "window" on Noah's ark and the problem of ventilation have escalated largely because the Hebrew word translated window (*tsohar*) in Genesis 6:16 appears only here in the Old Testament, and linguistic scholars are unsure as to its exact meaning (see Hamilton, 1990, p. 282). Translators of the KJV and NKJV use the word "window" to translate *tsohar*; however, according to Old Testament commentator Victor Hamilton, they "do so on the basis of the word's possible connection with *sahorayim*, 'noon, midday,' thus an opening to let in the light of day" (p. 282). Hebrew scholar William Gesenius defined *tsohar* in his Hebrew lexicon as simply "light," and translated Genesis 6:16 as "thou shalt make light for the ark" (1847, p. 704). He then surmised that this "light" represented, not **a** window, but **windows** (plural). The ASV translators also preferred "light" as the best translation for *tsohar*. Still more recent translations, including the RSV, NIV, and ESV, have translated Genesis 6:16 as "Make a **roof**" for the ark, instead of make a "window" or "light."

Such disagreement among translations is, admittedly, somewhat discouraging to the person who wants a definite answer as to how *tsohar* should be translated. What is clear, however, is that the word translated "window" two chapters later, which Noah is said to have "opened" (8:6), is translated from a **different** Hebrew word (*challôwn*) than what is used in Genesis 6:16. The word *challôwn* (8:6) is the standard Hebrew word for "window" (cf. Genesis 26:8; Joshua 2:18). Yet, interest-ingly, this is **not** the word used in 6:16. One wonders if these were two different entities, or if in 8:6, Noah opened one of a plurality of aligned windows that God instructed him to make in 6:16?

Another assumption often brought into a discussion re-garding the "window" (*tsohar*) of 6:16 is that it was one square cubit. Although many people have imagined Noah's ark as having one small window 18 inches high by 18 inches wide, the phrase "you shall finish it to a cubit from above" (6:16, NKJV; cf. RSV) does not give the Bible reader any clear di-mensions of the opening. The text just says that Noah was to "finish it to a cubit from the top" (NASV; "upward," ASV). The simple truth is, the **size** of the lighting apparatus men-tioned in this verse is unspecified. The text seems to indicate only the distance the opening was from the top of the ark, rather than the actual size of the window. Thus we cannot form a definite picture of it. But, we do know that nothing in the text warrants an interpretation that the "window" was just a "small opening" (as skeptic Dennis McKinsey alleged). A more probable theory, which aligns itself appropriately with the text, is that the opening described in Genesis 6:16 extended around the ark's circumference 18 inches from the top of the ark with an undeterminable height. According to geologist John Woodmorappe, such an opening would have provided sufficient light and ventilation for the ark (1996, pp. 37-44). [For further reading on this subject, I recommend Woodmorappe's book, *Noah's Ark: A Feasibility Study*.]

When reading the Bible, it always is important to remem-ber that many details about the events it records often are **not** revealed to the reader. So it is with the plans recorded in the Bible regarding Noah's ark. As Henry Morris commented, "It was obviously not the intention of the writer to record the complete specifications for the ark's construction, but only enough to assure later readers that it was quite adequate for its intended purpose…'to preserve life on the earth' " (1976, p. 182). Truly, absolute certainty regarding the openings on the ark cannot be determined. We know of an opening mentioned in Genesis 6:16 (*tsohar*), as well as one (*challôwn*) mentioned in 8:6. And, since Noah, his family, and the animals on the ark survived the Flood, it is only logical to conclude that God made proper ways to ventilate the ark in which they lived during the Flood. Although nothing in Scripture demands that those of us living millennia after the Flood need to know how it was ventilated, lighted, etc., it is very likely that He used the opening mentioned in Genesis 6:16.

HOW LONG DID THE FLOOD LAST?

Although some have accused the Genesis text of error in regard to how long the Flood waters were upon the Earth, a careful reading of the Flood account indicates that the Deluge lasted approximately one year. The chronology would have included the following:

   40 days of rain (Genesis 7:4)

  110 additional days of water "prevailing on the earth," for a total of 150 days (Genesis 7:24)

   74 days until mountains were viewed (This was from the 17th day of the seventh month to the 1st day of the tenth month. $13 + 30 + 30 + 1$) [Genesis 8:5]

    7 days elapsed before Noah sent out the raven (Genesis 8:6-7)

    7 days elapsed before Noah sent out the dove for the first time (Genesis 8:8)

    7 days elapsed before Noah sent out the dove for the second time (Genesis 8:10)

    7 days elapsed before Noah sent out the dove the final time (Genesis 8:12)

29   days elapse to correlate with the date of 601st year, 1st month, 1st day (Genesis 8:13)

57   days elapse before Noah and the animals disembark (Genesis 8:14-16)

371 days total

I once read where an individual writing for *Newsweek* magazine ridiculed the inerrancy of the book of Genesis because it (allegedly) indicates that the Flood lasted both "40 days and 40 nights" and "a whopping 370 days and nights" (Andrews, 2004, p. 28). The elementary explanation to this alleged conundrum, which it seems most anyone with a cursory knowledge of the Genesis Flood account would know, is that God caused it "to **rain** on the earth forty days and forty nights" (Genesis 7:4), but the land was still covered with water, and Noah was not allowed out of the ark, for another 331 days (Genesis 7:24; 8:5-16). Obviously, there is a difference between how long it **rained** on the Earth, and how long the floodwaters actually remained upon the Earth. Considering that a five year old can make this distinction, one wonders why some Bible critics cannot?

WHERE DID ALL OF
THE FLOOD WATERS GO?

According to evolutionist Bill Butler, "The greatest geologic fiction that the Creationists adhere to is Noah's Flood" (2002). The idea that water ever covered the entire Earth, including the highest hills and mountains (Genesis 7:19-20), supposedly is unthinkable (and impossible). As seen throughout this chapter, evolutionists propose several questions when expressing their unbelief in the Noahic Flood. Another question was raised by Butler in his article, "Creationism = Willful Ignorance." He asked: "If the earth's surface were covered by an additional 29,000+ feet of water, how do you get rid of it?" If Mt. Everest reaches a height of over 29,000 feet, then the Bible allegedly indicates that the Flood waters reached even higher–approximately 23 feet higher than the peak of Mt. Everest (Genesis 7:20). If such is the case, where did all of the water go?

First, the Bible is more specific about **who** caused the waters to subside, than **where** exactly all of the waters went. Genesis 8:1,3 says, "**God made** a wind to pass over the earth, and the waters subsided…. And the waters receded continually from the earth." Years later, the prophet Isaiah recorded how Jehovah compared a promise He made to Israel with His promise "that the waters of Noah would no longer cover the earth" (Isaiah 54:9). Although these passages do not tell us exactly where the waters went, for the Christian who believes that the Bible is God's inspired Word, such revelation should be adequate–**God did something** with the Flood waters.

Second, the skeptic's assertion (that there presently is not enough water on the Earth for there ever to have been the kind of flood described in Genesis 6-8) is based upon invalid assumptions. The truth is, we are unaware how high the mountains were in Noah's day, nor do we know the depth of the ocean valleys. Thus, one cannot know how much water was on the Earth during the Noahic Flood. Psalm 104:6-8 indicates that, at some time in the past, God established **new** heights and depths for the Earth's mountains and valleys. While directing his comments to Jehovah, the psalmist proclaimed:

> You covered it [the Earth–EL] with the deep as with a garment; the waters were standing above the mountains. At Your rebuke they fled, at the sound of Your thunder they hurried away. **The mountains rose; the valleys sank down to the place which You established for them**" (NASV, updated version, emp. added).

Just as God miraculously altered the Earth's topography during the Creation week (Genesis 1:9-13), and just as He miraculously sent flood waters upon the Earth, it appears that God miraculously caused the waters to subside. In all likelihood, the antediluvian world was vastly different from the Earth of today (cf. 2 Peter 3:6). It seems probable (and reasonable to believe) that the mountains of Noah's day were much smaller than, say, such peaks as Mt. Everest or Mt. McKinley that are so well known to us. Thus, the Flood did not have to rise to levels of 29,000+ feet to cover everything on the Earth. We know, according to the Scriptures, that the waters rose above the mountaintops; however, we simply cannot know the heights reached by the antediluvian mountains. (Interestingly, marine fossils have been found near the top of Mt. Everest.)

Where did all of the Flood waters go? The most logical answer in light of the Scriptures appears to be that God made room for the waters by adjusting the Earth's topography. Much of the water from the Flood likely has retreated into the deeper ocean trenches—valleys that, in places, are over seven miles deep.

[NOTE: In an attempt to defend his criticism of the Noahic Flood, and to discredit anyone (like me) who would argue that the Earth's topography after the Flood was likely very different than it was before the Flood, evolutionist Bill Butler (mentioned above) has suggested the following. First, he emphatically stated that since, "The Tigris/Euphrates valley existed in its present form before the flood," the topography of the Earth could not have changed that much during (and after) the Flood. Second, he argued that "the text specifically states the flood covered 'all the high mountains.' If the mountains were low at this time, the word 'high' would not be used" (2002).

Notice, however, the faulty reasoning involved in both points Butler made. First, there is **no proof** that "The Tigris/Euphrates valley existed in its present form before the flood." In fact, according to Genesis 2:10-14, there was one river that went out of Eden that then parted and became four rivers. The Tigris and Euphrates rivers of today, however, do not branch from a common source, but arise from separate sources in the Armenian mountains. The rivers of the same name in Genesis 2 are different than those that exist today by the same name. (It is very possible that the people who left the ark, as well as their descendants, used familiar names for the new rivers they found.) Second, simply because Genesis 7:19-20 stresses that the Flood waters covered "all the **high** hills/mountains," does not mean these mountains could not have been somewhat lower than the mountains of today. Butler stated: "If the mountains were low at this time, **the word 'high' would not be used.**" Question: Who is to say that the word "high" would not be used? If in a particular class of dwarfs, some were taller than others, could the instructor not speak of certain "tall dwarfs" in his class? Who is to say that he could not use the word "tall" when speaking of a few particular dwarfs who might be much taller than others? Similarly, just because Genesis 7:19-20 uses the word "high," does not mean that mountains before the Flood were at the height they are currently. Truthfully, however tall the mountains were before the Flood, some would have reached "higher" than others, and thus could be referred to as the "high mountains."]

THE IMPORTANCE OF FLOOD LEGENDS

Although for many years skeptics have rejected the factuality of the Bible's account of a worldwide flood, interestingly, anthropologists who study legends and folktales from different geographical locations and cultures consistently have reported corroboration from secular flood stories in practically every civilization. Legends have surfaced in hundreds of cultures throughout the world that tell of a huge, catastrophic flood that destroyed most of mankind, and that was survived by only a few individuals and animals. Although most historians who have studied this matter estimate that these legends number into the 200s, according to evolutionary geologist Robert Schoch, "Noah is but one tale in a worldwide collection of at least **500 flood myths**, which are the most widespread of all ancient myths and therefore can be considered among the oldest" (2003, p. 249, emp. added). Schoch went on to observe:

> Narratives of a massive inundation are found all over the world.... Stories of a great deluge are found on every inhabited continent and among a great many different language and culture groups (pp. 103,249).

Over a century ago, the famous Canadian geologist, Sir William Dawson, wrote about how the record of the Flood

> is preserved in some of the oldest historical documents of several distinct races of men, and is indirectly corroborated by the whole tenor of the early history of most of the civilized races (1895, pp. 4ff.).

Legends have been reported from nations such as China, Babylon, Mexico, Egypt, Sudan, Syria, Persia, India, Norway, Wales, Ireland, Indonesia, Romania, etc.–comprising a list that could go on for many pages (see Perloff, 1999, p. 167). Although the vast number of such legends is surprising, the similarity between much of their content is equally amazing. James Perloff noted:

> In 95 percent of the more than two hundred flood legends, the flood was worldwide; in 88 percent, a certain family was favored; in 70 percent, survival was by means of a boat; in 67 percent, animals were also saved; in 66 percent, the flood was due to the wickedness of man; in 66 percent, the survivors had been forewarned; in 57 percent, they ended up on a

mountain; in 35 percent, birds were sent out from the boat; and in 9 percent, exactly eight people were spared (p. 168).

American Indian Legends

The Aztecs tell of a worldwide global flood in a story with striking parallels to the biblical deluge. "Only two people, the hero Coxcox and his wife, survived the flood by floating in a boat that came to rest on a mountain" (Schoch, p. 103). Then, soon after the flood, giants constructed a great pyramid in an endeavor to reach the clouds. Such ambition is said to have angered the gods, who scattered the giants with fire sent from the heavens (cf. Genesis 11:1-9).

In the ancient land we now refer to as Mexico, one tribe of Indians, known as the Toltecs, told of a great flood. In their legend, a deluge destroyed the "first world" 1,716 years after it was created. Only a few people escaped this worldwide flood, and did so in a "toptlipetlocali" (a word that means "closed chest"). After these few people exited the closed chest, they wandered about the Earth, and found a place where they built a "zacuali" (a high tower) in case another flood came upon the Earth. At the time of the "zacuali," the Toltecs' languages were confused and they separated to different parts of the Earth.

Another ancient tribe of Mexico told the story of a man named Tezpi who escaped the deluge in a boat that was filled with animals. Similar to Noah, who sent out a raven (a scavenger bird) that never returned, and a dove that came back with an olive leaf, "Tezpi released a vulture, which stayed away, gorging on cadavers. Then he let a hummingbird go, and it returned to him bearing a twig" (Schoch, p. 104).

Ancient Greek Mythology

According to the Greek legend of the deluge, humans became very wicked. Zeus, the leader of the many gods in Greek mythology, wanted to destroy humans by a flood, and then raise up another group. However, before he could do this, a man by the name of Deucalion, and his wife Pyrrha, were warned of the impending disaster. This fortunate couple was placed in a large wooden chest by one of the immortals named Prometheus. For nine days and nights, the floodwaters covered almost all of the Earth. Only a few mountain peaks remained. The wooden chest came to rest on the peak of Mount Parnassus. Later, after leaving the wooden chest, Deucalion sacrificed to Zeus.

Chinese and Asian Legends

In the land of China, there are many legends about a great flood. One of those comes from a group of people known as the Nosu. According to their legend, God sent a personal messenger to Earth to warn three sons that a flood was coming. Only the youngest son, Dum, heeded the messenger. He constructed a wooden boat to prepare for the coming flood. When the waters arrived, Dum entered his boat, and was saved. After the waters began to recede, the boat landed on the mountains of Tibet, where Dum had three sons who repopulated the Earth. Interestingly, even the Chinese character for "boat" possibly reveals the story of Noah and the other seven people on the ark. The three elements used to symbolize a boat are:

舟 + 几 + 口 = 船

vessel   eight   mouth (or people)   boat

The Iban people of Sarawak tell of a hero named Trow, who floated around in an ark with his wife and numerous domestic animals (Schoch, p. 252). Natives from India tell a story about a man named Manu who built an ark after being warned of a flood. Later, the waters receded, and he landed on a mountain (Schoch, p. 250).

Ancient Babylonian Mythology

Possibly the most famous flood account (aside from the biblical record of Noah and the Flood) comes from the ancient Babylonian empire. The *Gilgamesh Epic*, written on twelve clay tablets that date back to the seventh century B.C., tells of a hero named Gilgamesh. In his search for eternal life, Gilgamesh sought out Utnapishtim, a person who was granted eternal life because he saved a boatload of animals and humans during a great flood. On the eleventh tablet of this epic, a flood account is recorded that parallels the Genesis account in many areas. According to the story, the gods instructed Utnapishtim to build a boat because a terrible flood was coming. Utnapishtim built the boat, covered it with pitch, and put animals of all kinds on it, as well as certain provisions. After Utnapishtim entered the boat with his family, it rained for six days and nights. When the flood ended, the boat rested on Mount Niser. After seven days, Utnapishtim sent out a dove to see if the waters had receded. The dove came back, so he sent a swallow, which also returned. Finally, he sent out a raven—which never returned. Utnapishtim and his family finally exited the boat and sacrificed to their gods (see Roth, 1988, pp. 303-304).

What is the significance of the various flood legends? The answer seems obvious: (a) we have well over 200 flood legends that tell of a great flood (and possibly more than 500—Schoch, p. 249); (b) many of the legends come from different ages and civilizations that could not possibly have copied any of the similar legends; (c) the legends were recorded long before any missionaries arrived to relate to them the Genesis account of Noah; and (d) almost all civilizations have some sort of flood legend. The conclusion to be drawn from such facts is that in the distant past, there was a colossal flood that forever affected the history of all civilizations.

Those living soon after the Flood did not have the book of Genesis to read to their descendants. (Genesis was not written until several hundred years after the Flood.) The account of the Flood was passed from one generation to the next. Many parents and grandparents told their children and grandchildren about the huge ark, the wonderful animals, and the devastating Flood, long before the Genesis record ever existed. Over the years, the details of the story were altered, but many of the actual details remained the same. Alfred Rehwinkel wrote:

> Traditions similar to this record are found among nearly all the nations and tribes of the human race. And this is as one would expect it to be. If that awful world catastrophe, as described in the Bible, actually happened, the existence of the Flood traditions among the widely separated and primitive people is just what is to be expected. It is only natural that the memory of such an event was rehearsed in the ears of the children of the survivors again and again, and possibly made the basis of some religious observances (1951, pp. 127-128).

Harold W. Clark, in his volume, *Fossils, Flood and Fire*, commented:

> Preserved in the myths and legends of almost every people on the face of the globe is the memory of the great catastrophe. While myths may not have any scientific value, yet they are significant in indicating the fact that an impression was left in the minds of the races of mankind that could not be erased (1968, p. 45).

After the "trappings" are stripped away from the kernel of truth in the various stories, there is almost complete agreement among practically all flood accounts: (a) a universal destruction by water of the human race and all other living things occurred; (b) an ark, or boat, was provided as the means of escape for some; and (c) a seed of mankind was provided to perpetuate humanity. As Furman Kearley once observed: "These traditions agree in too many vital points not to have originated from the same factual event" (1979, p. 11). In volume three of his multi-volume set, *The Native Races of the Pacific Slope–Mythology,* H.H. Bancroft wrote: "There never was a myth without a meaning;...there is not one of these stories, no matter how silly or absurd, which was not founded on fact" (1883).

Among the noted scholars of days gone by who have studied these matters in detail are such men as James G. Frazer (*Folklore in the Old Testament*) and William Wundt (*Elements of Folk Psychology*). Wundt, who did his utmost to find some kind of reasonable case for independent origins of the various flood sagas (and who had no great love for the biblical evidence), was forced to admit:

> Of the combination of all these elements into a whole (the destruction of the earth by water, the rescue of a single man and seed of animals by means of a boat, etc.), however, we may say without hesitation, it could not have arisen twice independently (1916, p. 392, parenthetical comment in orig.).

Or, as Dawson concluded more than a century ago:

> [W]e know now that the Deluge of Noah is not mere myth or fancy of primitive man or solely a doctrine of the Hebrew Scriptures.... [N]o historical event, ancient or modern, can be more firmly established as matter of fact than this (1895, pp. 4ff.).

Chapter 5

ALLEGED CHRONOLOGICAL CONTRADICTIONS

Since the Bible begins at the Creation with Genesis–the book of beginnings–and ends with the book of Revelation (which many scholars believe was the last recorded book of the Bible), students of the Scriptures often assume that the Bible was compiled chronologically. Many students approach their reading of the Bible with the mindset that everything in Scripture is arranged "from A to Z." Since Genesis records what took place at the beginning of time, and it is the first book of the Bible, then the rest of the Bible follows suit, right? Actually, what the diligent student eventually finds is that the Bible is **not** a book of strict chronology. All sixty-six books of the Bible are not arranged in the order in which they were written. Furthermore, all of the events contained within each book also are not recorded chronologically.

Consider the following arrangement of books in the Bible:

- Although the books of Haggai and Zechariah have been placed near the end of the Old Testament, these men prophesied during the days of Ezra and Nehemiah (cf. Ezra 5:1; 6:14). Twenty books separate Haggai and Zechariah from the book of Ezra, yet the events recorded in each book were occurring at the same time. Obviously, these books are not arranged in chronological order.

- Even though 2 Chronicles appears before the book of Job, the events recorded in Job took place long before those that are recorded in 2 Chronicles. In fact, if the Bible were a book of strict chronology, the events recorded in Job would be placed somewhere within the book of Genesis, likely somewhere after chapter nine (cf. Job 22:15-16; 42:16-17).

- In the New Testament, one might assume that since 1 Thessalonians comes after the book of Acts, that Luke penned Acts earlier than Paul penned his first letter to the church at Thessalonica. The truth is, however, 1 Thessalonians was written years before the book of Acts was completed.

In addition to the books of the Bible not being arranged chronologically, inspired writers did not always record information in a strictly chronological sequence. Making the assumption that the entire Bible was written chronologically hinders a proper understanding of the text. As you will see throughout this chapter, several alleged contradictions are resolved simply by acknowledging that many times Bible writers did not record events in a strict sequential order.

ONLY ONE LANGUAGE BEFORE BABEL?
Genesis 10:5,20,31; 11:1

According to some skeptics, Genesis 10 verses 5, 20, and 31 contradict what is stated in Genesis 11:1. Supposedly, since Moses recorded that the descendants of Shem, Ham, and Japheth spoke different languages in Genesis 10, and yet he indicated that "the whole earth had one language and one speech" in Genesis 11:1, then a discrepancy exists. Obviously, before the dispersion of man at Babel, the whole Earth could not have both **many** languages and **only one** language at the same time.

The explanation to this "problem" is that the events recorded in Genesis 10-11 were not written chronologically. Genesis 10 is more of an overview, while Genesis 11 speaks of one event within Genesis 10. Some of the things recorded in chapter 10 occurred before the tower of Babel, while others occurred sometime later. Consider that Genesis 2:5-25 does not pick up where chapter 1 left off; rather, it provides more detailed information about some of the events mentioned in chapter one. (Whereas Genesis 1 is arranged chronologically, Genesis 2 is organized topically.) Several of the events in Genesis 38 involving Judah and Tamar occurred while the things recorded in chapter 39 (and those that follow) took place. Similar to a teacher who is telling her class a story, and inserts information into it about something the main character did in the past or will do in the future, Moses "jumps" ahead of himself at times by inserting parenthetical material like that found in Genesis 10.

Aside from the languages mentioned in Genesis 10, there is another "clue" in the text that reveals the events recorded in chapter 11 occurred **before** the descendants of Noah began speaking different languages and spreading throughout the Earth. Genesis 10:25 mentions a man named Peleg (meaning "division") who received such a name because "in his days the earth was divided." More than likely, this is a reference to the confusion of languages at the tower of Babel described in chapter 11. The "Earth" (i.e., people; cf. 11:1) divided when God confused the languages (11:7-8). Thus, the division in Peleg's day is linked contextually to the linguistic segregation at Babel (Genesis 11:1-9).

When Genesis 10 and 11 are read with the understanding that not all events are recorded chronologically, one clearly sees how the events revealed in these chapters are entwined tightly with one another—so tightly in fact that those who seek contradictions are doomed to fail. Linguistically speaking, there was no pre-Babel confusion; only one language was in existence (Genesis 11:1).

DID SAUL KNOW DAVID PRIOR TO GOLIATH'S DEATH?
1 Samuel 16:14-23; 17:58

Following the account of Samuel's visit to Bethlehem to anoint David as the future king of Israel, the book of 1 Samuel indicates that David became the harp player and armor bearer for King Saul (16:14-23). Subsequent to this information, the reader is told of David's magnificent triumph over Goliath (1 Samuel 17), which then is followed by an "interrogation" by King Saul, who asked David, "Whose son are you, young man?" (17:58). A general reading through the text of 1 Samuel 16-17 has led some Bible believers to question why Saul (it seems) knew David, then did not know David, and then got to know him again. Skeptics, likewise, have inquired about the consistency of this story (see Morgan, 2003a; Wells, 2001; "Inerrancy," n.d.). Paul Tobin, in an article titled "Internal Contradictions in the Bible," summed up the skeptic's argument by stating that 1 Samuel 16 "clearly shows that David...was known to Saul. Yet a little later, after David's fight with Goliath, Saul is made to enquire from his chief captain as to the identity of the giant slayer (I Samuel 17:56). And he is again made to inquire from David who he is, when he should have known this all along" (2000). Allegedly, the Bible's portrayal of Saul's ignorance of David **after** Goliath's death is proof of the Bible writers' imperfection when penning the Scriptures.

First, it is imperative for one to recognize that, as with other Bible passages, nowhere in 1 Samuel 16-17 are we told that all of these events occurred in chronological order. Although throughout 1 Samuel, there is a general, sequential progression, such does not demand that **every** event recorded in the book must be laid out chronologically. In fact, within chapter 17 there is evidence that this is not the case. For example, the events recorded in 17:54 (i.e., David putting his armor in his tent, and taking the head of Goliath to Jerusalem) postdate the conversations mentioned in verses 55-58 (as verse 57 makes clear). More precisely, verses 55-56 synchronize with verse 40, while verses 57-58 could be placed immediately following verse 51 (Youngblood, 1992, 3:703). And, regarding chapter 16, who can say for certain that David was not already playing the harp for Saul before Samuel anointed him? First Samuel 17:15 indicates that "David occasionally went and returned from Saul to feed his father's sheep at Bethlehem." Perhaps it was during one of these furloughs that he was anointed as the future king of Israel (16:1-13). Unless the text clearly distinguishes one event as occurring before or after another, a person cannot conclude for certain the exact chronology of those events. Just because one historical event recorded in the Bible precedes another, does not mean that it could not have occurred at a later time (or vice versa). Truly, the ancients were not as concerned about chronology as is the average person in twenty-first-century America.

Aside from the fact that one cannot be certain about the exact sequence of events recorded in 1 Samuel 16-17, several possible explanations exist as to why Saul appeared not to recognize David after his triumphal victory over Goliath. First, enough time could have lapsed so that David's appearance changed significantly since the last time he appeared before King Saul. William M. Thomson, a missionary in Syria and Palestine for nearly half of the nineteenth century, once described the sudden changes in the physical development of Eastern youths in his book titled *The Land and the Book.*

> They not only spring into full-grown manhood as if
> by magic, but all their former beauty disappears; their
> complexion becomes dark; their features hard and
> angular, and the whole expression of countenance
> stern and even disagreeable. I have often been ac-
> costed by such persons, formerly intimate acquain-
> tances, but who had suddenly grown entirely out of
> my knowledge, nor could I without difficulty recog-
> nize them (1859, 2:366).

Few would deny that young men can change quickly over a
relatively short period of time. Facial hair, increased height
and weight, larger, more defined muscles, darker skin, a
deeper voice, as well as the wearing of different apparel,
may all factor into why a person may say to someone that he
or she knows, but has not seen for some time, "I hardly recognized you. You've changed." Surely, it is more than possible that between the time David served Saul as a harpist,
and the time he slew Goliath, he could have experienced
many physical changes that prevented a "distressed" king
from recognizing his former harpist.

A second reason Saul might have failed to recognize David
is because he may have lapsed into another unreliable mental state. Saul's intermittent deviation from normalcy is seen
throughout the book of 1 Samuel (cf. 16:14-23; 18:9-12; 19:
22-24; 22:6-19), and it is possible 17:54-58 is another allusion
to his defective perception. In his discussion of 1 Samuel 17,
biblical commentator Robert Jamieson mentioned this possibility, saying, "The king's moody temper, not to say frequent
fits of insanity, would alone be sufficient to explain the circumstance of his not recognizing a youth who, during the time
of his mental aberration, had been much near him, trying to
soothe his distempered soul" (1997).

Third, it could be that Saul did, in fact, remember David,
but because of jealousy over David's momentous victory (cf.

1 Samuel 18:8-11), and perhaps on hearing that Samuel had been to Bethlehem to anoint him as the next king (1 Samuel 16:1-13), Saul simply wanted to **act** like he did not know David. Such a scenario is not difficult to envision. Today, a teacher or coach might inquire about a student whom he or she already knows, yet in hopes of instilling more submission into the arrogant teen, the faculty member acts somewhat aloof. One textual indication that such may be the explanation of 1 Samuel 17:54-58 is that Saul still referred to David, the bear-killing, lion-slaying, Goliath-demolisher, as a "stripling" (Hebrew `elem–17:56, ASV) and "young man" (Hebrew na`ar–17:55,58). Although these two words do not necessarily carry a belittling connotation, neither designation seems very appropriate for a man who had just tried on the armor of King Saul–a man once described as "shoulders upward...taller than any of the people" (1 Samuel 9:2)–and had just killed one of the fiercest enemies of Israel. Truly, Saul's supposed ignorance of David and his family may well have been a "performance" instigated by what physician Herman van Praag once called, "haughtiness fed by envy" (1986, 35:421).

Finally, one must realize that the text does not even actually say that Saul did not know **David**. It only records that Saul asked, "Whose son is this youth?" (1 Samuel 17:55; cf. vss. 56,58). It is an assumption to conclude that Saul did not recognize David. The king simply could have been inquiring about David's family. Since Saul had promised to reward the man who killed Goliath by giving "**his father's house** exemption from taxes in Israel" (17:25), Saul might have been questioning David in order to ensure the identity of David's family. Furthermore, 18:1 seems to presuppose an extended conversation between the two, which would imply that Saul wanted even more information than just the name of David's father.

Truly, any of these possibilities could account for Saul's examination of David. The burden of proof is on the skeptic to show otherwise. As respected law professor Simon Greenleaf concluded regarding the rule of municipal law in relation to ancient writings:

> Every document, apparently ancient, coming from the proper repository or custody, and bearing on its face no evident marks of forgery, **the law presumes to be genuine, and devolves on the opposing party the burden of proving it to be otherwise** (1995, p. 16, emp. added).

Until skeptics logically negate the above possible solutions to the questions surrounding 1 Samuel 16-17, and are able to prove beyond doubt that the Bible writer made a genuine mistake, one does not have to doubt the integrity of the biblical text.

KINGLY CHRONOLOGY
IN THE BOOK OF EZRA
Ezra 4:7-23; 4:24-6:15

As if the spelling and pronunciation of Ahasuerus and Artaxerxes were not problematic enough for the average Bible student, one must also consider these Persian kings in light of the order in which they are mentioned in the book of Ezra. According to history, the Persian kings reigned in the following order: Cyrus (560-530 B.C.), Cambyses (530-522), Smerdis (522), **Darius I** (522-486), Ahasuerus (486-465), **Artaxerxes I** (465-424), Darius II (423-405), and Artaxerxes II (405-358) [see Cook, 1983, p. 350]. The difficulty that presents itself in the book of Ezra is that events surrounding letters which King Artaxerxes received from, and wrote to, the enemies of the Jews (see Ezra 4:7-23) are mentioned **before** the reign of Darius I (Ezra 4:24-6:15). If it is a proven fact that Darius served as king before Artaxerxes, why is the kingship of Darius recorded in the book of Ezra subsequent to the reign of Artaxerxes (recorded in Ezra 4:7-23)?

First, it needs to be pointed out that the Darius of the book of Ezra was in fact Darius I and not Darius II. The second Darius lived too late in history to have been contemporary with the rebuilding of the temple. Thus, one cannot solve the question at hand simply by suggesting that the Darius cited in Ezra was really Darius II, who lived after Artaxerxes I.

Second, some may attempt to solve this difficulty by alleging that Artaxerxes II was the king who reigned during the days of Ezra and Nehemiah's return to Jerusalem, while Artaxerxes I was the king mentioned prior to Darius' reign (Ezra 4:7-23). This solution is unacceptable, however, since Artaxerxes II lived several years after the events recorded in Ezra and Nehemiah.

So what is the answer? Why is the kingship of Darius recorded in the book of Ezra following events connected with the kingship of Artaxerxes (Ezra 4:7-23)–a king who is thought to have reigned after Darius? One possible solution to this difficulty is that Ahasuerus and Artaxerxes of Ezra 4:6,7-23 were respectively Cambyses (530-522) and Smerdis (522)–kings of Persia (listed above) who reigned before Darius I. Since Persian kings frequently had two or more names, it is not unfathomable to think that Cambyses and Smerdis also may have gone by the names Ahasuerus and Artaxerxes (see Wilson, 1996; see also Fausset, 1998).

Another explanation to this perceived dilemma is that the information concerning the kings of Persia in Ezra 4 is grouped according to theme rather than by chronology. Instead of having a record where everything in chapter four is in sequential order, it is reasonable to conclude that verses 6-23 serve as a parenthetical comment and that Ahasuerus and Artaxerxes (4:6-7) are indeed Ahasuerus (486-465) and Artaxerxes I (465-424) of history (rather than the aforementioned Cambyses and Smerdis).

Bible students must keep in mind that just as there is more than one way to write a book in the twenty-first century, ancient writers frequently recorded events chronologically while occasionally inserting necessary non-sequential material (e.g., Genesis 10-11; Matthew 28:2-4). It would have been natural for the writer of the book of Ezra to follow a discussion of the problems related to rebuilding the Jerusalem **temple** (4:1-5) with information on a similar resistance the Jews encountered while rebuilding the **walls** of Jerusalem (4:6-23). Although the details in verses 6-23 initially may puzzle our chronologically preconditioned mindset, they actually fit very well in their arrangement with the overall theme of the chapter. In verse 24, the story picks up where it left off in verse 5. The writer returns to his focus on the problems with the rebuilding of the temple, which lingered until "the second year of the reign of Darius king of Persia" (Ezra 4:24).

Regardless of which explanation one accepts for the inclusion of verses 6-23 in Ezra 4, they both provide a sufficient answer to the perceived difficulty. It is my judgment that the second of these two possibilities serves as the best, and most logical, explanation.

TO THE WILDERNESS—OR A WEDDING?
Mark 1:12; John 1:19-2:1

Those people who have done much study from the synoptic gospel accounts generally are aware that following the baptism of Jesus, He "then" (Matthew 4:1; Luke 4:1) "immediately" (Mark 1:12) was sent out by the Spirit into the wilderness where He fasted for forty days while being tempted by the devil. Skeptics likewise are "well informed" of this story. In fact, some skeptics presume to know about this time in Jesus' life so well, they have argued that the apostle John contradicted the synoptic writers (see "Inerrancy;" "Contradictions;" Wells, 2001). Allegedly, John placed Jesus at the wedding in Cana of Galilee just three days following His baptism (John 1:19-2:1), whereas Mark indicated that Jesus went into the desert for forty days "immediately" following His baptism. Is this a real chronological contradiction, as some suppose?

Like so many of the other occasions when skeptics contend that two or more passages of Scripture are at odds with one another, this is just another example of where a particular text has been misunderstood. John 1 does not teach (as has been alleged) that "three days after the events where Jesus and John the Baptist meet [and when Jesus was baptized–EL]…, Jesus was attending a wedding in Cana" ("Inerrancy"). Notice that the first chapter of John's gospel account actually teaches the following:

- Verses 19-25 contain John the Baptizer's testimony regarding who he is. ("Now this is the testimony of John, when the Jews sent priests and Levites from Jerusalem to ask him, "Who are you?"–vs. 19.)

- In verses 26-27, John explains to the priests and Levites that there is One Who is greater than him–Jesus.

- "The next day," John sees Jesus and proclaims, "Behold! The Lamb of God who takes away the sin of the world!" (vs. 29). John then explains to those around him that this Man is the One about Whom he was speaking the previous day (vs. 30).

- In verse 31, John the Baptizer explains to his listeners how Jesus was "revealed to Israel" at His baptism (vs. 31). Then, in the following three verses, John bears witness about that baptism, saying,

> I **saw** the Spirit descending from heaven
> like a dove, and He **remained** upon Him.
> I did not know Him, but He who sent me
> to baptize with water said to me, "Upon

whom you see the Spirit descending, and
remaining on Him, this is He who baptizes with the Holy Spirit." And I have
seen and testified that this is the Son of
God (32-35, emp. added).

- Verses 35-37 indicate that the day after John revealed
  the above facts to his listeners, he saw Jesus again,
  and two of John's disciples began following Jesus that
  very day.

- The next day, Philip and Nathanael began following
  the Lord.

- Then, "on the third day" following John's **testimony**
  of Jesus' baptism and the Spirit Who descended upon
  Him, Jesus and His disciples are said to be at a wedding in Cana of Galilee (John 2:1ff.)

Nowhere in John 1 does a person learn that Jesus and His
disciples are in Galilee at a wedding three days **after His
baptism**. The gospel of John does not even contain the actual account of Jesus' baptism. The apostle John recorded only
what John the Baptizer testified about the baptism of Jesus,
which occurred some time in the past (exactly when, we are
not told). While John and the others looked at Jesus, he related to them (in the past tense) the event of Jesus' baptism
and its significance. It is erroneous to assume that His baptism actually was taking place at the very time John the Baptizer was speaking the words recorded in John 1:29-34. Thus,
the apostle John, in writing his gospel account, did not "deny"
(as Steve Wells alleged) what the other gospel writers wrote
concerning the days immediately following Jesus' baptism.
He merely supplemented the synoptic gospels by revealing
to his readers that sometime after Jesus' baptism and wilderness temptations, He saw John the Baptizer again—and three
days later went to a wedding in Cana of Galilee.

IN WHAT ORDER DID
SATAN TEMPT JESUS?

Matthew 4:1-11; Luke 4:1-13

If you have ever compared Matthew's account of Satan tempting Jesus in the wilderness with Luke's account, you likely noticed that there is a difference in the sequence of the recorded events (Matthew 4:1-11; Luke 4:1-13). Both Matthew and Luke record first that Satan tested Jesus by challenging Him to turn stones to bread. However, while the two disciples of Jesus agree on the content of the next two tests, the second and third temptations recorded by Matthew are "flip-flopped" in Luke's account. Matthew recorded that Satan's second temptation involved him trying to persuade Jesus to throw Himself down off the pinnacle of the temple. The third temptation listed by Matthew was Satan's attempt to get Jesus to worship him. Even though Luke mentioned the same two events, he listed them in the reverse order—Satan first desired adoration from Jesus, and then he challenged Him to throw Himself down off the pinnacle of the temple. Based upon this difference, skeptics claim we have a clearcut discrepancy.

The problem with this allegation is that it is based upon an assumption. Those who claim that the "disorder" of temptations is a contradiction, presuppose that history always is written (or spoken) chronologically. However, common sense tells us otherwise. Open almost any world history textbook and you will see that even though most events are recorded chronologically, some are arranged topically. For example, in one chapter you may read about the European civilization in the late Middle Ages (A.D. 1000-1300). Yet, in the very next chapter you might learn about Medieval India (150 B.C.-A.D. 1400). Authors arrange textbooks thematically in order to reduce the confusion that would arise if every event in world history textbooks was arranged chronologically. Even when we rehearse life experiences to friends and family, oftentimes we speak climactically rather than chronologically. A teenager may return home from an amusement park and tell his father about all of the roller coasters he rode at Six Flags. Likely, rather than mentioning all of them in the order he rode them, he will start with the most exciting ones and end with the boring ones (if there is such thing as a "boring" roller coaster).

Had Matthew and Luke claimed to arrange the temptations of Jesus chronologically, skeptics would have a legitimate case. But, the fact of the matter is, neither Matthew nor Luke ever claimed such. Either one of the two gospel writers recorded these events in the order they happened, or both of them wrote topically. Most biblical scholars believe that Matthew was concerned more with the order of events in this story because of his use of words like "then" (4:5, Greek *tote*) and "again" (4:8, Greek *palin*). These two adverbs seem to indicate a more sequential order of the temptations. Luke simply links the events by using the Greek words *kai* and *de* (4:2, 5-6, translated "and"). [The NKJV's translation of *kai* as "then" in Luke 4:5 is unwarranted. It should be translated simply "and" (cf. KJV, ASV, NASV, and RSV)]. Similar to the English word "and" not having specific chronological implications, neither do the Greek words *kai* and *de* (Richards, 1993, p. 230).

THE CURSING OF THE FIG TREE
Matthew 21:18-20; Mark 11:12-14,20-21

As is evident from the number of alleged chronological contradictions within the four gospel accounts, people who study these accounts frequently misconstrue matters of chronology that are contained therein. Bible students need to keep in mind that the gospel writers never claimed to have recorded all of the events of Jesus' life in the exact order in which they occurred. Unless an action or event is denoted by a specific marker (such as "the next day," "on the morrow," "on the

Sabbath," etc.), there can be time gaps between the verses. One example of this is the account of the withered fig tree in Mark 11:12-14,20-21 and Matthew 21:18-20.

> And on the morrow, when they were come out from Bethany, he hungered. And seeing a fig tree afar off having leaves, he came, if haply he might find anything thereon: and when he came to it, he found nothing but leaves; for it was not the season of figs. And he answered and said unto it, "No man eat fruit from thee henceforward for ever." And his disciples heard it....
>
> And as they passed by in the morning, they saw the fig tree withered away from the roots. And Peter calling to remembrance saith unto him, "Rabbi, behold, the fig tree which thou cursedst is withered away" (Mark 11:12-14,20-21, ASV).
>
> Now in the morning as he returned to the city, he hungered. And seeing a fig tree by the way side, he came to it, and found nothing thereon, but leaves only; and he saith unto it, "Let there be no fruit from thee henceforward for ever." And immediately the fig tree withered away. And when the disciples saw it, they marvelled, saying, "How did the fig tree immediately wither away?" (Matthew 21:18-20, ASV).

In Mark, the Lord cursed the fig tree, but the account does not say **when it withered**. The disciples saw it withered the next day, and Peter remembered what the Lord had said. Matthew's account says that the Lord cursed the tree, and it withered immediately, but it does not say **when the disciples saw it**. Matthew 21:20 merely says, "And **when** the disciples saw it...," with no regard to the exact time. Based on the wording, the disciples could have seen it withered at the exact time Jesus cursed it, the next day, the next month, or even the next year. The verse in Matthew provides no time span between when it withered and when the disciples noticed.

However, Mark 11:12,19-20 does give the exact span of time between the curse and the time the disciples noticed it—one day. Since the gospels do not claim to be in exact chronological order, both Matthew and Mark offer a portion of the story. The best thing to do is to extrapolate—from both passages—exactly what happened. Both Mark 11:12 and Matthew 21:18 record that Jesus was hungry, and both recount how He approached a fig tree and, finding no figs, cursed it. Matthew then records that it withered immediately (21:19); Mark records that the disciples heard Jesus curse the tree, but he does not say whether or not they noticed the tree withered at that time (11:14). Next, Mark continues the narrative of Jesus cleansing the temple in Jerusalem (11:15-19). Both writers then recount the astonishment of the disciples at seeing the fig tree withered, with Mark designating it as the next day (11:20-21), and Matthew not specifying how much time passed between 21:19 and 21:20.

Another question to consider (and perhaps the one that is addressed most often in a discussion of the withered fig tree) is whether or not Jesus cursed the tree **before** or **after** the temple was cleansed. Since Matthew records this event before the cursing of the fig tree (21:12-19), and Mark places the cleansing of the temple after Jesus cursed the tree (11:15-19), it is supposed that one of the two writers was mistaken. The truth is, however, Matthew's account is more of a summary, whereas Mark's narrative in this instance is more detailed and orderly. Christ actually made two trips to the temple (Mark 11:11,15), and He cursed the fig tree on His second trip. Mark reveals that the cleansing of the temple "did not take place on the day that he [Jesus—EL] entered Jerusalem in triumph, but on the day following" (Barnes, 1997). Matthew, on the other hand, "addresses the two trips of Christ to the temple as though they were one event," which "gives the impression that the first day Christ entered the temple He drove out the buyers and sellers as well" (Geisler and Howe, 1992, p. 354). Mark's more-detailed account reveals that Jesus really made two trips to the temple. Thus, as Albert Barnes noted: "Mark has stated the order more particularly, and has 'divided' what Matthew mentions together" (1997). It would be like saying, "Last year my family and I went to Disney World," but then supplementing this statement at a later time by saying, "Last year my family and I went to Disney World, left for a two-day deep-sea fishing trip in the Gulf, and then went back to Disney World for a few more days."

When viewed in this light, these alleged contradictions between Matthew and Mark are seen simply as a matter of Matthew's account being more condensed than Mark's. And while Matthew has no timetable for the events, Mark shows that the disciples noticed the withered fig tree on their return from the temple.

WHEN DID JESUS CLEANSE THE TEMPLE?

John 2:13-22; Matthew 21:12-13; Mark 11:15-17; Luke 19:45-46

One of the most popular alleged Bible discrepancies pertaining to chronology—and one that skeptics are fond of citing in almost any discussion on the inerrancy of Scripture—is whether or not Jesus cleansed the temple **early** in His ministry, or near the **end**. According to Matthew, Mark, and Luke, Jesus cleansed the temple during the final week leading up to His death on the cross (Matthew 21:12-13; Mark 11:15-17; Luke 19:45-46). John, however, places his record of the temple cleansing in chapter 2 of his gospel account, between Jesus' first miracle (2:1-12) and His conversation with Nicodemus (3:1-21). How should John's gospel account be understood in light of the other three writers placing the event near the end of Jesus' ministry? Skeptics question, "Did Jesus enter the temple and drive out the money changers early in His ministry, or near the end?"

Most often, it seems, the explanation heard regarding this difficulty is that there was only one temple cleansing—near the end of Jesus' life—and John's placement of this event at an earlier time is the result of his "theological," rather than "chronological," approach to writing his account of the life and teachings of Jesus. The problem with this explanation is that, although overall John may have been a little less concerned with chronology than were the other writers, a straightforward reading of the text favors the position that this particular clearing of the temple was not something that occurred near the end of Jesus' life. The record of Jesus' first miracle, beginning in John 2:1, begins with the phrase, "On the third day…." This section ends with John writing the words, "After this…" (2:12, Greek *meta touto*). Following verse 12, John then begins his account of the temple cleansing saying, "Now the Passover of the Jews was at hand…" (2:13). It certainly would appear to be "out of the ordinary" for John to jump ahead nearly three years in the life of Jesus to an event that occurred in Jerusalem during the last week of His life, only then to backtrack to a time prior to "the second sign Jesus did when He had come out of Judea into Galilee" (John 4:54). Admittedly, John would not have erred in writing about the temple cleansing early on in his gospel account if the Holy Spirit saw fit to mention the event at that time. (Perhaps this would have been to show from the outset of Jesus' ministry that He "repudiated what was central to the Temple cults, and further that his death and resurrection were critically important"—Morris, 1995, p. 167.) A better explanation of this alleged contradiction exists, however: There were two temple cleansings.

Why not? Who is to say that Jesus could not have cleansed the temple of money-hungry, hypocritical Jews on two separate occasions—once earlier in His ministry, and again near the end of His life as He entered Jerusalem for the last time? Are we so naïve as to think that the temple could not have been corrupted at two different times during the three years of Jesus' ministry? Jesus likely visited the temple several times during the last few years of His life on Earth (especially when celebrating the Passover—cf. John 2:13,23; 6:4; 11:55), likely finding inappropriate things going on there more than once. Do churches in the twenty-first century sometimes have problems that recur within a three-year span? Have church leaders ever dealt with these problems in a public manner multiple times and in similar ways? Of course. ("How soon men forget the most solemn reproofs, and return to evil practices"—Barnes, 1956a, p. 196.)

What evidence does a person possess, which would lead him to conclude that Jesus cleansed the temple only once? There is none. While Matthew, Mark, and Luke recorded a temple cleansing late in Jesus' ministry, much evidence exists to indicate that John recorded an earlier clearing of the temple. It is logical to conclude that the extra details recorded in John 2 are not simply supplemental facts (even though the writers of the gospels did supplement each others' writings fairly frequently). Rather, the different details recorded by John likely are due to the fact that we are dealing with two different temple cleansings. Only John mentioned (1) the oxen and sheep, (2) the whip of cords, (3) the scattering of the money, (4) Jesus' command, "Take these things away," and (5) the disciples' remembrance of Psalm 69:9: "Zeal for Your house has eaten Me up" (2:17). Furthermore, John did not include Jesus' quotation of Isaiah 56:7, which is found in all three of the other accounts, and stands as a prominent part of their accounts of the temple cleansing.

In view of the major differences in wording, in setting, and in time, as well as the fact that, apart from the work of John the Baptizer, nothing in the first five chapters of John's gospel account is found in Matthew, Mark, or Luke, "we will require more evidence than a facile assumption that the two similar narratives must refer to the same event" (Morris, 1995, p. 167). There is no chronological contradiction here.

WHEN DID THE TEMPLE VEIL TEAR?
Matthew 27:50-51; Luke 23:44-46

A few years ago, a journal dedicated to revealing (alleged) Bible errors petitioned its readers to submit their "best" biblical questions and arguments that "they have found through actual experience to be exceptionally effective vis-à-vis biblicists...and they will probably be published for all to see and use" (McKinsey, 1988a, p. 6). The first response printed in this journal (two months later) was from a man who listed among his top five "Bible contradictions" a question of whether or not the veil of the temple was torn in two "before" (Luke 23:44-46) or "after" (Matthew 27:50-51) Jesus died on the cross. The skeptic stated that this question was one of his favorites to ask because it elicited "such ludicrous rebuttals from Christian apologists" (McKinsey, 1988b, p. 6).

Before taking the skeptic's word at face value as to what these scriptures actually say (or do not say), compare the passages for yourself.

> And Jesus cried again with a loud voice, and yielded up his spirit. And behold, the veil of the temple was rent in two from the top to the bottom (Matthew 27: 50-51, ASV; cf. Mark 15:37-38).

> And it was now about the sixth hour, and a darkness came over the whole land until the ninth hour, the sun's light failing: and the veil of the temple was rent in the midst. And Jesus, crying with a loud voice, said, "Father, into thy hands I commend my spirit": and having said this, he gave up the ghost (Luke 23: 44-46).

Do you read anything in either Matthew or Luke's account that says the veil was torn "before" or "after" Jesus died (to use the skeptic's own words)? Granted, Luke did mention the rending of the veil before he recorded that Jesus died,

and Matthew mentioned it after recording His death, but neither made any direct statements that would indicate exactly
when the rending took place. Simply because one Bible writer
recorded something before, or after, another writer does not
mean that either writer is attempting to establish a chronological timeline. Unless the skeptic can point to a verse by
both writers that says these events occurred in the precise order in which they are recorded, then no case can be made for
these two passages being incompatible.

Consider for a moment the "to do list" that many of us make
either daily or weekly. If someone peeked at your list and saw
where you crossed off the first four things, but the things that
you had marked off were not in the same order in which you
accomplished them, would you be guilty of lying (to yourself
or to a colleague)? No. Imagine also that you returned home
after work one day, and told your children some of the things
you had accomplished at the office. Then, you told your spouse
the same things you told your children, only in a somewhat
different order. Would your children have any right to call
you a liar if they overheard this second conversion between
you and your spouse? Of course not. The only way your children would be justified in calling you a liar is if you had told
both them and your spouse that every event you rehearsed
happened in the precise order in which you mentioned them.

The only way a skeptic could prove that Matthew 27:50-
51 and Luke 23:44-46 are contradictory is if he or she could
establish that both writers claimed to be writing all of these
events in precisely the same order in which they occurred.
Since, however, the critic cannot prove such intended chronology, he is left with another **alleged** and **unproven** "contradiction." Interesting, is it not, that this fairly simple "problem" was listed as a "top-five" question with which to "stump"
a Christian? Truly, using a little common sense proves helpful when studying the Bible.

TO GALILEE OR JERUSALEM?
Matthew 26:32; 28:7,10,16; Luke 24:33-43,49

Three times in the gospel of Matthew, the writer recorded where certain disciples of Jesus were instructed to meet the Lord in Galilee after His resurrection. During the Passover meal that Jesus ate the night of His betrayal, He informed His disciples, saying, "After I have been raised, I will go before you to Galilee" (Matthew 26:32). Three days later, on the day of Jesus' resurrection when Mary Magdalene and the other women came to the empty tomb of Jesus, Matthew recorded how an angel told them to notify the disciples of Jesus' resurrection, and to tell them exactly the same thing they were told three days earlier: "He is going before you into Galilee; there you will see Him" (28:7). Then, only three verses later, as the women were on their way to inform the disciples of Jesus' resurrection and the message given to them by the angel, Matthew recorded how Jesus appeared to them and said: "Rejoice!... Do not be afraid. Go and tell My brethren to go to Galilee, and there they will see Me" (28:9-10). Sometime thereafter, "the eleven disciples went away into Galilee, to the mountain which Jesus had appointed for them," and "worshipped Him" (28:16).

According to Matthew, Jesus unquestionably wanted to meet with His disciples in Galilee following His resurrection. However, some skeptics and sincere Bible students have asked why, according to Luke, Jesus met with His disciples in Jerusalem (24:33-43), and then commanded them to stay there until they were "endued with power from on high" (24:49). Does Luke's account contradict Matthew's? According to one Bible antagonist,

> Matthew, Mark, and John have Jesus saying the disciples are to rendezvous with him in Galilee, northern Israel, about three days journey away. In contradiction to this, Luke's two books–The Gospel of Luke and The Book of Acts, have Jesus planning to rendezvous in Jerusalem....

> In the real world, people cannot be in two places at the same time, and to claim otherwise is to be caught up in a contradiction…. The Bible, like the cheating husband, has been caught in a contradiction, exposed as a liar, and therefore can't be trusted to tell the truth (Smith, 1995).

Is the skeptic right? Is the Bible at fault in this instance? Does it place the same people in two different places "at the same time"? Where exactly did Jesus intend to meet with His disciples—in Galilee or Jerusalem?

The truth is, Jesus met with His disciples in both places, but He did so at **different** times. One of the reasons so many people allege that two or more Bible passages are contradictory is because they fail to recognize that mere differences do not necessitate a contradiction. For there to be a bona fide contradiction, not only must one be referring to the same person, place, or thing in the same sense, but **the same time period** must be under consideration. If a person looks at a single door in the back of a building and says, "That door is shut," but also says, "That door is open," has he contradicted himself? Not necessarily. The door may have been shut at one moment, but then opened the next by a strong gust of wind. Time and chronology are important factors to consider when dealing with alleged errors in the Bible.

Consider another illustration that more closely resembles the alleged problem posed by the skeptic. At the end of every year, the professional and managerial staff members at Apologetics Press travel to Birmingham, Alabama, for a two-day, end-of-the-year meeting. Suppose the Executive Director reminds us of this event three days beforehand, saying, "Don't forget about our meeting in Birmingham beginning Thursday," and then calls our homes on the morning of the meeting as another reminder, saying, "Don't forget about our meeting today in Birmingham." Would someone be justified in concluding that our Executive Director had lied about the meeting if, on that Thursday morning, all of the staff members at Apologetics Press (including the Executive Director) showed up at work in Montgomery, and carried out some of the same tasks performed on any other workday? Not at all. Actually, on the day the staff at Apologetics Press leaves for the end-of-the-year meeting, it is common for everyone to work until about 10:30 a.m., and then depart for the meeting in Birmingham. If someone asked whether we went into work in **Montgomery** on Thursday, one honestly could say, "Yes." If someone else asked if we traveled to **Birmingham** on Thursday for a two-day meeting, again, one could truthfully say, "Yes." Both statements would be true. We met at both places on the same day, only at **different** times.

Similarly, Jesus met with His disciples **both** in Jerusalem and in Galilee, but at different times. On the day of His resurrection, He met with all of the apostles (except Thomas) in Jerusalem, just as both Luke and John recorded (Luke 24:33-43; John 20:19-25). Since Jesus was on the Earth for only forty days following His resurrection (cf. Acts 1:3), sometime between this meeting with His apostles in Jerusalem and His ascension more than five weeks later, Jesus met with seven of His disciples at the Sea of Tiberias in Galilee (John 21:1-14), and later with all eleven of the apostles on a mountain in Galilee that Jesus earlier had appointed for them (Matthew 28:16). Sometime following these meetings in Galilee, Jesus and His disciples traveled back to Judea, where He ascended into heaven from the Mount of Olives near Bethany (Luke 24:50-53; Acts 1:9-12).

None of the accounts of Jesus' post-resurrection appearances contradicts another. Rather, each writer supplemented what a different writer left out. Jesus may have appeared to the disciples a number of times during the forty days on Earth after His resurrection (cf. 1 Corinthians 15:1-7), while the New Testament writers mentioned only the more prominent instances in order to substantiate the fact of His resurrection.

Still, one may ask, "Why did Jesus command His apostles to 'tarry in the city of Jerusalem' on the day of His resurrection until they were 'endued with power from on high' (Luke 24:49), if He really wanted them to meet Him in Galilee?" Actually, it is an assumption to assert that Jesus made the above statement on the same day that He arose from the grave. We must keep in mind as we study the Bible is that it normally is not as concerned about chronology as modern-day writings. Frequently (especially in the gospel accounts), writers went from one subject to the next without giving the actual time or the exact order in which something was done or taught (cf. Luke 4:1-3; Matthew 4:1-11). In Luke 24, the writer omitted the post-resurrection appearances of Jesus in Galilee (mentioned by both Matthew and John). However, notice that he never stated that Jesus remained **only** in Jerusalem from the day He rose from the grave until the day He ascended into heaven.

According to Luke 24 verses 1,13,21,29, and 33, the events recorded in the first forty-three verses of that chapter all took place on the very day of Jesus' resurrection. The last four verses of Luke 24 (vss. 50-53), however, took place (according to Luke) more than five weeks later (cf. Acts 1:1-12). But what about verses 44-49? When were these statements made? The truth is, no one can know for sure. Luke gives no indication (as he did in the preceding verses) that this particular section took place "on the first day of the week" (24:1), or on "the third day" since Jesus' crucifixion (24:21). All we know is that verses 44-49 took place sometime before He ascended into heaven (vss. 50-51). Simply because Luke used the Greek conjunctive particle *de* [translated "and" (ASV), "then" (NKJV), and "now" (NASV)] to begin verse 44, does not necessarily denote a close connection between the two verses, but only a general continuation of the account and a brief statement of what Jesus said. Even though many twenty-first-century readers assume that the events recorded in Luke 24:44-49 occurred on the very day Jesus rose from the grave, the text actually is silent on the matter.

The burden of proof is on the Bible critic to verify his allegation. Although the skeptic quoted earlier compared the Bible to a "cheating husband" who "has been caught in a contradiction," one must remember how equally deplorable it is to draw up charges of marital unfaithfulness when there is no proof of such. In reality, the Bible should be likened to a faithful husband who has been wrongfully accused of infidelity by prejudiced, overbearing skeptics whose case is based upon unproven assumptions.

WHEN DID PAUL GO TO JERUSALEM?
Acts 9:22-26; Galatians 1:16

Three times in the book of Acts, the Bible student is informed that after Saul's conversion to Christ in Damascus, he departed for Jerusalem. According to Acts chapter 9, Saul (also called Paul) "increased all the more in strength" following his baptism into Christ, and "confounded the Jews who dwelt in Damascus" (vs. 22). Then, when "many days were past…the disciples took him by night and let him down through the wall in a large basket" for fear of the Jews (vss. 23,25). Immediately following these verses, the text reads: "**And when Saul had come to Jerusalem**, he tried to join the disciples; but they were all afraid of him, and did not believe that he was a disciple" (vs. 26, emp. added). Add to these verses Paul's respective statements to the Jerusalem mob (Acts 22:17) and to King Agrippa (Acts 26:20) regarding his journey from Damascus to Jerusalem, and Bible students get the impression that shortly after Paul's conversion in Damascus, he journeyed to Jerusalem. The problem with this reasoning is that Paul later wrote to the churches of Galatia, and indicated that he "did not immediately…go up to Jerusalem" following his calling to Christ (Galatians 1:16). Rather, he went to Arabia, back to Damascus, and then **after three years** he went up to Jerusalem (1:17-18). [NOTE: "Arabia" generally is taken as a reference to the vast peninsula which bears that name. Its northwestern boundaries reached almost to Damascus–Pfeiffer, 1979, p. 203.] Concerned Bible students want to know how these passages are harmonized? Did Paul go straight to Jerusalem shortly after his conversion, or three years later?

Although Acts chapters 9, 22, and 26 all indicate that Paul went from Damascus to Jerusalem after he became a Christian, one must realize that none of these passages specifically says that Paul went **straight** from Damascus to Jerusalem. It only says, "And **when** Saul had come to Jerusalem...." The writer of Acts gives no time limitations here. In fact, nowhere in the New Testament will a person find a statement denying that three years expired between Paul's conversion and his first trip to Jerusalem as a Christian. Although rarely emphasized, what the Bible does **not** say regarding Paul's journeys is very important–it proves that the alleged contradiction is based only on speculation, and not on a fair representation of the Scriptures.

Some question why Paul did not mention his trip to Arabia to preach among the Gentiles when he spoke to the Jewish mob in Jerusalem, and later to King Agrippa. Was it not a vital piece of information? Did he just "forget" about this part of his life? Actually, Paul had a good reason for not mentioning his trip to Arabia–he was speaking to Jews who were "seeking to kill him" because of his dealings with Gentiles (Acts 21: 28-31). As a way of comparison, we can understand why a college football player who transferred from a rival school may not talk to his current teammates about his former college experiences, or why a new sales representative who transferred from a competing company may refrain from talking to current customers and/or coworkers about the three years he spent with the rival company. In a similar way, it did not aid

Paul's cause to mention at the very outset of his speech that some of his first work for the Lord was done among the Gentiles. (The Jews hated Paul for his dealings with the Gentiles. The events recorded in Acts 21 alone are proof of such hatred.) Certain situations simply warrant silence on a subject, rather than an exhaustive detailing of historical facts. Paul did not lie (to the Jerusalem mob or to King Agrippa) about his past experience working with the Gentiles for a time; he merely **omitted** this piece of information in his efforts to show his fellow Jews that the very people among whom he had been a loyal persecutor were those to whom he now preached.

The twenty-first-century reader must remember that a Bible writer (or a speaker whom a Bible writer quotes) may be writing/speaking from one point of view, and raise a point that may not be made in another situation. Neither Paul in his speeches, nor Luke in penning the book of Acts to Theophilus, saw a need to mention Paul's journey to Arabia. In his letter to the churches of Galatia, however, Paul was dealing with Judaizers who taught that one had to keep the Law of Moses to be saved, and who wished to discredit Paul as an apostle. Paul thus wrote to tell them that after his conversion, he preached among the Gentiles for an extended amount of time **before ever meeting with another apostle**. Paul did not hurry off to Jerusalem to get instruction and approval from the Twelve. In defense of his apostolic credentials to the churches of Galatia, Paul mentioned his delayed journey to Jerusalem in order to emphasize (among other things) his genuine apostleship, whose message and authority came from Almighty God, and not from the twelve apostles, or any other person.

Chapter 6

ALLEGED ETHICAL CONTRADICTIONS

ISRAELITE PLUNDERING, AND A MISSING DONKEY

Exodus 3:21-22; 12:35-36; 20:15; Matthew 21:1-7

Numerous passages of Scripture teach—either explicitly or implicitly—about the sinfulness of thievery. One of the Ten Commandments that God gave to Israel was: "You shall not steal" (Exodus 20:15). In the book of Leviticus, one can read where "the Lord spoke to Moses, saying, 'Speak to all the congregation of the children of Israel, and say to them... You shall not steal, nor deal falsely, nor lie to one another.... You shall not cheat your neighbor, nor rob him' " (19:1-2,11,13). If a thief was found breaking into a house at night and was struck so that he died, the old law stated that there would be "no guilt for his bloodshed" (Exodus 22:2). Under the new covenant, the apostle Paul wrote to the church at Ephesus, saying, "Let him who stole steal no longer, but rather let him labor, working with his hands what is good, that he may have something to give him who has need" (4:28). And to the Christians at Corinth, Paul wrote that thieves "will not inherit the kingdom of God" (1 Corinthians 6:9-11). Thus, God obviously considers stealing to be a transgression of His law.

Skeptics, however, question the consistency of the above Bible verses when compared to other passages of Scripture, which they feel often are overlooked in a discussion on the biblical view of thievery. One of these alleged inconsistencies is found in the book of Exodus, and centers on how the Israelites "plundered" the Egyptians during the Exodus. When God spoke to Moses at the burning bush about the Exodus from Egypt, He said: "It shall be, when you go, that you shall not go empty-handed. But every woman shall ask of her neighbor, namely, of her who dwells near her house, articles of silver, articles of gold, and clothing; and you shall put them on your sons and on your daughters. **So you shall plunder the Egyptians**" (Exodus 3:21-22, emp. added). Then, as the Exodus became a reality, the Bible tells how "the children of Israel had done according to the word of Moses…and **plundered the Egyptians**" (Exodus 12:35-36, emp. added). According to skeptic Steve Wells, "God tells the Hebrew women to break the eighth commandment…and encourages the Israelites to steal from the Egyptians" (2001).

A second Bible story frequently used by skeptics in defense of their belief in the errancy of Scripture is that of Jesus' disciples allegedly "stealing" a donkey and a colt. According to the gospel of Matthew, before entering Jerusalem during the final week of His life, Jesus instructed His disciples, saying, "Go into the village opposite you, and immediately you will find a donkey tied, and a colt with her. Loose them and bring them to Me. And if anyone says anything to you, you shall say, 'The Lord has need of them,' and immediately he will send them" (Matthew 21:1-3). Luke added: "So those who were sent went their way and found it just as He had said to them. But as they were loosing the colt, the owners of it said to them, 'Why are you loosing the colt?' And they said, 'The Lord has need of him.' Then they brought him to Jesus" (Luke 19:32-35). Regarding this story, Dennis McKinsey asked: "Are we to believe this isn't theft? Imagine seeing a stranger driving your car away while claiming the lord needed it" (1985, p. 1). Another infidel by the name of Dan Barker commented on this passage in his book, *Losing Faith in Faith: From Preacher to Atheist*, saying, "I was taught as a child that when you take something without asking for it, that is stealing" (1992, p. 166). Did Jesus really encourage His disciples to **steal** a donkey and a colt? And what about the Israelites plundering the Egyptians? Can these passages be explained logically in light of the numerous statements throughout Scripture that clearly condemn thievery?

A Proper Plundering, or an Unholy Heist?

Concerning the Israelites' plundering of the Egyptians, the Bible student first needs to recognize that Exodus 3:22 is a reconfirmation of a prophecy made centuries earlier when God spoke to Abraham, saying, "Your descendants will be strangers in a land that is not theirs, and will serve them, and they will afflict them four hundred years. And also the nation [Egypt–EL] whom they serve I will judge; **afterward they shall come out with great possessions**" (Genesis 15:13-14, emp. added).

Next, the honest Bible reader must concede that the Israelites' "plundering" was not comparable to the forceful plundering that an armed thief might undertake. The kind of plundering done by the Israelites is described within the text. God told Moses, "I will give this people [the Israelites–EL] **favor** in the sight of the Egyptians…. But every woman shall **ask** of her neighbor, namely, of her who dwells near her house, articles of silver, articles of gold, and clothing; and you shall put them on your sons and on your daughters" (Exodus 3:21-22). When it finally came time for the Exodus, the texts states:

> Now the children of Israel had done according to the word of Moses, and they had **asked** from the Egyptians articles of silver, articles of gold, and cloth-

ing. And the Lord had given the people **favor** in the sight of the Egyptians, so that **they granted them what they requested**. Thus they plundered the Egyptians (Exodus 12:35-36, emp. added).

Who but a biased skeptic would call this stealing? The actual circumstances were such that the Israelites merely **requested** various articles, which were then granted by the Egyptians. The "plundering" described in the book of Exodus was nothing more than receiving that for which the Israelites asked. [NOTE: The word "plundered" in these two passages is not the normal Hebrew term used for what soldiers do to the enemy at the conclusion of a battle. In Exodus, the word "plundered" (from the Hebrew word *natsal*) is used figuratively to mean that the Israelites accomplished the same thing as if they had taken them in battle—due to the extenuating circumstances of the plagues motivating the Egyptians to fear the Israelites and their God (see Archer, 1982, p. 110).]

But suppose for a moment that the Israelites **had** "plundered" the Egyptians (**at the Lord's command**), in the sense that they took various possessions **by force**. Would this have been unjust? Surely not, since Jehovah recognized that the Israelites had provided slave labor for the Egyptians for many years (the descendants of Jacob [Israel] had been in Egypt for more than 200 years). During this time, the Egyptians afflicted them "with burdens" and made them "serve with rigor" (Exodus 1:11,13). Pharaoh "made their lives bitter with hard bondage" (1:14), and, upon seeing the tremendous growth of the Israelites, even commanded that every son born of the Israelites be killed (1:22). In reality, the "plundering" that took place at the end of Israel's stay in Egypt (even had it been by force at the command of God) was a rather small compensation for the many years of agonizing slave labor they provided for the Egyptians.

Were Jesus' Disciples "Colt Crooks"?

Even if the skeptic is somewhat pacified by the above explanation of the Israelites' plundering, he likely will still want to know about the case in the New Testament of Jesus instructing two of His disciples to go into a village, locate a donkey and a colt, and to bring them back to Him. "Are we to believe this isn't theft?" asked Dennis McKinsey (1985, p. 1). Allegedly, "Jesus told people to take a colt…without the owners' permission." And that, says McKinsey, is "commonly known as stealing" (2000, p. 236).

Question: If I e-mailed my wife and asked her to walk to a neighbor's house and pick up his truck so that I could use it to haul an old furnace to the junkyard, would someone who read this same e-mail (perhaps finding a hard copy of it crumpled up in the trash) be justified in concluding that I asked my wife to steal the truck? Certainly not. Since the e-mail had no other information in it than the request to my wife concerning a neighbor's truck, a person reading the note would have to have access to additional information in order to come to the conclusion that my wife and I were guilty of theft. This person may be ignorant of the fact that I had prearranged such a pick-up with my neighbor the previous day. Or, perhaps my neighbor had told me at some earlier time that I could use his truck whenever I needed it.

What Mr. McKinsey and other skeptics never seem to take into consideration in their interpretation of Scripture is that the Bible does not record every single detail of every event it mentions (cf. John 21:25). The Bible was not intended to be an exhaustive chronological timeline citing every detail about the lives of all of the men and women mentioned within it. The New Testament book of Acts covers a period of about thirty years, but it actually is only about **some** of the acts of some of the early Christians. There were many more things that Paul, Peter, Silas, Luke, and other first-century Christians did that are not recorded therein. For example (as discussed in the previous chapter), Paul spent three years in Arabia and Damascus after his conversion (Galatians 1:16-18), yet Luke did not mention this detail, nor the many things Paul accomplished during these three years.

The case of Jesus telling His disciples to go locate the donkey and colt does not prove thievery, any more than Jesus' disciples inquiring about and occupying an "upper room" makes them trespassers (cf. Mark 14:13-15). When sending His two disciples to get the requested animals, Jesus told them exactly where to go and what to say, as if He already knew the circumstances under which the donkey and colt were available. Jesus may very well have prearranged for the use of the donkeys. Neither Mr. McKinsey nor any other skeptic can prove otherwise. Similar to how I am not obligated to go home from work every night and rehearse to my wife **everything** I did **each hour** at work, the Bible is not obligated to fill in every detail of every event, including the one regarding the attainment of two donkeys. No contradiction or charge of wrong is legitimate if unrelated circumstantial details may be postulated that account for explicit information that is given.

Furthermore, the innocence of Jesus and His disciples is reinforced by the fact that the disciples were able to leave with the donkeys. Had the disciples really been stealing the animals, one would think that the owners would not have allowed such to happen. Also, nothing is said in the text about what happened to the animals after Jesus rode them into Jerusalem. For all we know, Jesus' disciples could have immediately taken the animals back to their owners. [NOTE: For a rebuttle to the charge that Matthew and Mark contradict each other in regard to the **number** of donkeys Jesus rode into Jerusalem, see chapter nine.]

Skeptics who charge that the Bible contains contradictory teachings concerning the act of stealing have no firm ground on which to stand. The Israelites did not "steal" the Egyptians' clothing and jewels, they "asked" for them, and the Egyptians "granted them what they requested" (Exodus 12:35-36). And until it can be proven that Jesus' disciples took the donkeys by force (and without prior permission), justice demands that the accusations of guilt must be withdrawn. There are no justifiable contradictions here.

DOES GOD CONDONE LYING?
Joshua 2:1-21

One of the best-known stories in the Old Testament concerns the unusual manner in which the Israelites conquered the city of Jericho while they were in the process of inhabiting the land of Canaan (Joshua 2,6). A woman named Rahab not only provided sanctuary in her house for two Israelite spies but, when asked by the king's men about the matter (2:3), lied in order to protect them (2:5). Later, the lives of Rahab and her household were spared when Jericho was destroyed (2:14; 6:22-25)—a fact that has provided grist for the mill of Bible critics who suggest that this account establishes God's approval of situation ethics (cf. Hebrews 11:31; James 2:25). Their argument is as follows. Rahab lied. But the situation required that she do so for good reason—to protect the spies. Rahab was blessed, and her household was spared certain death. Thus, God must approve of situation ethics (e.g., lying under certain conditions). How should the Bible believer respond to such a suggestion? Does God approve of lying under some circumstances?

In addressing the critics' allegations, let us first admit the obvious. Rahab **did** lie—not once, but twice. When the king's emissaries came to interrogate her, she lied when she feigned ignorance about the spies being Israelites. She then lied a second time when she told the intermediaries that the spies had left the city through the main gate under cover of darkness. Let us also freely admit that Rahab and her household were the only ones saved during the assault upon Jericho (Joshua 6:17).

The question is not whether Rahab lied. She did. The question is not whether she was saved during Jericho's destruction. She was. The questions that must be addressed are these: (1) Did God bless Rahab **as a result of her lie**?; and (2) Is "situation ethics" acceptable? That is to say, can a person lie on certain occasions (if the situation warrants it), and still be pleasing to God?

First, notice what the Bible has to say about lying. Of the Ten Commandments, the ninth forbade lying (Exodus 20:16). And, in both the Old and New Testaments the telling of a falsehood is condemned (Leviticus 19:11; Proverbs 6:16-19; Ephesians 4:25; Colossians 3:9). As one writer stated the matter, "Just as there are no exceptions to the adultery commandment, there is none for the Ninth Commandment" (Webster, 1993, p. 2). God has denounced explicitly any form of lying, and has made it clear that those who commit such a sin without repenting shall spend eternity "in the lake which burns with fire and brimstone which is the second death" (Revelation 21:8).

Second, a close examination of the actual events of Joshua 2 is in order. Note, for example, that the spies never asked Rahab to lie for them. In fact, there is no indication in the text that the spies even knew Rahab **had** lied. Since they were hiding on the roof (Joshua 2:8), it is highly unlikely that they had any knowledge of her sin. It is wrong to suggest that Rahab received God's blessings as **a result of her lie**. The two New Testament passages that mention Rahab do not commend her for the sin of lying. Quite the opposite, in fact. The writer of Hebrews placed Rahab in the great "hall of fame of faith" (Hebrews 11) because "she received the spies with peace" (vs. 31). James acknowledged that she was "justified by works when she received the messengers" (2:25). Nowhere in Scripture is Rahab's sin of lying spoken of approvingly. Instead, it is her faith and her righteous works that are commended and approved. As one writer observed:

> What she is commended for is her faith or that which prompted her to deliver the spies from her townspeople, **not** the means by which she accomplished it. She had heard about God's dealings with Egypt and how He had delivered Israel through the parting of the Red Sea. So, the word of hearing profited her, because it was united by faith (Heb. 4:2). James did not write, "...was not Rahab the harlot justified by lying, in that she spoke an untruth to the king's men and sent the spies out another way?" Her faith was evidenced in the work of receiving the spies and sending them out another way (Lloyd, 1990, p. 357, emp. added).

Furthermore, it is important to consider the entire context of Rahab's life and vocation. She was a prostitute, living in a pagan city. As Wayne Jackson has observed:

> The case of Rahab is an example of where God honored a person due to their obedient faith in spite of a personal character flaw. Consider the following facts about this incident. Rahab was from a pagan environment. Her concept of morality and her personal lifestyle (she was a harlot) needed considerable refining. In spite of this sordid background, she had developed a genuine faith in Jehovah (Josh. 2:9ff.). She referred to Him as "God in heaven above, and on earth beneath...." Accordingly, when the spies approached her, she was not "disobedient" as were the others of Jericho, who perished in the destruction of the city, for she, through faith in God and His promises, received the spies in peace (Heb. 11:31), hid them, and sent them out another way (Jas. 2:25) [1986, 22: 23].

Should we be surprised that a prostitute, living in pagan surroundings, would lie to governmental authorities? Hardly.

But she was not saved because she lied; she was saved from the destruction of Jericho **in spite** of her lying (and harlotry). Bible critics have isolated Rahab's lie from both the context of the story, and from the remainder of her life, including additional biblical commentary on that life.

The question arises: Why, then, was she honored within the great "hall of fame of faith" in Hebrews 11, and spoken of by James as having been "justified"? Surely, the answer to the question has to do with the fact that Rahab did not remain in her sinful state. Rahab was not mentioned favorably by the writers of the books of Hebrews and James because she told a lie at one point in her life. Rather, she was commended for a lifetime of righteousness that followed a previous life of sin.

Consider two other famous Old Testament characters who sinned, yet who overcame those sins and were counted as faithful in God's eyes. Noah, for example, was "righteous," "perfect in his generations," and a man who "walked with God" (Genesis 6:9). Yet after the Flood he became drunk in front of his sons, and as a result, his nakedness was exposed before one of them (Genesis 9:20-23). Was Noah permanently condemned for a temporary sin? Gary Grizzell addressed this issue when he wrote:

> There is absolutely no record of anyone reproving Noah for his sin. There is no record of his repentance. This is the extent of the Old Testament revelation of Noah's retirement years. Did Noah die in an unrepentant state? No, just as Rahab did not die a harlot and a liar.... In the twenty-seven books of the New Testament there is not one hint of the historical fact of his sin of drunkenness. The only logical conclusion is that this implies his repentance prior to his death (1986, 15:70).

We know this to be the case because, like Rahab, Noah is mentioned specifically in Hebrews 11:7, and even is referred to as having become "an heir of righteousness which is according to faith."

Consider also the example of Abraham. In Genesis 12:10-20, Abraham deceptively told an Egyptian pharaoh that Sarai was his sister, rather than admitting that she was also his wife. Later, he similarly deceived Abimelech, king of Gerar, regarding the same matter (Genesis 20:1-2). To protect his own life, Abraham intentionally deceived the two rulers, while at the same time offering his wife sexually to the potentates. What faithful husband would act in such a manner and allow his wife to be taken by another man, without at least letting that man know that she was, in fact, his wife? Nevertheless, in James 2:23, Abraham is referred to as "the friend of God."

In addressing these very matters, Walter Kaiser correctly observed: "...divine approval of an individual in one aspect or area of his life does not entail and must not be extended to mean that there is a divine approval of that individual in **all** aspects of his character or conduct" (1983, pp. 270-271, emp. added). Or, as Grizzell noted: "God judges a man by the whole of his life, not one act of sin in his life" (1986, 15:70). Neither Noah nor Abraham should be condemned permanently because of a temporary occurrence of sin. Both of these men stood accountable before God, each accepting personal responsibility for his actions. They became noteworthy characters in biblical history not because of their sinful mistakes, but because of their eventual repentance and lifetimes spent in God's service.

If critics of the Bible would consider the Scriptures in their entirety, rather than isolating individual passages in an attempt to justify their preconceived conclusion that the Bible contains contradictions and discrepancies, controversy over such matters would cease to exist. Furthermore, it reeks of inconsistency for the critic to "pick and choose" matters that at first glance appear to support his allegations, yet ignore the plain and simple passages that refute those same allegations.

Rahab—a prostitute from a pagan background—humbled herself before the God of Abraham, Isaac, and Jacob. When she cried out, "I know that...the Lord your God, He is God in heaven above and on earth beneath" (2:9), she confessed her willingness to acknowledge both His existence and His sovereignty. It was not enough, however, for her merely to express her faith verbally. Rather, she had to **act** upon it by: (a) keeping silent about the spies' mission (Joshua 2:14,20); (b) binding the scarlet cord in the window of her house (2:18); and (c) remaining inside that house, which would be the sole location of her deliverance when God destroyed Jericho (2:18-19).

IS GOD THE AUTHOR OF FALSEHOODS?
1 Kings 22:19-28; Titus 1:2

The question answered in the preceding section of this chapter dealt with whether or not God condones lying in certain situations. Now we turn our attention to a similar question, but one that focuses more on the nature of God, and His role in a particular event in the life of Ahab, king of Israel. In 1 Kings 22, the story is told of King Ahab requesting the assistance from Jehoshaphat, king of Judah, to go to war with Syria in order to recover the territory of Ramoth Gilead. Jehoshaphat immediately agreed to assist Ahab in this battle, but he also asked for Ahab to "inquire for the word of the Lord" (vs. 5). Ahab willingly granted Jehoshaphat's request, and gathered together nearly 400 of his prophets. After these false prophets approved of Ahab's plan of war, and assured him victory against the Syrians (vss. 6,10-12), Jehoshaphat (apparently sensing that all was not well) asked if there was another prophet that they might consult in order to get more counsel. Ahab bitterly acknowledged that there still was one man who could be consulted regarding his desire to reclaim Ramoth Gilead for Israel–Micaiah, the son of Imlah. As Ahab suspected, once Micaiah (a true prophet of the Lord) was brought before him, he predicted defeat for the confederation (vss. 17-23)–a prophecy that Ahab and Jehoshaphat ignored, but one that was fulfilled. The battle ended with Israel and Judah in retreat, and Ahab dead.

The problem that many people have with this passage has to do with the lying spirit that Micaiah mentioned as coming from Jehovah. The text reads as follows:

> Then Micaiah said, "Therefore hear the word of the Lord: I saw the Lord sitting on His throne, and all the host of heaven standing by, on His right hand and on His left. And the Lord said, 'Who will persuade Ahab to go up, that he may fall at Ramoth Gilead?' So one spoke in this manner, and another spoke in that manner. Then a spirit came forward and stood before the Lord, and said, 'I will persuade him.' The Lord said to him, 'In what way?' So he said, 'I will go out and be a lying spirit in the mouth of all his prophets.' And the Lord said, 'You shall persuade him, and also prevail. Go out and do so.' Therefore look! The Lord has put a lying spirit in the mouth of all these prophets of yours, and the Lord has declared disaster against you" (1 Kings 22:19-23).

Few narratives in the Old Testament have been the focus of more infidel criticism than 1 Kings 22, and particularly these five verses. How could God, Who is revealed in the Bible as being One Who "cannot lie" (Titus 1:2; cf. Hebrews 6:18), "put a lying spirit in the mouth" of Ahab's prophets (1 Kings 22:23)? What rational explanation can be given to this alleged discrepancy? Is God, or Satan, the "father of lies" (John 8:44)?

First, the honest Bible student must observe that the narrative involves a **vision** that is highly **symbolic**. Therefore, it would be unwise to press it as though it were a **literal** circumstance. Micaiah answered Ahab with two parabolic visions. "In the first, Israel was likened to shepherdless sheep scattered on the mountains, which must find their own way home (v. 17). In the second Micaiah described a heavenly scene in which the Lord and his hosts discussed the best way to get Ahab to Ramoth Gilead so that he might fall in battle (vv. 19-23)" (Patterson and Austel, 1988, p. 164). Commentator Adam Clarke wisely noted that this account is an illustration, and "only tells, in figurative language, what was in the womb of providence, the events which were shortly to take place, the agents employed in them, and the permission on the part of God for these agents to act" (n.d., 2:476). Another writer has observed: "Visions of the invisible world can only be a sort of parables; revelation, not of the truth as it actually is, but of so much of the truth as can be shown through such a medium. The details of a vision, therefore, cannot safely be pressed, any more than the details of a parable" (Cook, 1981, 2:619).

Second, there is a common Hebrew idiom used throughout the Old Testament by which the **permissive** will of God is expressed in forceful, active jargon. The Lord is said to have "hardened Pharaoh's heart" (Exodus 7:3,13; 9:12; 10:1; et al.), "incited David against" Israel (2 Samuel 24:1), "deceived" His people (Jeremiah 4:10), and given them "statutes that were not good" (Ezekiel 20:25). In the New Testament, God is characterized as sending a strong delusion that some might believe a lie and be condemned (2 Thessalonians 2:11-12). Even Jesus used "commands" at times in a permissive sense. For example, He commanded the demons to "go" into the herd of pigs (Matthew 8:32), yet the preceding verse informs the reader that the demons begged Jesus to let them enter the swine. Thus, He was not the initiator of the demons' move (from inhabiting man to dwelling in pigs), He merely permitted them to do so. Similarly, when Jesus told Judas, "What you do, do quickly" (John 13:27), He was not giving Him a direct command, or forcing Judas to betray Him. Rather, Jesus **permitted** Judas' actions, and (since He knew what Judas was about to do) even encouraged him to do it quickly. All of these passages basically indicate that when men are determined to disobey their Creator, He allows them to follow the base inclination of their own hearts (cf. Romans 1:24-25). Such was the case with Ahab and his false prophets. God knew their hearts. He knew Ahab was going to go to war before he ever consulted with his prophets (1 Kings 22:3-4). He knew that the prophets were accustomed to telling the king whatever he wanted to hear (cf. 22:8), and He knew that they were also going to tickle Ahab's "itching ears" on this occasion (cf. 2 Timothy 4:3-4). Although God's will was made known to Ahab and his prophets in this case (i.e., Micaiah warned Ahab of the impending doom), He permitted their hardened hearts to believe a lie.

In 1 Kings 22:19-23, and numerous other verses of similar import, the Bible merely expresses what God **allows**, not what He **initiates** or **forces to happen**. Walter Kaiser rightly remarked that "many biblical writers dismiss secondary causes and attribute all that happens directly to God, since he is over all things. Therefore, statements expressed in the imperative form of the verb often represent only what is permitted to happen" (1988, p. 119). This account, therefore, should not trouble the sincere student of God's Word.

JEPHTHAH'S SACRIFICE
Judges 11:29-40

In Judges 11, the story is told of Jephthah the Gileadite sacrificing his only daughter to the Lord. Jephthah had vowed to God that if he were victorious in battle against the Ammonites, he would give to the Lord whatever came through the doors of his house upon his return from battle. Sadly, for Jephthah, his family, and for all of Israel, the one to greet him first when he arrived home was his only daughter.

The question has been asked many times (by both Bible believers and skeptics), "Did Jephthah really offer his daughter as a human sacrifice?" Skeptics also are fond of citing Jephthah's vow as proof that the ethics of God and the Bible are shown to be substandard. What can be said in response to such questions?

In the first place, if, in fact, Jephthah offered a human sacrifice, he did something that was strictly forbidden by Mosaic law and that is repugnant to God (Leviticus 18:21; 20:2-5; Deuteronomy 12:31; 18:10). It would be a bit bizarre for Jephthah to think that he could elicit God's favor in battle by promising to do something that was in direct violation of the will of God—i.e., offering a human sacrifice. Such a proposal would be equivalent to a person requesting God's blessing and assistance by offering to rape women or rob banks. God certainly would not **approve** of such an offer—though He may go ahead and assist the individual (11:32). [NOTE: God allows people to make wrong choices, even while He works out His own higher will in the midst of their illicit actions. He even can use such people to achieve a higher good (consider, as one example, Judas). When Israel clamored for a king—in direct opposition to God's will—He nevertheless allowed them to proceed with their intentions, and even lent His assistance in the selection (1 Samuel 8:7,18-19; 10:19; 12:19; cf. Psalm 106:14-15; Hosea 13:11; Acts 13:21).]

Second, if Jephthah offered his daughter as a human sacrifice, no indication is given in the text that God actually approved of the action. The Bible records many illicit actions carried out by numerous individuals throughout history, without an accompanying word of condemnation by the inspired writer. We must not assume that silence is evidence of divine approval. Even the commendation of Jephthah's faith in the New Testament does not offer a blanket endorsement to **everything** Jephthah did during his lifetime. It merely commended the faith that he demonstrated when he risked going to war. Similarly, the Bible commends the faith of Samson, and Rahab the prostitute (as seen earlier in this chapter), without implying that their behavior was always in harmony with God's will.

Third, Jephthah's action may best be understood by recognizing that he was using the term burnt offering (*'olah*) in a figurative sense. We use the term "sacrifice" in a similar fashion when we say, "I'll sacrifice a few dollars for that charity." Jephthah may have been offering to sacrifice a member of his extended household to permanent, religious service associated with the Tabernacle. Lest you think such "sacrifices" were not made, recall how the firstborn sons of Israel were also to be consecrated to Jehovah as a sacrifice (cf. Exodus 13:11-16; Number 18:14-16). Obviously, these sacrifices were not in the manner of the heathen, by a literal slaying and burning of human flesh upon the altar, "but by presenting them to the Lord as living sacrifices, devoting all their powers of body and mind to His service" (Keil and Delitzsch, 1996). Similarly, today, all Christians are commanded to present their bodies "as a living sacrifice" (Romans 12:1). The Bible also indicates that non-priestly religious service was available under the old law at the tabernacle or (later) at the temple, particularly to women who chose to so dedicate themselves (e.g., Exodus 38:8; 1 Samuel 2:22). Even in the first century, Anna must have been one woman who had dedicated herself to the Lord's service, since she "did not depart from the temple" (Luke 2:37).

Several contextual indicators support this conclusion. First, the two-month period of mourning that Jephthah granted to his daughter was not for the purpose of grieving over her impending loss of life, but over the fact that **she would never**

be able to marry. She bewailed her virginity—not her death (11:37). Second, the text goes out of its way to state that Jephthah had no other children: "[S]he was his only child. Besides her he had neither son nor daughter" (11:34). For his daughter to be consigned to perpetual celibacy meant the extinction of Jephthah's family line—an extremely serious and tragic matter to an Israelite (cf. Numbers 27:1-11; 36:1ff.). Third, the sacrifice is treated as unfortunate—again, not because of any concern over her death, but because **she would not become a mother**. After stating that Jephthah "did with her according to his vow which he had vowed," the inspired writer immediately adds that she "knew no man" (11:39). This statement would be a completely superfluous remark if she had been put to death. Fourth, the declaration of Jephthah's own sorrow (11:35) follows immediately after we are informed that he had no other children (11:34). Jephthah, it seems, was not upset because his daughter would **die** a virgin. He was upset because she would **live and remain** a virgin.

DEALING WITH ALLEGED
MORAL ATROCITIES

Skeptics frequently attack the Scriptures by citing what they believe to be moral discrepancies. They presume that if the Bible can be shown to contain a sordid morality, then people will reject it as a mere human (as opposed to divine) invention. They read of events such as the conquest of Canaan, and question how a loving God could be so cruel as to call for the destruction of entire nations. The thought of God ordering the deaths of women and innocent children so outraged Thomas Paine that he said such was sufficient evidence in itself to cause him to reject the divine origin of the Bible (1795, p. 90). Like many others, he self-righteously condemned the Bible for its alleged moral atrocities, and even went to the extreme of blaming the Bible for virtually every moral injustice ever committed.

> Whence arose the horrid assassinations of whole nations of men, women, and infants, with which the Bible is filled; and the bloody persecutions, and tortures unto death and religious wars, that since that time have laid Europe in blood and ashes; whence arose they, but from this impious thing called revealed religion, and this monstrous belief that God has spoken to man? (p. 185).

When confronted with alleged ethical discrepancies, one would do well to ask at least four questions. First, has the critic set **himself** up as the standard of right and wrong? Skeptics often place themselves in a precarious position. They spurn God's **objective** standard, and condemn the Bible according to their own **subjective** standard. But what makes **their** code worthy of acceptance or defense? If morality is so subjective, **who should decide** whose judgment is valid?

Second, does the charge of wrongdoing arise from the critic's ignorance of biblical teaching? For example, to allege that the God of the Bible is a monster for ordering Israel to destroy the Canaanites shows a lack of Bible knowledge. God did not arbitrarily choose to punish the Canaanites; rather, the Scriptures make clear that the inhabitants of Canaan were driven out of the land because of their great "wickedness" (Deuteronomy 9:4). Before entering into the land of Canaan, Moses spoke to the Israelites, saying:

> When you come into the land which the Lord your God is giving you, you shall not learn to follow the abominations of those nations. There shall not be found among you anyone who makes his son or his daughter pass through the fire, or one who practices witchcraft, or a soothsayer, or one who interprets omens, or a sorcerer, or one who conjures spells, or a medium, or a spiritist, or one who calls up the dead. For all who do these things are an abomination to the

> Lord, and **because of these abominations the Lord your God drives them out from before you**. You shall be blameless before the Lord your God. For these nations which you will dispossess listened to soothsayers and diviners; but as for you, the Lord your God has not appointed such for you (Deuteronomy 18:9-14, emp. added).

The inhabitants were so evil that the Creator no longer could bear their corruption. Like the millions of people who lost their lives in the worldwide Flood of Noah's day because "the wickedness of man was great in the earth," and "every intent of the thoughts of his heart was only evil continually" (Genesis 6:5), the Canaanites suffered as the result of their own wickedness. Similar to a father who warns his child of the consequences of disobedience, and then is true to his word at the event of infraction, God punished the Canaanite people for their evil deeds. Unfortunately, even though clear-thinking people consider a father disciplining his rebellious son as being a noble act, critics ask us to view God as an ogre for following a comparable course of action. Truly, the discrepancy is not with the Almighty, but with His critics. [NOTE: Those who ponder Jehovah's order to destroy innocent children must realize that these children were spared an even worse fate of being reared as slaves under the tyranny of sin. Instead of having to endure the scourge of a life of wickedness, followed by an eternity in hell, these innocent ones were ushered early into the rest and bliss of Paradise. For more reading on this subject, see Butt, 2004.]

Third, if the Bible is blamed for the savage acts that men commit, we must ask: "Do the Scriptures truly authorize the act in question?" For example, blame for the Crusades and the Inquisition often is laid upon the Bible; but where in the Bible is there any justification for either? Jesus removed the motive for the Crusades when He announced, "My Kingdom is not of this world" (John 18:36). And the bigotry and wick-

edness that were typical of the Inquisition are expressly forbidden in Scripture (1 John 3:15). Simply because people claim
to do something in the name of Christianity, does not mean
that God actually authorized their actions.

Fourth, a Bible student would do well to examine whether
the critic simply projected his own immoral thoughts into the
text in question. Close examination of moral criticisms often
reveals the predisposition of the skeptic to find what he wants
to find, and nothing else. Consider this telling statement by
Thomas Paine:

> ...I come to the book of Ruth, an idle, bungling story,
> foolishly told, nobody knows by whom, about a stroll-
> ing country-girl creeping slily to bed to her cousin
> Boaz. Pretty stuff indeed to be called the word of God.
> It is, however, one of the best books in the Bible, for it
> is free from murder and rapine (p. 110).

Such a perverse portrayal of the innocent act of Ruth is the
epitome of a depraved mind. One has but to read the book
of Ruth to see that such a picture is completely foreign to the
actual event and characters involved.

The alleged moral incongruities of Scripture cited so frequently by skeptics are only the distorted delusions of men
who wish to find fault with the faultless God of eternity. God
has set the standard for morality, and the Bible consistently
pictures Him acting in agreement with it.

Chapter 7

ALLEGED CONTRADICTIONS PERTAINING TO SALVATION

"CALLING ON THE NAME OF THE LORD"
Matthew 7:21; Acts 2:21; Romans 10:13

Considering how many people within "Christendom" teach that an individual can be saved merely by professing a belief in Christ, it is not surprising that skeptics claim that the Bible contradicts itself in this regard. Although Peter and Paul declared, "Whoever calls on the name of the Lord shall be saved" (Acts 2:21; Romans 10:13; cf. Joel 2:32), skeptics quickly remind their readers that Jesus once stated: "Not everyone who says to Me, 'Lord, Lord,' shall enter the kingdom of heaven, but he who does the will of My Father in heaven" (Matthew 7:21; cf. Luke 6:46). Allegedly, Matthew 7:21 clashes with such passages as Acts 2:21 and Romans 10:13 (see Morgan, 2003a; Wells, 2001). Since many professed Christians seem to equate "calling on the name of the Lord" with the idea of saying to Jesus, "Lord, save me," Bible critics feel even more justified in their pronouncement of "conflicting testimonies." How can certain professed followers of Christ claim that they were saved by simply "calling out to Christ," when Christ Himself proclaimed that a mere calling upon Him would not save a person?

The key to correctly understanding the phrase "calling on the name of the Lord," is to recognize that more is involved in this action than a mere verbal petition directed toward God. The "call" mentioned in Acts 2:21, Romans 10:13, and Acts 22:16 (where Paul was "calling on the name of the Lord"), is not equated with the "call" ("Lord, Lord") of which Jesus spoke in the Sermon on the Mount (Matthew 7:21).

First, it is appropriate to mention that even in modern times, to "call on" someone frequently means more than simply making a request for something. When a doctor goes to the hospital to "call on" some of his patients, he does not merely walk into the room and say, "I just wanted to come by and say, 'Hello.' I wish you the best. Now pay me." On the contrary, he involves himself in a service. He examines the patient, listens to the patient's concerns, gives further instructions regarding the patient's hopeful recovery, and then oftentimes prescribes medication. All of these elements may be involved in a doctor "calling upon" a patient. In the mid-twentieth century, it was common for young men to "call on" young ladies. Again, this expression meant something different than just "making a request" (Brown, 1976, p. 5).

Second, when an individual takes the time to study how the expression "calling on God" is used throughout Scripture, the only reasonable conclusion to draw is that, just as similar phrases sometimes have a deeper meaning in modern America, the expression "calling on God" often had a deeper meaning in Bible times. Take, for instance, Paul's statement recorded in Acts 25:11: "I appeal unto Caesar." The word "appeal" (*epikaloumai*) is the same word translated "call" (or "calling") in Acts 2:21, 22:16, and Romans 10:13. But, Paul was not simply saying, "I'm calling on Caesar to save me." As James Bales noted:

> Paul, in appealing to Caesar, was claiming the right of a Roman citizen to have his case judged by Caesar. He was asking that his case be transferred to Caesar's court and that Caesar hear and pass judgment on his case. In so doing, he indicated that he was resting his case on Caesar's judgment. **In order for this to be done Paul had to submit to whatever was necessary in order for his case to be brought before Caesar.** He had to submit to the Roman soldiers who conveyed him to Rome. He had to submit to whatever formalities or procedure Caesar demanded of those who came before him. All of this was involved in his appeal to Caesar (1960, pp. 81-82, emp. added).

Paul's "calling" to Caesar involved his submission to him. "That, in a nutshell," wrote T. Pierce Brown, "is what 'calling on the Lord' involves"–obedience (1976, p. 5). It is not a mere verbal recognition of God, or a verbal petition to Him. Those whom Paul (before his conversion to Christ) sought to bind in Damascus–Christians who were described as people "who call on Your [Jehovah's] name"–were not people who only prayed to God, but those who were serving the Lord, and who, by their obedience, were submitting themselves to His authority (cf. Matthew 28:18). Interestingly, Zephaniah 3:9 links one's "calling" with his "service": "For then I will restore to the peoples a pure language, **that they all may call on the name of the Lord, to serve Him with one accord**" (emp. added). When a person submits to the will of God, he accurately can be described as "calling on the Lord." Acts 2:21 and Romans 10:13 (among other passages) do not contradict Matthew 7:21, because to "call on the Lord" entails more than just pleading for salvation; it involves submitting to God's will. According to Colossians 3:17, every single act a Christian performs (in word or deed) should be carried out by Christ's authority. For a non-Christian receiving salvation, this is no different. In order to obtain salvation, a person must submit to the Lord's authority. This is what the passages in Acts 2:21 and Romans 10:13 are teaching; it is up to us to go elsewhere in the New Testament to learn **how** to call upon the name of the Lord.

After Peter quoted the prophecy of Joel, and told those in Jerusalem on Pentecost that "whoever calls on the name of the Lord shall be saved" (Acts 2:21), he told them **how** to go about "calling on the name of the Lord." The people in the audience in Acts 2 did not understand Peter's quotation of Joel to mean that an alien sinner must pray to God for salvation. [Their question in Acts 2:37 ("Men and brethren, what shall we do?") indicates such.] Furthermore, when Peter responded to their question, and told them what to do to be saved, he did not say, "I've already told you what to do. You can be saved by petitioning God for salvation through prayer. Just call on His name." On the contrary, Peter had to explain to them what it meant to "call on the name of the Lord." Instead of repeating this statement when the crowd sought further guidance from the apostles, Peter commanded them, saying, "Repent, and let every one of you be baptized in the name of Jesus Christ for the remission of sins" (2:38). Notice the parallel between Acts 2:21 and 2:38:

Acts 2:21	Whoever	Calls	On the name of the Lord	Shall be saved
Acts 2:38	Everyone of you	Repent and be baptized	In the name of Jesus Christ	For the remission of sins

Peter's non-Christian listeners learned that "calling on the name of the Lord for salvation" was equal to obeying the Gospel, which approximately 3,000 did that very day by repenting of their sins and being baptized into Christ (2:38, 41).

But what about Romans 10:13? What is the "call" mentioned in this verse? Notice Romans 10:11-15:

> For the Scripture says, "Whoever believes on Him will not be put to shame." For there is no distinction between Jew and Greek, for the same Lord over all is rich to all who call upon Him. For **"whoever calls on the name of the Lord shall be saved." How then shall they call on Him in whom they have not believed?** And how shall they believe in Him of whom they have not heard? And how shall they hear without a preacher? And how shall they preach unless they are sent? As it is written: "How beautiful are the feet of those who preach the gospel of peace, who bring glad tidings of good things!" (emp. added).

Although this passage does not define precisely what is meant by one "calling on the name of the Lord," it does indicate that an alien sinner cannot "call" until after he has heard the Word of God and believed it. Such was meant by Paul's rhetorical questions: "How then shall they call on Him in whom they have not believed? And how shall they believe in Him of whom they have not heard?" Paul's statements in this passage are consistent with Peter's proclamations in Acts 2. It was only **after** the crowd on Pentecost believed in the resurrected Christ Whom Peter preached (as is evident by their being "cut to the heart," and their subsequent question, "Men and brethren, what shall we do?") that Peter told them how to call on the name of the Lord and be saved (2:38).

Perhaps the clearest description of what it means for an alien sinner to "call on the name of the Lord" is found in Acts

22. As the apostle Paul addressed the mob in Jerusalem, he spoke of his encounter with the Lord, Whom he asked, "What shall I do?" (22:10; cf. 9:6). The answer Jesus gave Him at that time was not "call on the name of the Lord." Instead, Jesus instructed him to "arise and go into Damascus, and there you will be told all things which are appointed for you to do" (22:10). Paul (or Saul–Acts 13:9) revealed his belief in Jesus as he went into the city and waited for further instructions. In Acts 9, we learn that during the next three days, while waiting to meet with Ananias, Paul fasted and prayed (vss. 9,11). Although some today might consider what Paul was doing at this point as "calling on the name of the Lord," Ananias, God's chosen messenger to Paul, did not think so. He did not tell Paul, "I see you have already called on God. Your sins are forgiven." After three days of fasting and praying, Paul was still **lost in his sins**. Even though he obviously **believed** at this point, and had prayed to God, he had yet to "call on the name of the Lord" for salvation. When Ananias finally came to Paul, he told him: "Arise and be baptized, and wash away your sins, **calling on the name of the Lord**" (22:16, emp. added). Ananias knew that Paul had not yet "called on the name of the Lord," just as Peter knew that those on Pentecost had not done so before his command to "repent and be baptized." Thus, Ananias instructed Paul to "be baptized, and wash away your sins." The participial phrase, "calling on the name of the Lord," describes what Paul was doing when he was baptized for the remission of his sins. Every non-Christian who desires to "call on the name of the Lord" to be saved, does so, not simply by crying out, saying, "Lord, Lord" (cf. Matthew 7:21), or just by wording a prayer to God (e.g., Paul–Acts 9; 22; cf. Romans 10:13-14), but by obeying God's instructions to "repent and be baptized...in the name of Jesus Christ for the remission of your sins" (Acts 2:38).

This is not to say that repentance and baptism have always been (or are always today) synonymous with "calling on the name of the Lord." Abraham was not baptized when he "called upon the name of the Lord" (Genesis 12:8; cf. 4:26), because baptism was not demanded of God before New Testament times. And, as mentioned earlier, when the New Testament describes people who are already Christians as "calling on the name of the Lord" (Acts 9:14,21; 1 Corinthians 1:2), it certainly does not mean that Christians continually were being baptized for the remission of their sins after having been baptized to become a Christian (cf. 1 John 1:5-10). Depending on when and where the phrase is used, "calling on the name of the Lord" includes: (1) obedience to the Gospel plan of salvation; (2) worshiping God; and (3) faithful service to the Lord (Bates, 1979, p. 5). However, it is never used in the sense that all the alien sinner must do in order to be saved is to cry out and say, "Lord, Lord, save me."

Thus, the skeptic's allegation that Matthew 7:21 contradicts Acts 2:21 and Romans 10:13 is unsubstantiated. And, the professed Christian who teaches that all one must do to be saved is just say the sinner's prayer, is in error.

TAKING POSSESSION OF
WHAT GOD GIVES
Ephesians 2:8-9

Relatively few within Christendom would deny that eternal salvation is a free gift from God. The New Testament is replete with statements stressing this point. The most oft'-quoted verse in all of Scripture teaches this very fact: "God so loved the world that He gave His only begotten Son…" (John 3:16). God did not offer the gift of eternal life to the world because of some great accomplishment on the part of mankind. Rather, as Paul wrote to the church at Rome, "God demonstrates His own love toward us, in that while we were still sinners, Christ died for us" (5:8). Later, in that same chapter in Romans, Paul spoke of the **"free gift"** of spiritual life through Christ (5:15-21). He wrote to the church at Corinth, indicating that it is God "who **gives us** the victory through our Lord Jesus Christ" (1 Corinthians 15:57, emp. added). And earlier in this epistle, Paul expressed gratitude for the Corinthians and their salvation, saying, "I thank my God always concerning you for **the grace of God** which was **given** to you by Christ Jesus" (1:4, emp. added). Truly, God gives His grace away to anyone who will humbly accept it (James 4:6; 1 Peter 5:5; cf. Revelation 22:17). It is, as so many have noted, **unmerited** favor.

A Case Study in "Receiving" What God "Gives"

Unfortunately, much misunderstanding exists in the religious world today concerning how mankind freely receives salvation from God. This subject also is a favorite of many skeptics. They attempt to point out inconsistencies in the Bible concerning how man is saved. Is it by grace, by faith, or by works?

To better understand the relationship between God's gifts and man's reception of those gifts, it is helpful to study one particular gift from God—one that is mentioned in the Old Testament more times than any other thing God is ever said to have given. If a person were to open a concordance and look up the word "give" or one of its derivatives (i.e., gave, given, giving, etc.), he would find that whenever this word is found in conjunction with something God does, or has done, it is used more in reference to the land of Canaan (which God **gave** to the descendants of Abraham) than with any other subject. Although the Old Testament mentions numerous things that God gave the Israelites (e.g., manna, quail, water, rest, etc.), the gift of God cited most frequently (especially in Genesis through Joshua) is that of God giving the Israelites the land of Canaan. He promised to **give** this land to Abraham almost 500 years before his descendants finally "received" it (Genesis 12:7; cf. 13:15,17; 15:7; 17:8). While the Israelites were still in Egyptian bondage, God spoke to Moses, and said: "I will bring you into the land which I swore to give to Abraham, Isaac, and Jacob; and **I will give it to you** as a heritage: I am the Lord" (Exodus 6:8, emp. added). After the Exodus from Egypt, God instructed Moses to send twelve men "to spy out the land of Canaan, which I am **giving** to the children of Israel" (Numbers 13:2, emp. added). In the book of Leviticus, one can read where Jehovah gave the Israelites laws concerning leprosy—laws that He introduced by saying, "When you have come into the land of Canaan, **which I give you as a possession**…" (Leviticus 14:33-34, emp. added). During the years of wilderness wanderings, God reminded Israel of this gift numerous times—and it **always** was spoken of as a gift, never an earned possession.

Notice, however, some of the things that the Israelites still had to do in order to "take possession" (Numbers 13:30; Joshua 1:15) of this gift. They had to prepare provisions (Joshua 1:11), cross the Jordan River (Joshua 3), march around the city of Jericho once a day for six days, and seven times on the seventh day (Joshua 6:1-4), blow trumpets and shout (Joshua 6:5), and then utterly destroy all that was in Jericho (Joshua 6:21). They also proceeded to do battle with the inhabitants of Ai (Joshua 8). Joshua 10 records how the Israelites "chased" and "struck" the inhabitants of the southern part of Canaan (Joshua 10:10). They then battled their way up to the northern part of Canaan, and took possession of it, too (Joshua 11). Finally, after the land on both sides of the Jordan had been divided among the Israelites, the Bible records how Caleb courageously drove out the giant descendants of Anak from Hebron. He **seized** the land **given** to him by God (Joshua 14:6-15; 15:13-19; Judges 1:9-20). Such is an overriding theme throughout the first six books of the Bible—"**The Lord gave**

to Israel all the land of which He had sworn to give to their fathers, and **they [Israel] took possession of it**" (Joshua 21: 43, emp. added).

Perhaps the truth that God **gave** this land to the Israelites was never made clearer than when Moses spoke to them just prior to their entrance into Canaan.

> So it shall be, when the Lord your God brings you into the land of which He swore to your fathers, to Abraham, Isaac, and Jacob, to give you large and beautiful cities which you did not build, houses full of all good things, which you did not fill, hewn-out wells which you did not dig, vineyards and olive trees which you did not plant—when you have eaten and are full—then beware, lest you forget the Lord who brought you out of the land of Egypt, from the house of bondage…. He brought us out from there, that He might bring us in, to give us the land of which He swore to our fathers (Deuteronomy 6:10-12,23).

God did not award this land to the Israelites because of some mighty work on their part. This land, which flowed "with milk and honey" (Numbers 13:27), was not a prize handed out to them because of some great achievement by the Israelites (cf. Deuteronomy 7:7). They did not deserve it. The Israelites did not purchase it from God with any kind of earned income. They did not earn the right to be there. God, Who owns everything (Psalm 24:1; 89:11), **gave** it to them as a gift. **It was free.** God described it as a gift when He first promised it to Abraham (Genesis 12:7), and He described it as a gift after Israel inhabited it hundreds of years later (Joshua 21:43). It was unmerited. The Israelites' acceptance of God's gift, however, did not exclude **effort** on their part.

When it comes to the **spiritual** Promised Land that God has freely offered to anyone who will "take" it (Revelation 22:17; Titus 2:11; cf. Matthew 11:28-30), some have a difficult time accepting the idea that man must **put forth effort** in order to receive it. Many today have come to the conclusion that effort **cannot** be part of the equation when the Bible speaks of God's gracious gifts. The idea is: "Since God's grace cannot be earned or merited, then anyone who claims that human effort is involved in its acceptance is in error." Clearly, though, many scriptures indicate that man's efforts are not always categorized as works of merit. God **gave** the Israelites freedom from Egyptian bondage, but they still had to put forth some effort by walking from Egypt, across the Red Sea, and into the Wilderness of Shur (Exodus 15:22; cf. Exodus 16:32; Joshua 24:5). Israel did not "earn" Canaan, but they still exerted much effort (i.e., they **worked**) in possessing it. God **gave** the Israelites the city of Jericho (Joshua 6:2). But, He gave it to them only **after** they followed His instructions and encircled the city for seven days (Hebrews 11:30). Furthermore, Israel did not deserve manna from heaven; it was a free gift from God. Nevertheless, if they wanted to eat it, they were required to put forth effort in gathering it (Exodus 16; Numbers 11). These Old Testament examples clearly teach that something can be a gift from God, even though conditions must be met in order for that gift to be received.

This point can also be understood effectively by noting our attitude toward physical gifts today. If a friend wanted to give you $1,000,000, but said that in order to receive the million dollars you had to pick up a check at his house, take it to the bank, sign it, and cash it, would any rational person conclude that this gift was earned? Of course not. Even though some effort was exerted to receive the gift, the effort was not a work of merit. Similarly, consider the young boy who is on the verge of drowning in the middle of a small lake. If a man heard his cries, and then proceeded to save the boy by running to the edge of the lake, inflating an inner tube, tying some rope around it, and throwing it out to the young boy who was struggling to stay afloat, would any witness to this event describe the young boy as "saving himself" (or earning his rescue) because he had to exert the energy to grab the inner tube and hold on while being pulled onto the bank by the passerby? No. A gift is still a gift even when the one receiving it must exert a certain amount of effort in order to possess it.

"Taking Possession" of Salvation

The New Testament leaves no doubt that the grandest of all gifts (salvation through Christ–a spiritual gift that was in God's mind "before the foundation of the world"–Ephesians 1:4; 3:11) is not the result of any kind of meritorious work on the part of man. The apostle Paul stressed this point several times in his writings. To the Christians who made up the church at Ephesus, he wrote: "For by grace you have been saved through faith, and that not of yourselves; it is the gift of God, not of works, lest anyone should boast" (Ephesians 2:8-9). In his epistle to Titus, Paul emphasized that we are saved, "not by works of righteousness which we have done, but according to His mercy" (3:5). Then, again, while writing to young Timothy, Paul highlighted the fact that we are saved by the "power of God," and "not according to our works" (2 Timothy 1:8-9). This truth cannot be overly stressed; however, it can be, and has been, perverted and misrepresented.

Unfortunately, some have come to the conclusion that man plays no part in his being saved from sin by God. They say: "Salvation is a gift of God that is from nothing we do ourselves" (Schlemper, 1998). Or, "Salvation is a gift from God–we do nothing to get it" (MacPhail, n.d.). "[W]e do nothing to become righteous...God did all that was necessary in His Son" ("The Godhead," n.d.). The truth is, however, when it comes to the gift of salvation that God extends to the whole world (John 3:16), there are requirements that must be met on the part of man in order for him to receive the gift. Contrary to what some are teaching, there is something that a person must

do in order to be saved. The Jews on Pentecost understood this point, as is evident by their question: "Men and brethren, what shall we **do**?" (Acts 2:37). Saul, later called Paul (Acts 13:9), believed that there was something else he needed to do besides experience a personal encounter with the resurrected Lord on his way to Damascus, for he asked Jesus, "Lord, what do You want me to **do**?" (Acts 9:6). And the jailor at Philippi, after observing the righteousness of Paul and Silas and being awakened by the earthquake to see the prison doors opened (Acts 16:20-29), "fell down trembling before Paul and Silas…and said, 'Sirs, what must I **do** to be saved?' " (Acts 16: 30). If those who responded to these questions (Peter in Acts 2, Jesus in Acts 9, and Paul and Silas in Acts 16) had the mindset of some today, they should have answered by saying, "There is nothing for you to do. Just wait, and salvation will come to you." But their responses were quite different from this. All three times the question was asked, a command to **do** something was given. Peter told those on Pentecost to "repent and be baptized" (Acts 2:38); Paul and Silas instructed the Philippian jailor and his household to "[b]elieve on the Lord Jesus Christ" (Acts 16:31); and Jesus commanded Saul to "[a]rise and go into the city, and you will be told what you must do" (Acts 9:6). Notice that none of them gave the impression that salvation involves us "doing **nothing**." Jesus told Saul that he **"must do"** something. When Saul arrived in Damascus as Jesus had directed him, he did exactly what God's spokesman, Ananias, commanded him to do (Acts 22:12-16; 9:17-18). Similar to how the land of Canaan was "received" by an active Israel, so the free gift of eternal life is received by man taking action.

Much controversy within Christendom is caused by disagreement on how much action an alien sinner should take. Since God has extended to mankind an indescribable (2 Corinthians 9:15), undeserved gift, we are told that the acceptance of such a gift can involve only the smallest amount of effort, else one might be accused of salvation by "works of righteousness." Usually, this action is said to involve nothing more than confessing faith in Jesus as the Son of God, and praying that He will forgive sins and come into a person's heart (see "Prayer of Salvation," n.d.). This, we are told, is man's way of taking possession of God's grace. Allegedly, all one must do in order to lay hold on the eternal life that God freely gives to all is to

> [a]ccept Christ into your heart through prayer and he'll receive you. It doesn't matter what church you belong to or if you ever do good works. You'll be born again at the moment you receive Christ. He's at the door knocking.... Just trust Christ as Savior. God loves you and forgives you unconditionally. Anyone out there can be saved if they accept Christ, now! Let's pray for Christ to now come into your heart (see Staten, 2001).

The prayer that the alien sinner is urged to pray frequently goes something like this:

> Lord Jesus, I need You. Thank You for dying on the cross for my sins. I open the door of my life and receive You as my Savior and Lord. Thank You for forgiving my sins and giving me eternal life. Take control of my life. Make me the kind of person You want me to be (see McDowell, 1999, p. 759).

According to *The Billy Graham Evangelistic Association* Web site, in an article titled, "How to Become a Christian," "[w]hen you receive Christ into your heart you become a child of God, and have the privilege of talking to Him in prayer at any time about anything" ("How to Become a Christian," n.d.). This is what many within Christendom believe one must do to "take possession" of God's grace. The overriding thought seems to be, "There can't be much involved in getting saved, because God saves, not man. We have to make it as easy and painless as possible so that no one will accuse us of 'salvation by works.' "

Contrary to the above statements, the New Testament gives specific prerequisites that must be followed before one can receive the atoning benefit of Christ's blood (Revelation 1:5; 1 John 1:7). These conditions are neither vague nor difficult to understand. A person must confess faith in Jesus Christ as the Son of God (John 8:24; Romans 10:9-10; cf. 1 Timothy 6:12), and he must repent of his past sins (Acts 26:20; Luke 13:3; Acts 2:38). Although these prerequisites are slightly different from those mentioned above by some modern-day denominational preachers, they are genuinely accepted among the Protestant world. By meeting these conditions, most people understand that a person is merely receiving God's grace (by following God's plan). Few, if any, would accuse a man who emphasizes these prerequisites of teaching "salvation by works of merit."

However, the Bible discusses yet another step that precedes salvation—a step that has become extremely controversial within Christendom—water baptism. It is mentioned numerous times throughout the New Testament, and both Jesus and His disciples taught that it **precedes** salvation (Mark 16:16; Matthew 28:19-20; Acts 2:38). The apostle Paul's sins were washed away only **after** he was immersed in water (Acts 22:16; cf. Acts 9:18). [NOTE: Even though it was on the road to Damascus that Paul heard the Lord, spoke to Him, and believed on Him (Acts 9), Paul did not receive salvation until he went into Damascus and was baptized.] The book of Acts is replete with examples of those who did not receive the gift of salvation until after they professed faith in Christ, repented of their sins, and were **baptized** (Acts 2:38-41; 8:12; 8:26-40; 10:34-48; 16:14-15; 16:30-34; 18:8). Furthermore, the epistles of Peter and Paul also call attention to the necessity of baptism (1 Peter 3:21; Colossians 2:12; Romans 6:1-4). If a person wants the multitude of spiritual blessings found "in Christ" (e.g., salvation–2 Timothy 2:10; forgiveness–Ephesians 1:7; cf. Ephesians 2:12; etc.), he must not stop after confessing faith in the Lord Jesus, or after resolving within himself to turn from a sinful lifestyle. He also must be "baptized into Christ" (Galatians 3:27; Romans 6:3) "for the remission of sins" (Acts 2:38).

So why, one might ask, if so many passages of Scripture teach the necessity of baptism, is there so much controversy about baptism being a condition of salvation? Several reasons could be mentioned here (e.g., "The thief on the cross was saved, yet not baptized. Thus, we don't have to be baptized to be saved." For a full refutation of this line of reasoning, see Miller, 2003b), but one that is extremely popular (and has been for some time) is the idea that baptism is a "work." And, since we are not saved by "works" (Ephesians 2:8-9), then, allegedly, baptism cannot be required in order to receive (or "take possession of"--cf. Revelation 22:17) salvation. Notice how some religionists have articulated these sentiments.

- In Part three of a series of articles on baptism, called the "FUD Series" (FUD standing for Fear, Uncertainty, and Doubt), Darrin Yeager wrote: "The act of baptism is a work (or ritual). Paul makes clear the point works do not (and cannot) save us. Even the faith we have is a gift of God. Since works cannot save us, baptism plays no part in the salvation of the believer" (2003). Yeager concluded this article by saying: "Its [sic] tragic baptism has become such a point of contention in the church. Considering the whole counsel of God several points become clear." Among those points was: "Baptism is a work, and the Bible is clear works to [sic] not save us…. [B]aptism is absolutely, positively **not** required for salvation" (emp. in orig.).

- In an article titled, "What Saves? Baptism or Jesus Christ?," Buddy Bryant cited Titus 3:5, and then wrote: "Baptism is a work of righteousness and we are not saved by works of righteousness which we have done" (n.d.).
- Under the heading, "Water Baptism is Not for Salvation," one church Web site exclaimed: "Water baptism **is** a 'work of righteousness'…. Our sins were not washed away by water, but by the Lord Jesus Christ…" (see "Water Baptism," n.d., emp. in orig.). Similarly, another church Web site ran an article titled, "Does Water Baptism Save?," declaring: "Water baptism is a **work** (something that man does to please God), and yet the Bible teaches again and again that a person is not saved by works" (see "Does Water," n.d., parenthetical item and emp. in orig.).

These statements summarize the feelings of many within Christendom concerning baptism: "It is a work, and thus not necessary for the person who wants to be saved." The truth of the matter is, however, when careful consideration is given to what the Bible teaches on this subject, one will find no discrepancy between the idea that man is saved "by grace… through faith" (Ephesians 2:8-9) and not by works, and at the same time is saved following baptism.

Part of the confusion concerning baptism and works is the result of being uninformed about the biblical teaching of works. The New Testament mentions at least four kinds of works: (1) works of the Law of Moses (Galatians 2:16; Romans 3:20); (2) works of the flesh (Galatians 5:19-21); (3) works of merit (Titus 3:4-7); and (4) works resulting from obedience of faith (James 2:14-24; Luke 17:10; cf. Galatians 5:6). The first three works mentioned here certainly do not lead to eternal life. The last category often is referred to as "works of God." This phrase does not mean works **performed by** God; rather, the intent is "works **required and approved by** God" (Thayer, 1977, p. 248, emp. added; cf. Jackson, 1997, 32:47). Consider the following example from Jesus' statements in John 6:27-29:

> Work not for the food which perisheth, but for the food which abideth unto eternal life.... They said therefore unto him, What must we do, that we may work the **works of God**? Jesus answered and said unto them, This is the **work of God**, that ye believe on him whom he hath sent (ASV, emp. add).

Within this context, Christ made it clear that there are works that humans must do to receive eternal life. Moreover, the passage affirms that **believing itself is a work** ("This is the **work** of God, that ye **believe** on him whom he hath sent"). It therefore follows that if one is saved **without any type of works**, then he is saved **without faith**, because **faith is a work**. Such a conclusion would throw the Bible into hopeless confusion!

Will anyone step forward and espouse the idea that faith is a meritorious work? Can a person "earn salvation" by believing in Christ? To this day, I have never heard anyone assert that belief is a work of merit. Although it is described in the Bible as being a "work," we correctly understand it to be a condition upon which one receives salvation. Salvation is still a free gift from God; it is the result of His grace and Jesus' work on the cross, not our efforts.

But what about baptism? The New Testament **specifically excludes** baptism from the class of human meritorious works unrelated to redemption. In fact, the two books where the apostle Paul condemns salvation by works the most vehemently (Romans and Galatians), are the very books that relate the fact that water baptism places a person "into Christ" (Romans 6:3; Galatians 3:27). Also, the fact that baptism is not a work of merit is emphasized in Titus 3:4-7.

> For we ourselves were also once foolish, disobedient, deceived, serving various lusts and pleasures, living in malice and envy, hateful and hating one another. But when the kindness and the love of God our Savior toward man appeared, not by works of righteousness which we have done, but according to His mercy He saved us, through the washing of regeneration and renewing of the Holy Spirit, whom He poured out on us abundantly through Jesus Christ our Savior, that having been justified by His grace we should become heirs according to the hope of eternal life.

This passage reveals at least three things. First, we **are not saved** by works of righteousness that we do by ourselves (i.e., according to any plan or course of action that we devised—see Thayer, 1977, p. 526). Second, we **are saved** by the "washing of regeneration" (i.e., baptism), exactly as 1 Peter 3:21 states (see also Ephesians 5:26). [NOTE: Even Baptist theologian A.T. Robertson believed that the phrase "washing of regeneration" refers specifically to water baptism (1931, 4:607).] Thus, in the third place, baptism is excluded from all works of human righteousness that men contrive, but is itself a "work of God" (i.e., required and approved by God) necessary for salvation.

When one is raised from the watery grave of baptism, it is according to the "working of God" (Colossians 2:12), and not any manmade plan. Although many have tried, no one can suggest (justifiably) that baptism is a meritorious work of human design, anymore than he can logically conclude that Naaman "earned" his physical cleansing of leprosy by dipping in the Jordan River seven times (see 2 Kings 5:1-19). When we are baptized, we are completely passive. If you really think about it, baptism is something that is done **to** a person, not **by** a person (thus, one hardly can have performed any kind of meritorious "work").

Taking Possession of Salvation "by Faith"

The Bible, in a multitude of passages, affirms that people are saved by, through, because of, or on account of, their faith. Paul wrote in the epistle to the Romans: "Therefore, having been justified by faith (*pistis*), we have peace with God through our Lord Jesus Christ" (5:1). A few chapters earlier, Paul declared: "Therefore we conclude that a man is justified by faith (*pistis*) apart from the deeds of the law" (3:28). The writer of the book of Hebrews concluded that "without faith (*pistis*) it is impossible to please Him, for he who comes to God must believe (*pisteuo*) that He is, and that He is a rewarder of those who diligently seek Him" (11:6). In Ephesians 2:8-9 we read: "For by grace you have been saved through faith (*pistis*), and that not of yourselves; it is the gift of God, not of works, lest anyone should boast." With this tiny sampling of verses about faith, it is easily seen that every person who is saved must have faith. But what is biblical faith?

The word translated "faith" in each of the above verses derives from the Greek noun *pistis* (the verb form of which is *pisteuo*). Respected Greek scholar Joseph Thayer said that the word *pistis* in the New Testament is used of "a conviction or belief respecting man's relationship to God and divine things, generally with the included idea of trust and holy fervor born of faith and conjoined with it" (1977, p. 512). When the verb form *pisteuo* is used "especially of the faith by which a man embraces Jesus" it means "a conviction, full of joyful trust, that Jesus is the Messiah—the divinely appointed author of eternal salvation in the kingdom of God, conjoined with obedience to Christ" (Thayer, p. 511).

The word *pisteuo* often is translated by the word "believe." For instance, in Acts 10:43, the apostle Peter spoke of Jesus, saying: "To Him all the prophets witness that, through His name, whoever believes (*pisteuo*) in Him will receive remission of sins." The apostle Paul wrote: "It pleased God through the foolishness of the message preached to save those who believe (*pisteuo*)" (1 Corinthians 1:21). Paul, in Romans 10: 11, made a similar statement when he declared: "For the Scripture says, 'Whoever believes (*pisteuo*) on Him will not be put to shame.' "

These verses, taken by themselves, seem to suggest that any person who maintains a mere mental conviction that Jesus is the Son of God has eternal life. Many people and denominations have taken such a position. Baptist scholar L.S. Ballard, in his debate with Thomas B. Warren, affirmed this position: "The Scriptures teach that faith in Christ procures salvation without further acts of obedience" (Warren and Ballard, 1965, p. 1). Herschel Hobbs declared: "Instantaneous salvation refers to redemption from sin (Acts 2:21; Romans 10:10). This experience occurs immediately upon one's believing in Jesus Christ as one's Saviour" (1964, p. 90). Albert Mohler, in discussing his particular denomination, stated: "We cherish the gospel of Jesus Christ as the means of salvation to all who believe. We know that there is salvation in the name of Jesus and in no other name. Sinners come to Christ by faith, and are justified by **faith alone**" (2001, p. 63, emp. added).

It is to those last two words that we must direct our attention—"faith alone." Mohler (and most of the denominational world) teaches that a person can be, and is in fact, saved by faith alone, or faith only. This idea of "faith only" was popularized by Martin Luther in the sixteenth century. The Catholic Church of Luther's day had grown corrupt, and was prescribing a host of unscriptural ways to obtain forgiveness. Forgiveness could be obtained, according to the Catholic Church, by purchasing indulgences, and a soul could be "bought" out of Purgatory if the proper funds flowed into the Church's coffers. In reaction to this "works-based" plan of forgiveness, Martin Luther developed his idea of a "faith-only" plan of salvation. He took this idea so far, in fact, that when he translated Romans 3:28, he inserted the word *alone* into the text so that it would read, "We reckon therefore that a man is justified by faith **alone** apart from the works of the law," even though the word **alone** is not found in the original text (see Lewis, 1991, pp. 353ff.). Luther's "faith only" doctrine has become a principal tenet in the thinking and teaching of most denominations.

[NOTE: Interestingly, even though Martin Luther often taught that salvation is based on faith alone, and is not received based upon a person's meritorious works, he did not take "faith alone" to mean that mere mental assent to Christ's deity was sufficient to obtain salvation. Luther's idea of faith alone does not conform to the modern-day idea that baptism is a work and cannot be required for salvation. According to Luther's own words, he believed wholeheartedly in the necessity of baptism as a requisite for salvation. In his *Large Catechism,* he wrote:

> [I] affirm that Baptism is no human trifle, but that it was established by God Himself. Moreover, **He earnestly and solemnly commanded that we must be baptized or we shall not be saved**. No one is to think that it is an optional matter like putting on a red coat. It is of greatest importance that we hold Baptism in high esteem as something splendid and glorious. The reason why we are striving and battling so strenuously for this view of Baptism is that the world nowadays is full of sects that loudly proclaim that Baptism is merely an external form and that external forms are useless…. Although Baptism is indeed performed by human hands, yet it is truly God's own action (1530, pp. 98-99, emp. added).

From Luther's comments about baptism, it is obvious that he viewed water baptism as essential for salvation. Many of the protestant denominations that attribute their ideas about "faith only" to Martin Luther seem to be unaware that Luther's concept of faith alone was not in opposition to works of God (like repentance and baptism), but in opposition to meritorious works by which a person believes that he or she "earns" salvation. Those today who teach that "faith alone" excludes baptism, and cite Martin Luther's name in their defense, need to consider what Luther meant by "faith alone." He stated:

> But our know-it-alls, the new spirit people, claim that faith alone saves and that human works and outward forms contribute nothing to this. We answer: It is of course true that nothing in us does it except faith, as we shall hear later. But these blind leaders of the blind refuse to see that faith must have something in which it believes, that is, something it clings to, something on which to plant its feet and into which to sink its roots. **Thus faith clings to the water and believes Baptism to be something in which there is pure salvation and life**, not through the water, as I have emphasized often enough, but because God's name is joined to it.... It follows from this that whoever rejects Baptism rejects God's word, faith, and the Christ who directs us to Baptism and binds us to it (1530, pp. 101-102, emp. added).]

Four primary lines of reasoning show that the Bible does not teach a "faith only" or "belief only" plan of salvation. First, numerous passages insist that other things besides belief in Christ are necessary to obtain salvation. Second, biblical faith involves not only mental assent, but also obedient action to God's commands. Third, the book of James explicitly says that no man is justified "by faith only." And fourth, the Bible contains examples of people who believed in Jesus (*pisteuo*), yet were still lost.

First, numerous Bible passages insist that something other than a mere belief in Christ is necessary to obtain salvation. Concerning confession, Paul wrote: "For with the heart one believes to righteousness, and with the mouth confession is made to salvation" (Romans 10:10). In Luke 13:3, Jesus declared to His audience: "Unless you repent, you will all likewise perish." The inspired historian, Luke, in the book of Acts, recorded that God had "also granted to the Gentiles repentance to life" (Acts 11:18). After healing the lame man, Peter instructed his audience to "repent therefore and be converted, that your sins may be blotted out" (Acts 3:19). We see in these verses that belief, confession, and repentance are required of all who desire to obtain salvation through Christ.

Another item that the New Testament writers included as necessary for salvation is obedience. Hebrews 5:9 states: "And having been perfected, He became the author of eternal salvation to all who obey Him." Peter made the statement: "For the time has come for judgment to begin at the house of God; and if it begins with us first, what will be the end of those who do not obey the gospel of God" (1 Peter 4:17). In the second epistle to the Thessalonians, Paul forewarned that Christ one day will execute judgment on those who "do not know God, and on those who do not obey the gospel of our Lord Jesus Christ" (1:8).

The list of things required of a person in order to obtain salvation could go on: hope (Romans 8:24), baptism (Acts 2:38; 1 Peter 3:21), and love (1 John 4:7-8) are just a small sampling. The point is, none of these things, in and of itself, saves anyone. Faith without confession does not save. Confession without hope cannot save. And obedience without love is powerless to obtain salvation. The "faith only" doctrine is in error because it bases its entire case for salvation on one aspect listed in the New Testament. Using that type of logic, a person could turn to 1 John 4:7-8–"Beloved let us love one another, for love is of God; and everyone who loves is born of God and knows God"—and say that love is the only thing necessary for salvation, apart from faith or repentance.

In several of these verses, we see the New Testament writers using one or more figures of speech. For instance, the figure of speech known as synecdoche, in which a part of a thing is used to describe the whole of the thing, is used often in passages that discuss salvation. Dungan wrote:

> This is many times the case with the salvation of sinners. The whole number of conditions are indicated by the use of one. Generally the first is mentioned—that of faith—because without it nothing else could follow. Men were to call on the name of the Lord, in order to be saved (Romans 10:17); they must believe on the Lord Jesus Christ (Acts 16:31); they must repent of their sins (Acts 17:30); they must be baptized in the name of the Lord (Acts 22:16). But it is common to have one of these mentioned, without any statement to the presence of any other (1888, p. 305).

E.W. Bullinger, arguably the most respected scholar in the world on figures of speech in the Bible, specifically mentioned 1 John 4:15 as an example of a biblical idiom. He commented that the phrase, "to confess," in this verse means more than a simple verbal statement. The phrase "is used of abiding in the faith, and walking according to truth" (1898, p. 828).

In truth, it would be possible to go to any number of verses and pick out a single thing that the verse says saves a person. According to the Bible, love, repentance, faith, baptism, confession, and obedience are but a few examples of the things that save. However, it would be dishonest, and poor Bible scholarship, to demand that "only" repentance saves, or "confession alone" saves, or that "baptism by itself" has the power to save. In the same sense, one cannot (justifiably) pick the verses that mention faith and belief, and demand that a person is saved by "faith only" or "belief alone."

Second, the biblical use of the word faith involves much more than mere mental assent to a certain fact. It also involves obedience to God's commands. Recalling Thayer's definition of the word, faith is "a conviction, full of joyful trust, that Jesus is the Messiah—the divinely appointed author of eternal salvation in the kingdom of God, **conjoined with obedience to Christ**" (1977, p. 511, emp. added). Throughout the New Testament, we see this definition of "obedient belief" used by the inspired writers. In 1 Peter 2:7, the apostle wrote: "Therefore, to you who **believe**, He is precious; but to those who are **disobedient**, 'The stone which the builders rejected Has become the chief cornerstone' " (emp. added). In this verse, Peter used disobedience as the opposite of belief. The Hebrews writer also equated unbelief and disobedience. In Hebrews 3:18-19, the Israelites were not allowed into the Promised Land because they "did not obey" (3:18). But the next verse states: "So we see that they could not enter in because of unbelief" (3:19). And Hebrews 4:6 also declares that they "did not enter because of disobedience."

Repeatedly, faith is coupled with action in the New Testament. In Galatians 5:6, we read that "faith **working** through love" is the process that avails for salvation. Hebrews 11, recognized by Bible students as "the faith chapter," shows this action process by using Old Testament examples of individuals who pleased God. By faith, Abel "offered" (vs. 4); by faith, Noah "prepared" (vs. 7); and by faith, Abraham "obeyed" (vs. 8). Verse 30 of this chapter demonstrates perfectly the relationship between belief and action. The verse states: "By faith the walls of Jericho fell down after they were encircled for seven days." Joshua and the Israelites believed that God would give them the city of Jericho, but that belief was effective only **after** they "encircled" the city for seven days.

Another good example of the biblical use of "belief coupled with action" is found in Acts 16. Paul and Silas were locked in prison, and were singing hymns when an earthquake loosed their chains. The Philippian jailer in charge of the prison thought his prisoners had escaped, and was about to kill himself, when Paul and Silas stopped him. Immediately, the jailer inquired: "Sirs, what must I do to be saved?" (vs. 30). Then they replied: "Believe on the Lord Jesus Christ, and you will be saved, you and your household" (vs. 31).

> Then they spoke the word of the Lord to him and to all who were in his house. And he took them the same hour of the night and washed their stripes. And immediately he and all his family were baptized. Now when he had brought them into his house, he set food before them; and he rejoiced, **having believed** in God with all his household (vss. 32-34, emp. added).

When the jailer asked what he needed to do to be saved, Paul and Silas told him to "believe (*pisteuo*) on the Lord Jesus Christ." Yet the passage does not say he "believed" until after he had been baptized. His belief was coupled with obedience. A similar situation is found in Acts 2. In that chapter, Peter's listeners asked him, "Men and brethren, what shall we do?" (vs. 37). "Then Peter said to them, 'Repent, and let every one of you be baptized in the name of Jesus Christ for the remission of sins' " (vs. 38). A few verses later, we read that about three thousand souls were obedient to Peter's plea and were baptized. Then, in verse 44 the Bible describes the obedient group of followers by saying, "Now all who believed were together."

But some object to this biblical usage and maintain that such a use contradicts passages like Romans 3:28 and Ephesians 2:8-9, which teach that a person is not saved by works. First, Romans 3:28 does not separate faith from all works; rather, it states: "Therefore we conclude that a man is justified by faith apart from the deeds **of the law**" (emp. added). The "law" discussed here is the Law of Moses, as is shown by Paul's references to circumcision in verse 30. This passage does not say that faith saves apart from all works, but apart from works of the Law of Moses. Ephesians 2:8-9 states that a person is saved "by grace through faith...not of works," yet verse 10 says Christians are created in Christ Jesus "for good works," and the rest of the chapter discusses how the Jews and the Gentiles were both justified because the "law of commandments" (i.e., the Law of Moses) had been abolished (2: 15). No person has ever been righteous enough to earn his or her salvation. Nor had any person been able to comply fully with the Law of Moses in order to earn salvation. But that does not mean that faith "apart from all action" saves a person. In fact, just the opposite is the case.

The second chapter of James deals a crushing blow to the doctrine of "faith only." Verses 14-26 systematically eliminate the possibility of a person being saved by "faith only." James wrote to the Christians, asking, "What does it profit, my brethren, if someone says he has faith but does not have works? Can faith save him?" These rhetorical questions demand a "No" answer. Then, in verse 17 he declared: "Thus also faith by itself, if it does not have works, is dead." He went on to say that Abraham "was justified by works when he offered Isaac his son on the altar. Do you see that faith was working together with his works, and by works faith was made perfect" (vss. 21-22)? Of course, Abraham did not earn his salvation, nor was he saved because of a sinless adherence to the Law. On the contrary, he was saved by "offering" and "working" exactly as God commanded him. Abraham first showed his active faith when He obeyed God's call to leave his homeland (Hebrews 11:8). He continued to show his active, living faith when he offered Isaac. Throughout his life, he was saved because he obeyed the "works of God"—works that God approved in order to obtain salvation.

James further commented: "You see then that a man is justified by works, and **not by faith only**" (vs. 24, emp. added). It is interesting to note that this is the only place in the entire New Testament where the words "faith only" are found together, and it **explicitly states that a person is not saved by faith only.** James concluded his chapter on faith with this statement: "For as the body without the spirit is dead, so faith without works is dead also." Faith without the "works of God" is a dead faith that cannot save. Abraham was justified after he "offered," the walls of Jericho fell by faith after they were "encircled," the Philippian jailer's belief was not complete until he was baptized, and Noah's faith caused him to "prepare." It is the case that if the Israelites had not walked around Jericho, the walls would not have fallen, regardless of their belief. It is the case that if Noah had not "prepared" the Ark, he would not have been saved from the Flood, regardless of what he believed about God's warning. And it is the case that if a person does not confess Christ, does not repent of his sins, and is not baptized for the remission of those sins, then that person will not be saved, regardless of what he or she believes about Christ.

In order to prove this last statement, we move to the fourth objection to the "faith only" doctrine–the Bible contains references to individuals who believed (*pisteuo*) that Jesus was the Son of God, yet who still were lost. In Mark 1:21-28, the Bible records an instance in which Jesus was confronted by a man with an unclean spirit. Upon contacting Jesus, the spirit "cried out, saying, 'Let us alone! What have we to do with You, Jesus of Nazareth? Did You come to destroy us? I know who You are–the Holy One of God' " (vss. 23-24). Certainly, it would not be argued that the demon was saved simply because he believed that Jesus was the "Holy One of God." Why not, one might ask? For the simple reason that, although the unclean spirit acknowledged the deity of Jesus, he was not willing to penitently obey Christ. James, in his chapter on faith, said as much when he stated: "You believe that there is one God. You do well. Even the demons believe–and tremble! But do you want to know, O foolish man, that faith without works is dead" (2:19-20)?

The inspired apostle John documents another example of a group of people who "believed in" Christ, but who were lost in spite of their belief. In John 12:42-43, the text reads: "Nevertheless even among the rulers many believed (*pisteuo*) in Him, but because of the Pharisees they did not confess Him, lest they should be put out of the synagogue; for they loved the praise of men more than the praise of God." Is it the case that these rulers of the Jews were saved because they believed in Jesus, even though they were too scared to confess him? To ask is to answer. They were lost, even though they "believed (*pisteuo*) in Him."

The Bible nowhere teaches that a person can be saved by "faith only." No mere mental consent to the deity of Christ can save (cf. Matthew 7:21). True, biblical faith in Christ is belief in His deity **conjoined with** obedience to His commandments. Saving faith always has been made complete and living only through obedience to God's commands. It is a living faith that "works through love" to accomplish the "works approved by God." It is a living faith that brings about repentance, confession, submission to water baptism, and love for God and one's fellow man. Similar to how Israel received the Promised Land from God after following His instructions, today, any alien sinner can "take possession" of the free gift of salvation at any time by taking these steps.

ONE QUESTION, THREE DIFFERENT ANSWERS
Acts 2:37-38; 9:6; 16:31

Three times in the book of Acts, Luke the physician recorded non-Christians asking what they needed to do to be saved, and three times a different answer was given. The heathen jailor from Philippi asked Paul and Silas, "Sirs, what must I do to be saved?," and was told: "**Believe on the Lord Jesus Christ**, and you will be saved" (16:31). The Jews on Pentecost asked the apostles, "Men and brethren, what shall we do?," and were instructed to **"repent and be baptized"** (2: 37-38). A few years later, Saul (later called Paul–Acts 13:9) asked Jesus, Who appeared to Saul on his way to Damascus, "Lord, what do you want me to do?" (9:6; 22:10). After being told to go into Damascus to find out what he "must do" to be saved, Ananias, the Lord's servant, commanded Saul to "[a]rise and **be baptized**, and wash away your sins, calling on the name of the Lord" (22:16). The question that many ask is: "Why are three different answers given to the same question?" Are these answers contradictory, or is there a logical explanation for their differences?

The reason that three different answers were given to the question of salvation is because on each occasion the questioners were at different "locations" on the road to salvation. The rationality of such answers can be illustrated by considering what a person is told in reference to his physical distance from a certain city. If a friend calls me to ask how far it is from his house in Jackson, Tennessee, to my parents' house in Neosho, Missouri, I would inform him that he is **475 miles** from Neosho. If he calls me back the next day, notifying me that he is now in Little Rock, Arkansas, and asks about the distance to Neosho, I would give him a different answer. He now would be **260 miles** from Neosho. If, later that evening, he called me one last time and asked how far Fort Smith is from Neosho, again I would give him a different answer–**130 miles**. No rational person would accuse me of contradicting myself, since each question was asked from a different reference point. Three different answers were given, but all three were correct. Likewise, the New Testament records three different answers given to the question, "What must I do to be saved," because the sinners who asked these questions were at different stages of understanding on the road to salvation.

The Philippian jailor was commanded to believe in Christ, because he had not yet heard and believed the saving message of Jesus (Acts 16:31-32; Romans 10:17). It would have been pointless for Paul and Silas to command the jailor to repent and/or be baptized when he had not yet even heard the Gospel. If today, a Muslim, Hindu, or Buddhist, asked a Christian the same question the Philippian jailor asked Paul and Silas, the same answer would need to be given. Before ever teaching a Muslim about the essentiality of repentance and baptism, he first must express belief in Jesus as the Son of God. If this step (i.e., believing) is never taken on the road to salvation, the other steps are meaningless. [NOTE: The Bible reveals that after Paul and Silas "spoke the word of the Lord" to the jailor and his household, they believed and "immediately" were baptized (Acts 16:33). By implication, Paul and Silas must have taught the jailor and his family about the essentiality of baptism after stressing the need to "believe on the Lord Jesus Christ" (cf. Acts 8:35-36,38). Question: If water baptism has nothing to do with salvation, then why were the jailor and his household immersed in water not long after midnight (cf. Acts 16:25,33)?]

The Jews on Pentecost had already heard Peter's sermon when they asked their question about salvation (Acts 2:37). Peter knew that they already believed, and that such belief came from hearing the message he preached (cf. Romans 10:17). The Jews had passed the point of belief (being "pricked in their heart"), and were told to "repent and be baptized" in order to obtain salvation (cf. Mark 16:16).

Still, someone might wonder why Ananias neglected to tell Saul to believe or repent when he informed him about how to have his sins washed away. The reason: Saul already was a penitent believer in Christ by the time he came in contact with Ananias. Saul did not need to be told to believe or repent, since he had already done so. He knew the Lord existed, having spoken directly with Him on the road to Damascus, and he expressed a penitent attitude by praying to God and fasting for three days (Acts 9:9,11). At this point, Saul lacked only one thing: he needed to be baptized (Acts 22:16).

The reason these sinners were told three different things regarding salvation was because they were at different starting points when given the various answers. It is as if the jailor were in Jackson, Tennessee, the Jews on Pentecost in Little Rock, Arkansas, and Saul in Fort Smith. All wanted to go to the same place, but were at different starting points when they asked the question, "What must I do to be saved?" The unbeliever was told to believe. The believers were told to repent. And the penitent believer was told to be baptized. The three statements may be different, but they are not contradictory. For a person to become a child of God, he or she must do all three (see John 8:24; Luke 13:3,5; Matthew 28:19; Mark 16:16).

THE BIBLE'S TEACHING ON BAPTISM: CONTRADICTORY OR COMPLEMENTARY?

1 Corinthians 1:14,16,17; John 4:2; Acts 2:38; Mark 16:16

According to numerous skeptics, the Bible contradicts itself regarding whether or not water baptism is essential for salvation (e.g., Drange, 1996; Morgan, 2003a; cf. Wells, 2001). In Dennis McKinsey's book, *Biblical Errancy* (2000), He lists several verses that teach the need for one to be baptized in order to be saved (Matthew 28:19; Mark 16:16; Acts 2:38; 1 Peter 3:21; etc.), but then he lists four verses (John 4:2; 1 Corinthians 1:14,16,17) which allegedly teach that baptism "is not a necessity" (p. 61). According to these men, Jesus and Paul were confused regarding the purpose of baptism—was it necessary, or not?

There is no doubt that Jesus and His apostles taught the essentiality of being immersed in water for salvation. After Jesus commissioned His apostles to "go into all the world and preach the gospel to every creature," He stated that "he who believes and is baptized will be saved; but he who does not believe will be condemned" (Mark 16:15-16; cf. Matthew 28: 19). The Jews who had murdered Christ, and to whom Peter spoke on the Day of Pentecost when he ushered in the Christian age, were told: "Repent, and let every one of you be baptized in the name of Jesus Christ for the remission of sins" (Acts 2:38). Before becoming a Christian, Saul of Tarsus was commanded to "arise and be baptized, and wash away your sins, calling on the name of the Lord" (Acts 22:16). The biblical solution to the problem of soul-damning sin is that the person who has heard the Gospel, who has believed its message, who has repented of past sins, and who has confessed Christ as Lord must then—in order to receive remission (forgiveness) of sins—be baptized. [The English word "baptize" is a transliteration of the Greek word *baptidzo*, meaning to immerse, dip, plunge beneath, or submerge (Thayer, 1958, p. 94).] According to Peter, "baptism," corresponding to Noah's deliverance through water, "now saves us…(not the removal of the filth of the flesh, but the answer of a good conscience toward God), through the resurrection of Jesus Christ" (1 Peter 3:21). Although baptism is no less, nor more, important than any other of God's commands regarding what to do to be saved, the New Testament clearly teaches that **water immersion is the point at which a person is saved by the resurrection of Jesus Christ**.

If it is the case then that baptism is essential for salvation, then why did the apostle John write: "Therefore, when the Lord knew that the Pharisees had heard that Jesus made and baptized more disciples than John (**though Jesus Himself did not baptize**, but His disciples), He left Judea and departed again to Galilee" (John 4:1-3, emp. added)? And why did the apostle Paul write to the church at Corinth: "**I thank God that I baptized none of you** except Crispus and Gaius, lest anyone should say that I had baptized in my own name…. **For Christ did not send me to baptize, but to preach the gospel**" (1 Corinthians 1:14-17, emp. added)? Do these statements indicate that baptism is **not** necessary for a person to be saved, as skeptics allege? No, they do not.

First, John did not indicate that Jesus thought baptism was unnecessary; he merely stated the fact that Jesus did not personally do the baptizing; rather, His disciples did (John 4:2). The phrase in 4:1 regarding Jesus "baptizing" more disciples than John is simply a figure of speech where a person is represented as doing something when, in fact, he merely supplies the means for doing it. For example, Joseph indicated on one occasion that his brothers sold him into Egypt (Genesis 45:4-5; cf. Acts 7:9), when actually they sold him to the Ishmaelites (who then sold him into Egypt). This is a well-known principle in law—a person who acts through another to break the law (e.g., paying someone to commit murder) is deemed by authorities to be guilty of breaking the law himself. Similarly, Jesus did not **personally** baptize anyone. But, **His teaching and influence** caused it to be done. Jesus, the subject, is mentioned, but it is the circumstance of His influence that is intended. His teaching was responsible for people being baptized. Thus, this passage actually implies that Jesus commanded that His listeners be baptized. It in no way contradicts teachings found elsewhere in the Bible.

Second, Paul's statements in his letter to the church at Corinth must be taken in their proper context in order to understand their true meaning. In 1 Corinthians 1:10-17, Paul was dealing with the division that was plaguing the Corinthian Christians. He had heard of the controversy in Corinth, and begged them to stand united, and to resolve their differences.

Now I plead with you, brethren, by the name of our
Lord Jesus Christ, that you all speak the same thing,
and that there be no divisions among you, but that
you be perfectly joined together in the same mind
and in the same judgment. For it has been declared to
me concerning you, my brethren, by those of Chloe's
household, that there are contentions among you.
Now I say this, that each of you says, "I am of Paul,"
or "I am of Apollos," or "I am of Cephas," or "I am of
Christ." Is Christ divided? Was Paul crucified for you?
Or were you baptized in the name of Paul?

I thank God that I baptized none of you except Crispus
and Gaius, lest anyone should say that I had baptized in my own name. Yes, I also baptized the household of Stephanas. Besides, I do not know whether I
baptized any other. For Christ did not send me to
baptize, but to preach the gospel, not with wisdom of
words, lest the cross of Christ should be made of no
effect (1 Corinthians 1:10-17).

Later, Paul added:

For where there are envy, strife, and divisions among
you, are you not carnal and behaving like mere men?
For when one says, "I am of Paul," and another, "I
am of Apollos," are you not carnal? Who then is Paul,
and who is Apollos, but ministers through whom you
believed, as the Lord gave to each one? I planted,
Apollos watered, but God gave the increase. So then
neither he who plants is anything, nor he who waters,
but God who gives the increase (1 Corinthians 3:3-
7).

When a person reads 1 Corinthians 1:14-17 in view of the
problem of division in Corinth that Paul was addressing in
chapter one and throughout this letter, he or she has a better
understanding of Paul's statements regarding baptism. He

was not indicating that baptism was unnecessary, but that people should not glory in the one who baptizes them. Some of the Corinthians were putting more emphasis on **who** baptized them, than on the **one body of Christ to which a person is added when he or she is baptized** (cf. Acts 2:41,47; Ephesians 4:4). Paul was thankful that he did not personally baptize any more Corinthians than he did, lest they boast in **his** name, rather than in the name of **Christ** (1:15). Likely, this is the same reason why "Jesus Himself did not baptize, but His disciples." As Albert Barnes surmised: "[I]f **he** [Jesus—EL] had baptized, it might have made unhappy divisions among his followers: those might have considered themselves most worthy or honoured who had been baptized by **him**" (1956a, p. 213, emp. in orig.). Paul understood that the fewer people he personally baptized, the less likely they were to rejoice in his name. [NOTE: In 1 Corinthians 1:13, Paul implied that the only way to be saved is to be baptized into the name of Christ, saying, "Was Paul crucified for you? Or were you baptized in the name of Paul?"] Paul's desire was for converts to tie themselves to the Savior, and not to himself. He knew that "there is salvation in no one else" but Jesus; "for there is no other name under heaven that has been given among men, by which we must be saved" (Acts 4:12). Paul concerned himself with preaching, and, like Jesus, left others to do the baptizing.

When Paul stated: "Christ did not send me to baptize, but to preach the gospel," he meant that preaching was his main work, and that others could immerse the converts. He did not mean by this statement that **baptism** is unimportant, but that the **baptizer** is inconsequential. Consider this: If Paul did not baptize, but preached, and, if others baptized those who heard Paul's teachings, what can we infer about the **content** of Paul's teachings? The truth is, at some point, he must have instructed the unsaved to be baptized (which is exactly what occurred in Corinth—read Acts 18:1-11; 1 Corinthians

6:11). Similar to how we logically infer from the Ethiopian eunuch's baptism (Acts 8:36-39), that when Philip "preached Jesus to him" (8:35), he informed the eunuch of the essentiality of baptism, we can truthfully affirm that Paul taught that baptism is essential for salvation. The allegation that Paul and Jesus ever considered baptism non-essential is simply unfounded.

Chapter 8

ALLEGED CONTRADICTIONS INVOLVING THE TWO TESTAMENTS

WRONGLY DIVIDING THE TRUTH
Exodus 20:8; Colossians 2:16

A glaring weakness in the skeptic's effort to discredit the Bible is the failure to understand that Old Testament laws no longer are binding upon men today unless they are reiterated under the new law of Christ. It is a common tactic among skeptics today to point to certain commands in the Old Testament, and then insist that they contradict various commands in the New Testament. For example, on page 166 of Dan Barker's book, *Losing Faith in Faith*, he poses the question, "Shall we keep the Sabbath?" He then cites Exodus 20:8 (among other Old Testament passages), which reads: "Remember the Sabbath day to keep it holy." In supposed contradiction to this verse, he quotes Colossians 2:16: "Let no man therefore judge you in meat, or in drink, or in respect of

an holy-day, or of the new moon, or of the Sabbath days."
According to Barker's logic, the Bible says in one place that
people should keep the Sabbath, but it says in another place
that the Sabbath does not necessarily have to be kept, therefore the Bible contradicts itself.

It is easy to see, however, that Barker refuses to recognize
one of the central tenets of the New Testament: The old law
(Old Testament) was specifically for the Jewish nation, it was
done away with at the death of Christ, and the new law (the
New Testament) replaced it. The New Testament books of
Hebrews and Galatians were written specifically to confirm
that very fact. Hebrews 8:13 explains that the Old Testament
laws had become obsolete at the time of the writing of the
book of Hebrews. If Dan Barker would have read just a few
verses before Colossians 2:16, he would have encountered
the fact that the old law had been "nailed" to the cross (2:14).
Also, Ephesians 2:14-17 explains that in His death, Jesus Christ
abolished the old law and brought in a new law. Under that
new law, people no longer are required to keep the Sabbath,
offer bulls and goats for sin sacrifices, or make yearly trips to
the temple. Although we still can learn numerous valuable
lessons and principles about how to live godly lives from the
old law (cf. Romans 15:4; 1 Corinthians 10:11), we are bound
by it no longer.

Any person who accuses the Bible of a contradiction in
this instance (and others similar to it) is guilty of misunderstanding two crucial issues: (1) the difference between the
Old Testament and New Testament in the Bible; and (2) the
law of contradiction. The law of contradiction states that two
opposing statements cannot be both true and not true in the
same respect at the **same time**. Barker's supposed contradiction about the Sabbath does not take into account that the
statements were written nearly 1,500 years apart, that the old
law already had been abolished, and that the new law con-

tains no commandment to keep the Sabbath. If skeptics would concern themselves more with learning how to rightly divide the word of truth (2 Timothy 2:15) than with seeing how many alleged contradictions they can rattle off on one printed page, assumed Bible contradictions like this one would become a thing of the past.

Sadly, a great deal of confusion exists even in the religious world concerning what spiritual law man is living under today. Some say the old law still is binding–all of it. Others say that most of it has been abolished, but that some of it still is in effect. Many simply pick and choose laws out of both testaments, and abide only by those that are appealing to them. Much of the confusion today about the old law and the new law is a result of the false teachings of the Seventh-Day Adventist Church. This intensely evangelistic group teaches that the Ten Commandments still are binding in the present age. Although most Christians readily agree that nine of the Ten Commandments either are stated explicitly or are implied in the New Testament (and thus are binding today because they are part of the new law), Seventh-Day Adventists actively teach that the Ten Commandments (including especially the command to observe the Sabbath day–Exodus 20:8) are part of "God's unchangeable law" (from the Seventh-Day Adventist's official Web site–www.adventist.org/beliefs). Whereas certain parts of the Old Testament have been abolished, they insist that God intended for the Ten Commandments to be an eternal covenant that all of His children must follow.

The Seventh-Day Adventists teach that God gave two laws on Mt. Sinai. They differentiate between the Ten Commandments and the ceremonial laws, saying that one (the Ten Commandments) is the Law of God, while the other (the ceremonial laws) is the Law of Moses. Moreover, they assert that all of the passages in the Bible that refer to the old law being abolished are speaking of the ceremonial laws and not the

Ten Commandments, which (they stress) were written with the very finger of God (Exodus 31:18).

Those who separate the "the Law of God" and "the Law of Moses" (in an attempt to find approval for continuing to follow portions of the old law, like keeping the Sabbath) fail to realize that the Bible does not make such a distinction. Ezra read from "the Book of the Law of Moses," which also was called "the Book of the Law of God" (Nehemiah 8:1,18). Luke recorded that after Mary gave birth to Jesus "when the days of her purification according to **the law of Moses** were completed, they brought Him to Jerusalem to present Him to the Lord (as it is written in **the law of the Lord**, 'Every male who opens the womb shall be called holy to the Lord'), and to offer a sacrifice according to what is said in **the law of the Lord**, 'A pair of turtledoves or two young pigeons' " (Luke 2:22-24, emp. added). The Law of Moses and the Law of the Lord were the same thing. When writing to the brethren in Rome, the apostle Paul quoted from the Ten Commandments, and taught that it was part of the old law to which they had "become dead...through the body of Christ" (Romans 7:4, 7). In his second epistle to the Corinthians, Paul wrote:

> [C]learly you are an epistle of Christ, ministered by us, written not with ink but by the Spirit of the living God, not on tablets of stone but on tablets of flesh, that is, of the heart.... But if the ministry of death, written and engraved on stones, was glorious, so that the children of Israel could not look steadily at the face of Moses because of the glory of his countenance, which glory was passing away, how will the ministry of the Spirit not be more glorious.... For even what was made glorious had no glory in this respect, because of the glory that excels. For **if what is passing away was glorious, what remains is much more glorious** (3:2-11, emp. added).

What was "passing away"? The law written on the "tablets of stone." What was the law "engraved on stones" that was given to Moses on Mt. Sinai? The Ten Commandments (Exodus 20). In this passage, Paul teaches the very opposite of what Seventh-Day Adventists teach—the Ten Commandments are **not** an eternal covenant.

The New Testament explicitly teaches that the old law has been abolished. Whether one is talking about the Ten Commandments or the ceremonial laws, the Law of Moses or the Law of God, all are considered the old law that no longer is in effect. Jesus Christ fulfilled that law, and nailed it to the cross forever (Matthew 5:17-18; Colossians 2:13-17).

NEW TESTAMENT WRITERS' USE OF OLD TESTAMENT PROPHECIES

Psalm 41:9; John 13:18; Jeremiah 31:15; Matthew 2:18

The New Testament writers did not always use Old Testament prophecy in a way that conforms to some people's idea of how they think it should be used. For this reason, many allege that the New Testament writers take Old Testament Scriptures out of context, or that they "reuse" or "warm over" already fulfilled Old Testament passages in order to make their point. However, in response to this idea, logical solutions can be contemplated that clarify and justify the New Testament writers' multiple uses of Old Testament prophecy.

First, could it not be the case that the Holy Spirit, knowing what would happen in the future, directed the Old Testament writers to pen phrases and statements that had an immediate application as well as a distant future application? Well did Wayne Jackson write:

> [I]s it not possible that the omniscient Holy Spirit, who guided both the Old Testament prophets and the New Testament inspired writers, could have directed certain prophecies to ancient Israel, but also

could have known that a future event would ultimately
fulfill the meaning of his words? What is wrong with
such a view? Absolutely nothing. It surely is possible
and preserves the integrity of the New Testament writers. Let me suggest an example to illustrate this point.

David declared: "Yea, mine own familiar friend, in
whom I trusted, who did eat of my bread, hath lifted
up his heel against me" (Psalm 41:9). During the last
supper, Christ quoted from this passage as follows:
"He that eateth my bread lifted up his heel against
me" (John 13:18), applying it to the treachery of Judas, and declaring that such fulfilled the statement in
David's psalm. The Lord, however, altered the quotation. He omitted, "whom I trusted," from the original source, the reason being, He never trusted Judas!
Jesus knew from the beginning who would betray Him
(John 6:64). It is clear, therefore, that Psalm 41:9 had
an immediate application to one of David's enemies,
but the remote and complete "fulfillment" came in
Judas' betrayal of the Son of God. (1988, 8:29)

Indeed, many New Testament quotations of Old Testament
prophecies could conceivably fall into the category of "remote fulfillment." Consider the situation of Matthew's use of
Jeremiah 31:15. In Jeremiah, the Old Testament prophet obviously was dealing with a fairly immediate point in the not-
too-distant future when the mothers of Israel would weep because of the captivity and punishment that the enemies of Israel would inflict upon them. However, Matthew employed
Jeremiah's prophecy—"A voice was heard in Ramah, weeping and great mourning, Rachel weeping for her children;
And she would not be comforted, because they are not" (Matthew 2:18)—to refer to the mothers who wept over King Herod's
vicious slaughter of the innocent male children of Bethlehem.
Taking Jackson's comments into consideration, it is not a dif-

ficult stretch to maintain that the Holy Spirit certainly could have foreseen the dastardly deeds of King Herod, and supplied Jeremiah with a prophetic utterance that could sufficiently describe the captivity and punishment in the Old Testament, as well as depict the gruesome scene related in Matthew. Richards added to this explanation by saying:

> The Jeremiah passage quoted is linked to this event. Jeremiah 31:15 portrays Rachel, the symbolic mother of the Jews, weeping as her descendants are torn from the Promised Land. Yet that prophecy is found in a context of the hope that despite the tears God promises the exiles will return. Now, despite the tears shed for the innocent victims of Herod's slaughter, their deaths underline the escape of the child Jesus, whose survival ultimately means restoration of humankind to a personal relationship with God. As tears intermingled with joy in Jeremiah's time, so tears and joy intermingle in Bethlehem (1993, p. 228).

It also is interesting to note that many times, Old Testament prophecies have not only immediate and remote applications, but also multiple, diverse uses. Jackson commented:

> Still again, we may note that, consistent with His own purposes, the Holy Spirit may give a prophecy multiple applications. Consider the case of Psalm 2:7, where Jehovah said: "Thou art my son; this day have I begotten thee." In the New Testament, this statement is applied to Christ in several different senses. First, it is employed to demonstrate that Christ is superior to the angels, for the Father never addressed any angelic being, saying, "You are my son, this day have I begotten thee" (cf. Hebrews 1:5). [This is a truth which the "Jehovah's Witnesses" (who claim that Christ was a created angel) would do well to learn.] Second, Psalm 2:7 is applied by Paul to Christ's resurrection

from the dead. The apostle argues that "God hath fulfilled the same unto our children, in that he raised up Jesus; as also it is written in the second psalm, Thou art my son..." (Acts 13:33). It was, of course, by His resurrection that Jesus was declared to be the Son of God with power (Romans 1:4). Thus, it was appropriate that the psalm be applied to the Lord's resurrection. Third, the writer of Hebrews uses the psalm to prove that Christ glorified not Himself to be made our high priest; rather, such a role was due to His relationship as the Son of God (Hebrews 5:5). Again, we absolutely must stress that the Holy Spirit, who inspired the original psalm, surely had all of these various thoughts in mind as is evidenced by His guidance of the New Testament writers as they employed His language (8:29-30, bracketed statement in orig.).

After looking closely at the different ways in which the New Testament writers used the Old Testament Scriptures, it cannot be argued effectively that there was error or discrepancy on their part. Although they might not have used certain passages in a way that some people might prefer, they did use the prophecies without contradiction or discrepancy in a manner consistent with the plan and purpose of the Holy Spirit.

WHO WAS MATTHEW QUOTING?
Matthew 27:9-10; Zechariah 11:12-13

After reporting in his gospel account about Judas' suicide and the purchase of the potter's field, Matthew quoted from the prophets as he had done many times prior to chapter 27. He wrote: "Then was fulfilled what was spoken by Jeremiah the prophet, saying, 'And they took the thirty pieces of silver, the value of Him who was priced, whom they of the children of Israel priced, and gave them for the potter's field, as the Lord directed me'" (27:9-10). For centuries, these two verses have been contemplated by Christians and criticized by skeptics. The alleged problem with this passage, as one modern-day critic noted, is that "this is not a quote from Jeremiah, but a misquote of Zechariah" (Wells, 2001). Skeptics purport that Matthew misused Zechariah 11:12-13, and then mistakenly attributed the quotation to Jeremiah. Sadly, even some Christians have advocated this idea (see Cukrowski, et al., 2002, p. 40). What can be said of the matter?

As with all alleged contradictions, critics and skeptics should have investigated further (i.e., study with diligence and handle the Scriptures correctly–2 Timothy 2:15) before making such boisterous claims that Matthew mishandled the prophets' words. Three considerations help clarify the situation. First, notice carefully that Matthew did not say that Jeremiah **wrote** this particular prophecy; rather, he indicated that this prophecy was **spoken** by Jeremiah. Similar to how Paul's quotation of Jesus (recorded in Acts 20:35–"It is more blessed to give than to receive") was from something Jesus verbally stated that never was recorded by one of the gospel writers, it may be that Jeremiah once spoke the prophecy in question, but never had Baruch, his amanuensis, put it in written form. Truly, one should not automatically expect to find a **written** account of a prophecy when the New Testament writer mentions it as having been spoken. Also, it should not be surprising to us if the Holy Spirit saw fit to inspire Jeremiah to speak these words, and then a few years later to inspire Zechariah to put a similar sentiment in written form.

Second, in Jesus' day, rabbinical practice entailed identifying quotations by the name of the first book in a group of books that had been clustered by literary genre. Writing in the journal *Bibliotheca Sacra* over a half a century ago, Charles Feinberg commented on this point, saying, "The Talmudic tradition [e.g., *Baba Bathra* 14b–EL] shows that the prophetic writings in order of their place in the sacred books was Jeremiah, Ezekiel, Isaiah, etc. This order is found in many Hebrew MSS.... Matthew, then quoted the passage as from the roll of the prophets, which roll is cited by the first book" (1945, p. 72). Furthermore, in all of the quotations from Zechariah in the New Testament, no mention is ever made of his name in conjunction with the prophecies (cf. Matthew 21:4; 26:31; John 12:14; 19:37). Thus, it is logical to conclude that Matthew merely referred to this whole division of the Old Testament by naming its first book (Jeremiah), just as Jesus referred to the "writings" section of the Old Testament by the name of its first book, Psalms (Luke 24:44). Jeremiah could have served as the designation for quotations from any of the included books. (Another example is found in Mark 1:2-3 where Isaiah 40:3 and Malachi 3:1 are blended and attributed to Isaiah.)

Third, and perhaps most important, Old Testament context is critical in sorting out the use of the Old Testament in the New Testament. New Testament writers frequently were guided by the Holy Spirit to weave the thought of several Old Testament contexts into a single application. Matthew referred to a series of details in the following order: the thirty pieces of silver (vs. 3); Judas threw the silver down in the temple (vs. 5); the chief priests took the silver and bought the potter's field (vs. 6-7); and the field was named (vs. 8).

Matthew then quoted from the Old Testament (vss. 9-10). Notice the comparison between Matthew's wording and the Old Testament references:

MATTHEW	ZECHARIAH
"And they took the thirty pieces of silver"	"So they weighed out for my wages thirty pieces of silver."

| "the value of him who was priced, whom they of the children of Israel priced" | "And the Lord said to me, 'Throw it to the potter'—that princely price they set on me." |
| "And gave them for the potter's field, as the Lord directed me" | "So I took the thirty pieces of silver and threw them into the house of the Lord for the potter." |

JEREMIAH
"Arise and go down to the potter's house...there he was, making something at the wheel" (18:2-3).
"Go and get a potter's earthen flask...and go out to the Valley of the Son of Hinnom" (19:1-2).
"Even so I will break this people and this city, as one breaks a potter's vessel" (19:11).
"Please buy my field that is in Anathoth.... So I bought the field...and weighed out to him the money—seventeen shekels of silver" (32:8-9).

Matthew's use of Zechariah is clearly paraphrastic, drawing from its wording while adjusting locus. In Matthew, the chief priests took the money returned by Judas; in Zechariah, Zechariah requested wages from the people. In Matthew, Judas threw the money on the ground before the chief priests; in Zechariah, Zechariah was told to throw the money "to the potter," which was achieved by throwing it into the house of the Lord for the potter. Matthew's greatest emphasis is on the acquisition of a potter's field. Zechariah says nothing about a field.

It is not until one peruses the pages of Jeremiah that one sees the striking resemblance, first to Zechariah, and then to Matthew's narrative. Zechariah's allusion to the potter harks back to the imagery and symbolism of Jeremiah. But Matthew's allusion to the potter's field harks back to Jeremiah—not Zechariah. So Matthew was demonstrating the overriding superintendence of the Holy Spirit, Who was combining and summarizing elements of prophetic symbolism both from Zechariah and from Jeremiah.

A superficial assessment of the surface tension between Matthew and Jeremiah fails to grasp the complexity and sophistication of the ultimate Mind behind Matthew's handling of the sacred text. The one who assumes error on the part of Bible writers inevitably fails to probe the depths of inspired writ to discover the ingenuity and power that reside there.

"THIS IS THE LAW
AND THE PROPHETS"
Matthew 5-7

Most people who are familiar with the Bible would agree that Matthew chapters 5-7, often referred to as the Sermon on the Mount, contain some of the most memorable sayings in the world. Jesus' list of beatitudes (5:3-12), His instruction to "do to others what you would have them do to you" (7:12, NIV), and His parable of the wise man and the foolish man (7:24-27) often are recalled even by those who rarely (if ever) read the Bible. When people implement these principles and rules that Jesus taught nearly 2,000 years ago, individuals grow stronger, families become more united, and society becomes a better place in which to live.

Sadly, however, the most famous "sermon" in the world also has become one of the most misunderstood and most abused sermons ever delivered. "Judge not, that you be not judged" (7:1) is quoted to "prove" that we never can judge anyone at any time (cf. John 7:24). The narrow and difficult way to heaven that **few** will find often is discounted by the idea that nearly **everyone** will have eternal life (7:13-14). And millions of people have changed Jesus' statement, "Not everyone who says to Me, 'Lord, Lord,' shall enter the kingdom of heaven" (7:21), to "Just accept Jesus into your heart and you will be saved."

Another misconception of the Sermon on the Mount revolves around some of the contrasts Jesus made. Six times in Matthew 5 it is recorded that Jesus contrasted what **"was** said" to what **"I** say." Many believe that Jesus was contrasting the old law of Moses (what "was said") with the new law of Christ (what "I say"). Whereas Jesus taught that it was wrong to be angry with a brother without a cause (5:22-26), many contend that the old law taught only murder as being wrong, and not the emotions (such as anger) that lead to murder (5:21). Supposedly, the law of Christ went a step farther than the Law of Moses. According to this line of thinking, the old law taught individuals to take personal retribution on those who wronged them (5:38) and to hate their enemies (5:43), while the new law taught to resist retaliation (5:39-42) and to love your enemies (5:44). In contrasting the Law of Moses and the righteousness of the kingdom that Jesus would require, the point frequently is made that the old law was concerned only with the **actions** of man, whereas the new law is concerned about the **heart** of man.

The first problem with this line of thinking is that Jesus never said He was contrasting His teachings with the old law. Instead, Jesus made statements such as: (1) "you have heard that it was said to those of old" (5:21,27); (2) "furthermore it has been said" (5:31); (3) "again you have heard that it was said to those of old" (5:33); and (4) "you have heard that it was said" (5:38,43). If Jesus were referring to what Moses had commanded in the old law itself, likely a different wording would have been used. For example, at other times, when Jesus definitely was referring to what the law actually said, He made such statements as "it is written" (Matthew 4:4,7,10) and "Moses commanded" (Matthew 8:4). [Notice that these phrases occur in the chapters immediately before and after the Sermon on the Mount.] Instead of using phrases like these to show that He was referring to the Law of Moses, Jesus repeatedly spoke about what "was said." He never mentioned who said it, only that it had been said.

Another dilemma that arises when one teaches that Jesus merely was contrasting the old law with the new law, is that Jesus referred to some statements that simply are not to be found in the Old Testament. For instance, in Matthew 5:21 He said, "You have heard that it was said to those of old, 'You shall not murder,' and whoever murders will be in danger of the judgment." The phrase "and whoever murders will be in danger of the judgment" is found nowhere in the Old Testament. Likewise, when Jesus stated, "You have heard that it was said, 'You shall love your neighbor and hate your enemy,'" He could not have been quoting from the old law because the old law never said to "hate your enemy."

So what was Jesus doing if He was not contrasting the old law with the new law? The answer to this question is found in the immediate context of this passage where Jesus stated: "Do not think that I came to destroy the Law or the Prophets, I did not come to destroy but to fulfill.... I say to you, that unless your righteousness exceeds the righteousness of the scribes and Pharisees, you will by no means enter the kingdom of heaven" (Matthew 5:17,20). The comparisons Jesus made throughout the rest of the chapter were between the **traditional/oral interpretation and application of the Law of Moses** (not the **revealed written Law of Moses**) and the righteousness of the kingdom that Jesus would require of His disciples (under the new law). In the Sermon on the Mount, Jesus expounded the **real** meaning of the original law as it was intended. He applied it correctly, and "the people were astonished at His teaching, for He taught them as one having authority, and not as the scribes" (Matthew 7:28-29). The scribes and Pharisees had failed in their attempts to explain the law correctly, whereas Jesus explained and applied its real meaning and exposed the error of the "learned." This point is illustrated perfectly by one of Jesus' statements recorded in chapter 7: "Therefore, whatever you want men to do to you, do also to them, for **this is the Law and the proph-**

ets" (vs. 12, emp. added). Jesus was not instituting a new commandment; rather, He was explaining that doing "to others what you would have them do to you" is a summary expression of all that the Old Testament required (Barnes, 1997).

Although many people in the religious world teach that in His oft'-quoted sermon Jesus simply was contrasting the old law with the new law, the context indicates that Jesus actually was reacting, not to the law itself, but to the way the law had been misinterpreted and abused. The Old Testament did not encourage or allow a person to be angry with his brother without a cause or to covet another's wife (cf. Proverbs 6:18; Exodus 20:17), but, sadly, many of the Jews had interpreted the law in such a way. In His masterful explanation of the law, Jesus exposed the error of the scribes and Pharisees, and preached the righteousness demanded of those who wish to enter the kingdom of heaven. Even though we no longer are under the old law today (Hebrews 8:7-13; Colossians 2:14; etc.), what a blessing it is to read it (cf. Romans 15:4) and to learn from the Master's perfect interpretation of it. Like Ezra and others from long ago, Jesus "gave the sense [of the law–EL], and helped them to understand the reading" (cf. Nehemiah 8:8).

IS THE NEW TESTAMENT "GIVEN BY INSPIRATION OF GOD"?
2 Timothy 3:16-17

In attempts to discredit the divine origin of the New Testament, some critics have accused Christian apologists of mishandling 2 Timothy 3:16-17. The argument goes something like this: "When the apostle Paul wrote, 'All Scripture is given by inspiration of God,' he was referring to the Old Testament, not the New Testament." As "proof," these individuals cite 2 Timothy 3:15 wherein Paul told Timothy, "From childhood you have known **the holy scriptures**, which are able to make you wise for salvation through faith which is in Christ Jesus" (emp. added). Since the "Scriptures" (ASV, "writings"; Greek *grámmata*) of which Paul spoke in this verse obviously referred to the Old Testament (since the New Testament writings would not have been around when Timothy was a child), then we are told that the "Scripture" (Greek, *grafeé*) mentioned in verse 16 also must refer **only** to the Old Testament. Furthermore, it is alleged, since "the New Testament was not written at the time Paul wrote 2 Timothy 3:16," supposedly "he could only be claiming inspiration for the Old Testament." Such statements are made by some in hopes to prove that the New Testament documents do not claim divine inspiration for themselves, but only for the Old Testament. And, skeptics assert, "if the New Testament does not claim inspiration for itself, then neither should we."

Primarily, when the term "Scripture(s)" is found in the New Testament, it is used in reference to the Old Testament. In fact, 52 times one can read the word "Scripture(s)" in the King James translation of New Testament, and nearly every time it is referring only to the Old Testament. However, at least two times this term is used when referring to both the Old Testament and the writings that eventually would become the New Testament. For example, Paul quoted Luke 10:7 as "Scripture" in his first epistle to Timothy (5:18). And in 2 Peter 3:16, Peter placed Paul's letters on a par with the Old Testament Scriptures when he compared them to "the rest of the Scriptures." Thus, it is incorrect to say that the New Testament does not claim inspiration for itself.

But what about 2 Timothy 3:16-17? Does it claim divine inspiration for the Old Testament alone? Is it inappropriate to quote this verse when defending the inspiration of the **whole** Bible, including the New Testament? All agree that 2 Timothy 3:16 applies to the Old Testament. Some scholars, however, teach that it applies **only** to the Old Testament. Adam Clarke stated in his commentary on 2 Timothy:

> The apostle is here [3:16–EL], beyond all controversy,
> speaking of the writings of the Old Testament, which,
> because they came by divine inspiration, he terms
> the Holy Scriptures, 2 Tim. 3:15; and it is of them
> **alone** that this passage is to be understood; and al-
> though all the New Testament came by as direct an
> inspiration as the Old, yet, as it was not collected at
> that time, not indeed complete, **the apostle could
> have no reference to it** (1996, emp. added).

Albert Barnes also accepted this understanding to some extent when he stated that 2 Timothy 3:16 "properly refers to
the Old Testament, and should **not** be applied to **any** part of
the New Testament, **unless** it can be shown that that part
was then written, and was included under the general name
of 'the Scriptures' " (1997, emp. added). Was a part of the
New Testament written by the time Paul penned this letter
to Timothy? Yes. As commentator Burton Coffman noted:
"A **great deal** of the NT had indeed already been written"
(1986, p. 270, emp. added). In fact, scholars believe that one
of Paul's earliest epistles (1 Thessalonians) was written approximately 15 years prior to this epistle to Timothy. Interestingly, in his first letter to the Thessalonian brethren, he
claimed the words he wrote were "by the word of the Lord"
(4:15). Thus, the notion that Paul did not consider his own
writings as Scripture is false.

Perhaps the Holy Spirit guided Paul to write "**all** Scripture
is" (in verse 16), rather than the "**holy** Scriptures are" (as in
verse 15) "given by inspiration of God," because He wanted
to differentiate between the Old Testament alone (that Timothy learned as a child), and the Old Testament combined with
the New Testament writings—some of which had been in cir-
culation for almost fifteen years. One may never know for
sure. However, it seems certain, considering all of the above
information: (1) that Paul had earlier quoted Luke 10:7 as Scrip-

ture; (2) that Peter referred to Paul's writings as "Scripture;" (3) that Paul indicated prior to his writing of 2 Timothy that he wrote "by the word of the Lord" (2 Thessalonians 4:15; cf. Galatians 1:12); and (4) that much of the New Testament already had been written. Thus, 2 Timothy 3:16-17 "can be interpreted as covering the NT as well as the Old" (Ward, 1974, p. 200).

The critics' efforts to discredit the reliability of the New Testament by alleging it does not even claim to be given by divine inspiration are to no avail. The fact is, it claims inspiration numerous times (cf. 1 Thessalonians 2:13; 1 Corinthians 2:10-13)–one example of which is 2 Timothy 3:16-17.

Chapter 9

MISCELLANEOUS ALLEGED CONTRADICTIONS

OH BROTHER...OR IS IT NEPHEW?
Genesis 14:12,14,16

I am constantly amazed at what "Bible contradiction" the skeptic will come up with next. A person would like to think that critics of the Bible's inerrancy might have some limits to their allegations, but, apparently they do not. Instead of taking a few moments with the Bible (and a concordance or a Bible dictionary) in order to learn how a particular word is used throughout Scripture, some skeptics simply look at a particular English word in one place, and if that particular word is used elsewhere in the Bible in a different sense, then they claim that there is an obvious "contradiction." Such is the case with the skeptics' treatment of Lot in the book of Genesis. Allegedly, Lot cannot logically be described as Abraham's "nephew" and his "brother" at the same time. Because Genesis 14:12 states that Lot was "Abram's brother's son" (NKJV; "nephew"–NIV), and Genesis 14:14 and 14:16 say that Lot was Abram's (or Abraham's—Genesis 17:5) "brother," skeptics allege that the writer of Genesis erred. The renowned Bible critic Dennis McKinsey has this alleged discrepancy listed three different times on his Web site. In one section simply titled "Contradictions," he states:

> If there is any area in which the Bible's imperfections and errancy is most apparent, it is that of inconsistencies and contradictions.... As incredible as it may seem, there are some individuals who still say, "The Bible is perfect and inerrant. There are no inaccuracies." So, for the benefit of these holdouts, I am going to provide a list of some **simple, straightforward problems** that even some well-known spokesmen for the fundamentalist position grudgingly concede (1983d, emp. added)

One of the "contradictions" McKinsey lists is that of Lot being described as both Abram's nephew and his brother. As he and numerous other skeptics (whose writings can be accessed easily on the Internet) see it, these verses represent a "simple, straight-forward problem" for the apologist who seeks to defend the inerrancy of the Bible.

The truth is, however, there is a "simple, straightforward" **solution** to the problem. In Genesis 14:12, the Hebrew terms *ben 'achi* are used to indicate that Lot literally was Abraham's "brother's son." Lot was Haran's son, and thus Abraham's nephew (Genesis 11:27; 12:5). At the same time, Lot was also Abraham's brother (Hebrew *'achiw*). He was not Abraham's brother in the literal sense we so often use this word today, but he was Abraham's brother in the sense that they were family. For the skeptic's argument to hold any weight, he first must prove that the term for brother (*'ach*) was used in the Bible **only** when speaking of a male sibling. But, they cannot prove that point. Although its basic meaning is male sibling (cf. Genesis 4:2), the Hebrew term for brother(s) appears about 629 times throughout the Old Testament in a variety of ways.

- Whether two males have the same mother and father, only the same father, or just the same mother, the term "brother" is used to describe their relationship (cf. Genesis 37:14; 42:3-4; Judges 8:19).

- In Genesis chapter 29, Laban is called Jacob's "brother": "And Laban said unto Jacob, 'Because **though art my brother**, shouldest thou therefore serve me for nought?'" (vs. 15, emp. added, KJV). Just before Laban's statement, "Jacob told Rachel that he was her father's [Betheul's] brother" (vs. 12, KJV). Considering that Jacob was only a cousin (or close kinsmen) to Laban and Betheul (28:5; 24:29-31,50-51,55; cf. 22:20-24), when these men used the term "brother" in discussions with (or about) each other, they merely were speaking of one another as blood relatives, and not actual male siblings.

- In another nuance, members of the same tribe are called "brethren" (*'acha*) in 2 Samuel 19:12.

- In Exodus 2:11, Moses' fellow Israelites are called "brethren" (cf. Acts 3:22; Hebrews 7:5). As is noted in A.R. Fausset's *Bible Dictionary*, the Israelites often "distinguished a 'brother' as an Israelite by birth, and a 'neighbor' a proselyte, and allowed neither title to the Gentiles" ("Brother," 1998).

- In the midst of his suffering, Job spoke of his friends (Eliphaz, Bildad, and Zophar) as "brothers" (NKJV, Hebrew *'acha*).

- In the New Testament, the term "brother(s)" (Greek *adelphos*) is used numerous times in reference to the relationship Christians have with one another as children of God (1 Corinthians 5:11; 6:6; 7:12; Philippians 2:25; et al.).

Dennis McKinsey and other skeptics who parade Genesis 14:12 and 14:14 in front of the world as a "simple, straight-forward problem" that allegedly has no solution are (as usual) guilty of misrepresenting the biblical writers. Every indication in Scripture leads the unbiased person to conclude that the term brother carries a wide variety of semantic shadings.

Considering the many ways in which the term brother was used in ancient times, and even the variety of ways it is used in twenty-first-century America, any sincere truth-seeker should be appalled at the blatantly false accusations made by McKinsey and others regarding Genesis 14 and the use of the term "brother."

WAS KETURAH ABRAHAM'S WIFE OR CONCUBINE?
Genesis 25:1,4; 1 Chronicles 1:32-33

Although Keturah is mentioned only four times in the Bible (in two different sections of Scripture–Genesis 25:1,4; 1 Chronicles 1:32-33), her relationship to Abraham has come under severe scrutiny. Skeptics have charged the Bible writers with erring in regard to their portrayal of Keturah. Allegedly, Genesis 25:1 and 1 Chronicles 1:32 are contradictory, because the first passage indicates Keturah was Abraham's "wife," while the other says she was "Abraham's concubine." Based upon the understanding of some that there is a distinction of the Hebrew words "wife" ('iššâ) and "concubine" (pileges) during the monarchic period, even some Bible believers may be somewhat perplexed at the different titles given to Keturah. Was she Abraham's wife, or was she his concubine? Many are aware that during David's reign as Israel's king, he had "wives" and "concubines" (2 Samuel 19:5). Also, during Solomon's kingship, "he had seven hundred wives, princesses, and three hundred concubines" (1 Kings 11:3). In these contexts, the terms "wives" ('iššâ) and "concubines" (pileges) are distinct terms that rarely, if ever, are used interchangeably. Such begs the question, "Why was Keturah called Abraham's wife in one passage, and his concubine in another?" Are these two sections of Scripture really contradictory, as Bible critics would have us believe?

First, for Genesis 25:1 and 1 Chronicles 1:32-33 to be a contradiction, one must know whether or not these passages are referring to the same time. It is possible that Keturah was Abraham's "concubine" in the beginning, and then became his "wife" at a later time. If such were the case, Bible writers could legitimately use both terms when describing her.

Second, although it might have been unusual for the terms "wives" and "concubines" to be used interchangeably during the monarchic period, evidence indicates that in patriarchal times, using these terms to refer to the same person was somewhat normal. Consider the following:

- Bilhah, Rachel's maid (Genesis 29:29), was one of Jacob's "concubines" (35:22). But, she also was called his "wife," both before and after she gave birth to two of Jacob's sons (30:4; 37:2).
- Genesis 16:3 calls Hagar Abraham's "wife" (*'iššâ*), while Genesis 25:6 implies that Hagar, Sarah's maidservant, also was his "concubine" (*pîlegeš*).
- Although Genesis 25:1 says, "Abraham again took a **wife**" (Keturah), verse 6 of that same chapter indicates Keturah also was his concubine.

> And Abraham gave all that he had to Isaac. But Abraham gave gifts to the sons of the **concubines** which Abraham had; and while he was still living he sent them eastward, away from Isaac his son, to the country of the east (25:5-6, emp. added).

> Isaac, son of Sarah, was set apart from all of Abraham's other sons, which were born to him by his **concubines**. By implication, Keturah, who was not the mother of Isaac, was described as a concubine (cf. 1 Chronicles 1:32).

Hebrew scholar Victor Hamilton believes this concubine-wife relationship to be dissimilar to what was seen during the days of David and Solomon. It is reasonable to conclude that this "coidentification" in Genesis indicates "that the concubines of Abraham and Jacob were not *pilagšim* [concubines–EL] in the later since, but that no term was available for that type of concubinage; thus *pilegeš* and *'iššâ* were used as synonyms to describe these women in the patriarchal narratives" (1990, p. 446). In an article that the late Semitist Dr. Chaim Rabin wrote regarding the origin of *pilegeš*, he stated: "By alternating the terms within the easily apprehended framework of a story, a similar impression of 'in-betweenness' was created" (1974, p. 362).

Keturah was a concubine-wife. It seems that she was more than a concubine (often considered a second-rate wife of servant status), but not on a par with Sarah, Abraham's first "wife" and mother of the promised son (Genesis 17:15-22). Just as Bilhah, Jacob's concubine-wife, did not rival Rachel or Leah, Keturah was not equivalent with Sarah. Thus, Bible writers were not mistaken when referring to Keturah and Bilhah as both wives and concubines; they simply used two words to indicate the "in-between" position the women held.

JACOB'S JOURNEY TO EGYPT
Genesis 46:27; Exodus 1:1,5; Acts 7:14

Three times in the Old Testament, it is stated that seventy people from the house of Jacob went down into Egypt. According to Genesis 46:27, "All the persons of the house of Jacob who went to Egypt were **seventy**." In the first few verses of the book of Exodus, Jacob's sons are named, and then again we are told, "All those who were descendants of Jacob were **seventy** persons" (Exodus 1:1,5). The third Old Testament reference to this number is found in Deuteronomy 10:22, where Moses spoke to the Israelites about the "great and awesome things" that God had done for them (10:21). He then reminded the children of Israel of how their "fathers went down to Egypt with **seventy** persons," which Jehovah made "as the stars of heaven in multitude" (Deuteronomy 10:22). The difficulty that Christians are challenged to resolve is how these verses can be understood in light of Stephen's statement recorded in Acts 7:12-14. Being "full of the Holy Spirit" (7:55) with a "face as the face of an angel" (6:15), Stephen reminded the Jews of their history, saying, "When Jacob heard that there was grain in Egypt, he sent out our fathers first. And the second time Joseph was made known to his brothers, and Joseph's family became known to the Pharaoh. **Then Joseph sent and called his father Jacob and all his relatives to him, seventy-five people**" (Acts 7:12-14, emp. added). Skeptics, as well as concerned Christians who seek to back their faith with reasonable answers, desire to know why Acts 7:14 mentions "seventy-five people," while Genesis 46:27, Exodus 1:5, and Deuteronomy 10:22 mention only "seventy persons." Exactly how many of Jacob's household went to Egypt?

Similar to how a person truthfully can give different degrees for the boiling point of water (100° Celsius or 212° Fahrenheit), different figures are given in the Bible for the number of Jacob's family members who traveled into Egypt. Stephen (in Acts 7:14) did not contradict the Old Testament passages where the number seventy is used; he merely computed the number differently. Precisely how Stephen calculated this number is a matter of speculation. Consider the following:

- In Genesis 46:27, neither Jacob's wife (cf. 35:19) nor his concubines is included in the seventy figure.

- Despite the mention of Jacob's "daughters and his son's daughters" (46:7), it seems that the only daughter included in the "seventy" was Dinah (vs. 15), and the only granddaughter was Serah (vs. 17).

- The wives of Jacob's sons are not included in the seventy (46:26).

- Finally, whereas only **two** descendants of Joseph are mentioned in Genesis 46 in the Masoretic text of the Old Testament, in the Septuagint, Joseph's descendants are calculated as being **nine**.

Taking into consideration how many individuals were omitted from "the seventy persons" mentioned in the Old Testament, at least two possible solutions to this alleged contradiction may be offered. First, it is possible that Stephen included Jacob's daughters-in-law in his calculation of seventy-five. Jacob's children, grandchildren, and great-grandchildren amounted to sixty-six (Genesis 46:8-26). If Jacob, Joseph, and Joseph's two sons are added, then the total number is seventy (46:27). If, however, to the sixty-six Stephen added the wives of Jacob's sons', he could have legitimately reckoned Jacob's household as numbering seventy-five, instead of seventy. [NOTE: Jacob is listed by Stephen individually.] Yet, someone might ask how sixty-six plus "twelve" equals seventy-five. Simple—not all of the wives were included. Joseph's wife obviously would not have been calculated into this figure, if Joseph himself were not. And, at least two of the eleven remaining wives may have been deceased by the time the family journeyed to Egypt. We know for sure that Judah's wife had already died by this time (Genesis 38:12), and it is reasonable to conclude that another of the wives had passed away as well. (In all likelihood, Simeon's wife had already died—cf. Genesis 46:10.) Thus, when Stephen stated that "Joseph sent and called his father Jacob and **all his relatives to him, seventy-five people**" (Acts 7:14), realistically he could have included the **living** wives of Joseph's brothers to get a different (though not a contradictory) number.

A second possible solution to this alleged contradiction is that Stephen quoted from the Septuagint. Although Deuteronomy 10:22 reads the same in both the Masoretic text and the Septuagint ("seventy"), Genesis 46:27 and Exodus 1:5 differ in the two texts. Whereas the Masoretic text says "seventy" in both passages, the Septuagint says "seventy-five." As R.C.H. Lenski concluded, however: "This is a mere matter of counting" (1961c, p. 270).

> The descendants of Jacob that went to Egypt were sixty-six in number (Gen. 46:26), but counting Joseph and his two sons and Jacob himself (Gen. 46:27), the number is seventy. In the LXX [Septuagint–EL] all the sons of Joseph who he got in Egypt were counted, "nine souls," which, with the sixty-six, made seventy-five (Lenski, p. 270).

Thus, instead of adding the nine living wives of Joseph's brothers (as proposed in the aforementioned solution), this scenario suggests that the number seventy-five is the result following the reading from the Septuagint—which includes the grandchildren of Joseph (cf. 1 Chronicles 7:14-21). [NOTE: The Septuagint and the Masoretic text may differ, but they do not contradict each other—the former simply mentions some of Joseph's descendants who are not recorded by the latter.] In Albert Barnes' comments concerning these differences, he appropriately noted:

> Why the Septuagint inserted these [Joseph's descendants–EL], it may not be easy to see. But such was evidently the fact; and the fact accords accurately with the historic record, though Moses did not insert their names. The solution of difficulties in regard to chronology is always difficult; and **what might be entirely apparent to a Jew in the time of Stephen, may be wholly inexplicable to us** (1956b, p. 123, emp. added).

One of the more "inexplicable" things regarding the 70 (or 75) "of the house of Jacob who went to Egypt," revolves around

the mention of some of Jacob's descendants who apparently
were not born until sometime **after** the journey to Egypt was
completed. If one accepts the Septuagint's tally of 75, including the grandchildren of Joseph, he also must conclude that
Manasseh and Ephraim (Joseph's sons) fathered these children sometime **after** Jacob's migration to Egypt, and possibly before Jacob's death seventeen years later (since Ephraim
and Manasseh still were very young when the house of Jacob
moved to Egypt). If one excludes the Septuagint from this
discussion, there still are at least two possible indications in
Genesis 46 that not all "seventy" were born before Jacob's
family arrived in Egypt. First, Hezron and Hamul (the sons
of Perez) are included in the "seventy" (46:12), yet the evidence strongly leans toward these great-grandsons of Jacob
not being born until **after** the migration. Considering that Judah, the grandfather of Hezron and Hamul, was only about
forty-three when the migration to Egypt took place, and that
the events recorded in Genesis 38 (involving his family) occurred over a number of years, it seems logical to conclude,
as did Steven Mathewson in his "Exegetical Study of Genesis
38," that "Judah's sons Perez and Zerah were quite young,
perhaps just a few months old, when they traveled to Egypt.
Therefore it would have been impossible for Perez to have
fathered Hezron and Hamul, his two sons mentioned in Genesis 46:12, before the journey into Egypt" (1989, 146:383).
He went on to note:

> A close look, however, at Genesis 46:12 reveals a vari-
> ation in the mention of Hezron and Hamul. The end
> of the verse reads: "And the sons of Perez were Hezron
> and Hamul." Yet throughout Genesis 46, the listing
> of descendants was done without the use of a verbal
> form. For example, verse 12a reads, "And the sons of
> Judah: Er and Onan and Shelah and Perez and Zerah"
> (146:383).

Hebrew scholar Umberto Cassuto commented on this "special phraseology," saying, "This external variation creates the impression that the Bible wished to give us here some special information that was different from what it desired to impart relative to the other descendants of Israel" (1929, 1:34). Cassuto also explained what he thought was the intention behind this special use of the verb "were."

> It intended to inform us thereby that the sons of Perez were not among those who went down to Egypt, but are mentioned here for some other reason. This is corroborated by the fact that Joseph's sons were also not of those who immigrated into Egypt, and they, too, are mentioned by a different formula (1:35).

A second indication that all "seventy" were likely not born before Jacob's family migrated to Egypt is that ten "sons" (descendants) of Benjamin are listed (46:21). If Joseph was thirty-nine at the time of this migration (cf. 41:46), one can figure (roughly) the age of Benjamin by calculating the amount of time that passed between their births. It was **after** Joseph's birth that his father, Jacob, worked his final six years for Laban in Padan Aram (30:25; 31:38,41). We know that Benjamin was more than six years younger than Joseph, because he was not born until sometime after Jacob discontinued working for Laban. In fact, Benjamin was not born until after Jacob: (1) departed Padan Aram (31:18); (2) crossed over the river (Euphrates–31:21); (3) met with his brother, Esau, near Penuel (32:22,31; 33:2); (4) built a house in Succoth (33:17); (5) pitched his tent in Shechem (33:18); and (6) built an altar to God at Bethel (35:1-19). Obviously, a considerable amount of time passed between Jacob's separation from Laban in Padan Aram, and the birth of Benjamin near Bethlehem. Albert Barnes conservatively estimated that Benjamin was thirteen years younger than Joseph (1997). Biblical commentator John T. Willis said Benjamin was likely about fourteen years younger than Joseph (1984, p. 433). Also, considering that Benjamin was referred to as "lad" ("boy"–NIV) eight times in Genesis chapters 43 and 44, which record events directly preceding Jacob's move to Egypt, one would not expect Benjamin to be any more than 25 or 26 years of age at the time of the migration. What is somewhat perplexing to the Bible reader is that even though Benjamin was by far the youngest son of Jacob, more of his descendants are named in Genesis 46 than any other son of Jacob. In fact, some of these descendants of Benjamin apparently were his **grandsons** (cf. Numbers 26:38-40; 1 Chronicles 8:1-5).

But how is it that ten of Benjamin's descendants, along with Hezron and Hamul, legitimately could appear in a list with those who traveled to Egypt, when all indications are that at least some were yet to be born? Answer: Because some of the names are brought in by prolepsis (or anticipation). Although they might not have been born by the time Jacob left for Egypt, they were in his loins–they "came from his body" (Genesis 46:26). Renowned Old Testament commentators Keil and Delitzsch stated: "From all this it necessarily follows, that in the list before us grandsons and great-grandsons of Jacob are named who were born afterwards in Egypt, and who, therefore, according to a view which we frequently meet with in the Old Testament, though strange to our modes of thought, came into Egypt *in lumbis patrum*" (1996). Jamieson, Fausset, and Brown agreed, saying:

> The natural impression conveyed by these words ["these are the names of the children of Israel which came into Egypt"–EL] is, that the genealogy which follows contains a list of all the members of Jacob's family, of whatever age, whether arrived at manhood or carried in their mother's arms, who, having been born in Canaan, actually removed along with him to Egypt.... A closer examination, however, will show

sufficient grounds for concluding that the genealogy was constructed on a very different principle—not that of naming only those members of Jacob's family who were natives of Canaan, but of enumerating those who at the time of the immigration into Egypt, and during the patriarch's life-time, were the recognized heads of families, in Israel, though **some of them, born after the departure from Canaan, could be said to have "come into Egypt" only in the persons of their fathers** (1997, emp. added).

While all seventy mentioned in Genesis 46 may not have **literally** traveled down to Egypt, Moses, writing this account more than 215 years later, easily could have used a figure of speech known as prolepsis to include those who would be born shortly thereafter, and who eventually (by the time of Moses) would have been "the recognized heads of families."

THE CANAANITES' IRON CHARIOTS

Joshua 17:18; Judges 1:19

Joshua 17:18: "But the mountain country shall be yours. Although it is wooded, you shall cut it down, and its farthest extent shall be yours; for you shall drive out the Canaanites, though they have iron chariots and are strong."

Judges 1:19: "So the Lord was with Judah. And they drove out the mountaineers, but they could not drive out the inhabitants of the lowland, because they had chariots of iron."

After reading the above two verses, it may look like they contradict each another. Did the children of Israel defeat the Canaanites with their chariots of iron as Joshua apparently had said they would, or were the chariots just too powerful for the people of Judah to overcome?

These two passages have several plausible ways of reconciliation, and we will deal with two of these. (Please remember that the **exact way** to reconcile any contradiction need not be pinpointed, as long as a **possible way** can be provided.) The first way to reconcile the passages is to show that Joshua was informing his listeners that they had the power to drive out the Canaanites **only if** they would follow God faithfully and be confident in His promises. Judges 2:1-3 says:

> Then the Angel of the Lord came up from Gilgal to Bochim, and said: "I led you up from Egypt and brought you to the land of which I swore to your fathers; and I said, 'I will never break My covenant with you. And you shall make no covenant with the inhabitants of this land; you shall tear down their altars.' But you have not obeyed My voice. Why have you done this? "Therefore I also said, 'I will not drive them out before you; but they shall be thorns in your side, and their gods shall be a snare to you.' "

God's promise through Joshua was not an unconditional guarantee that the children of Israel would possess all of the land they had been promised. It was conditional, based upon the faithfulness of the Israelites and their obedience to God's commandments. After all, God never would force the Israelites to clear the wooded areas against their will. Neither would He force them to conquer the iron chariots. The two verses under discussion easily could be dealing with land that God chose not to clear of its previous inhabitants because of the disobedience of the people of Judah.

A second possible solution could be that the children of Israel did conquer the mountain country, and succeeded in driving out its inhabitants for a brief time, but they were unable to maintain control of the cities. Thus, by the time referred to in Judges 1, the cities already could have been retaken by the chariots of iron.

As a final word, notice that Joshua said that "the mountain country" and "its farthest extents" were the promised possession of the Israelites. In Judges 1:19, the children of Israel did, indeed, drive out "the inhabitants of the mountains." Unless we force the phrase "its farthest extents" in Joshua 17: 18 to read "lowland" as in Judges 1:19, then there is absolutely no hint of a contradiction, and this entire explanation is unnecessary.

WHO WAS ABIJAH'S GRANDFATHER?
1 Kings 15:1-2; 2 Chronicles 13:1-2

Less than two decades following the split of the United Kingdom of Israel, Abijah (also called Abijam) began his reign as the second king of Judah–the Southern Kingdom. Following the death of his father, Rehoboam, Abijah reigned for about three years, and typically is remembered more for his God-given victory over Jeroboam and the Northern Kingdom than anything else (see 2 Chronicles 13). Some believe, however, that Abijah's name is better served as a reminder of one of the most obvious contradictions in the Bible (see McKinsey, 1998, pp. 1,3; Wells, 2001).

According to 1 Kings 15:1-2, "In the eighteenth year of King Jeroboam, the son of Nebat, Abijam became king over Judah. He reigned three years in Jerusalem; and his mother's name was Maacah **the daughter of Abishalom**" (1 Kings 15:1-2, NASV, emp. added)." Second Chronicles 13:1-2 indicates something different about Abijah's mother, Maacah (also called Micaiah). The chronicler recorded: "In the eighteenth year of King Jeroboam, Abijah became king over Judah. He reigned three years in Jerusalem; and his mother's name was Micaiah **the daughter of Uriel of Gibeah**" (13:1-2, NASV, emp. added). Although initially some might be disturbed by the three variant names listed in these verses (Abijam for Abijah, Maacah for Micaiah, and Abishalom for Absalom), skeptics generally focus their criticism upon the genealogy of Abijah. Was his mother the daughter of Absalom, son of David, or was she the daughter of Uriel of Gibeah?

If the term "daughter" was used only in one sense in the Bible—to mean strictly the direct, physical, female offspring of a parent—then Christians might have a legitimate problem on their hands. In this specific sense, Abijah's mother, Micaiah, could not be both the "daughter" of Absalom and the "daughter" of Uriel. The truth is, however, like the word "son," the term "daughter" is used in the Bible in a variety of ways. [NOTE: Aside from using the term "son" to signify son by actual birth, Bible writers used it to mean (1) son-in-law (1 Samuel 24:16; cf. 18:27), (2) grandson (Genesis 29:5; cf. 24:24,29), (3) descendant (Matthew 1:1), (4) son by creation, as in the case of Adam (Luke 3:38), (5) son by education (i.e., disciple—1 Samuel 3:6), etc.] The *International Standard Bible Encyclopaedia* lists several different ways that the term "daughter" is used in Scripture (in addition to the ordinary usage of the word), including: (1) daughter-in-law (Ruth 2:2); (2) female descendant (Luke 1:5; 13:16); (3) the women of a particular place taken collectively (Luke 23:28); (4) women in general (Proverbs 31:29); etc. Since the term "daughter(s)" is used in such a wide variety of ways in Scripture, a genuine contradiction cannot be shown to exist (in this case or in any other) unless it is proven that the same sense of the word is being used. Skeptics have no evidence that the term "daughter" can only be used in the strictest sense in 1 Kings 15:2, therefore the "contradiction" really is just an "allegation."

There simply is no way of knowing how many times in the Bible the terms "son(s)" and "daughter(s)" are used to mean grandchildren, great-grandchildren, or some other descendant. After reading Genesis 29:5, one might think that Laban was the son of Nahor, but Genesis 24 explains that he actually was Nahor's grandson (24:24,29; cf. 22:20-24). Consider also Mephibosheth. He is called the "son of Saul" in 2 Samuel 19:24, when actually he was "the son of Jonathan, the son of Saul" (2 Samuel 9:6; 4:4). He literally was Saul's grandson, though Scripture refers to him once simply as "son of Saul." These are only two examples where the Bible conveys to the reader that the term "son" was used to mean grandson. One can only wonder how many times the terms "son" and "daughter" are used this way throughout Scripture, and yet unlike the two aforementioned examples, were **not** fully explained as such.

Regarding Micaiah, most likely she was the **granddaughter** of Absalom and the **daughter** of Uriel. The first-century Jewish historian Josephus supports this understanding, saying that Micaiah "was a daughter of Absalom **by Tamar**" (*Antiquities*, 8:10:1, emp. added). Tamar was **not** Absalom's wife, but his daughter (2 Samuel 14:27), who was named for Absalom's beloved sister (2 Samuel 13:1). This would mean that Micaiah is actually the daughter of Tamar and Uriel, and the granddaughter of Absalom.

Unbelievers of all sorts are doing whatever they can to find "errors" within the Bible. The particular alleged contradiction regarding the identity of Abijah's grandfather (whether it is Absalom and Uriel) is merely one example where skeptics have pronounced guilt without sufficient evidence for such a verdict. It seems they could care less about how the Scriptures (and history) use and define biblical words, phrases, idioms, etc. If many skeptics exerted even a small amount of effort to understand the Bible, they would see their "contradictions" for what they really are—unsubstantiated accusations. As an example of the lack of effort exerted by some skeptics to understand the Bible, notice the following comment by Steve Wells, author of the *Skeptic's Annotated Bible*. He asked: "Who was Abijah's maternal **grandmother**? Uriel or Abishalom?" (2001, emp. added). At least four times on Wells' Web site the question regarding Abijah's maternal

grandmother is asked. The problem is, **neither** Uriel **nor** Abishalom were his grandmother. These were his **male** ancestors, not female.

If non-Americans interpreted American English words and phrases like skeptics interpret the Bible, can you imagine how frustrated Americans would get with them? Would a foreigner unaware of how many different ways the term "coke" is used in America be justified in calling a southerner a liar for saying that Dr. Pepper is a coke? People in the southeastern United States frequently refer to all sodas as cokes. When someone in Georgia says he wants a coke, it may mean that he wants a specific kind of coke–perhaps a Dr. Pepper. Consider also the non-American who hears three different people at a basketball game say, "That's my girl." If, based upon the fact that only one of the three people who made this comment could have been the girl's father, the foreigner concluded that one or more of those who used this phrase must have lied, would his accusation be foolproof? No. The reason: the phrase "That's my girl," has more than one meaning in American culture. A mother or father may use the phrase to mean, "That is my **daughter**." But, the expression might also be used by a young man to mean, "That's my **girlfriend**," or by a girl to mean, "That's my **good friend**." Until one can know for sure exactly how the phrase is used in a particular setting, a person is unjustified in his or her accusation of dishonesty.

If skeptics would only give the Bible writers some of the same consideration that they want people today to give them in their discussions and writings, we would not have to spend countless hours writing refutations that vindicate the Bible against unproven allegations.

DIFFERENT NAMES, SAME PERSON
Matthew 1:9; 2 Kings 15:7

Names can be rather confusing at times. A teacher might become puzzled on the first day of school when she finds out that half of her students do not immediately respond when she calls roll. The reason: they normally are called by another name than that which appears on the school records. A coach may not immediately recognize a certain player's identity, because his team only speaks of this player (on the opposing team) by using a nickname. After some investigation, however, the coach soon learns who the player actually is. Millions of individuals through the millennia have worn more than one name. Even at Apologetics Press, nearly half of my coworkers wear derivatives of their full, official name. James Monroe prefers to be called Jim. John Bradford simply goes by Brad. And David Lee is just Dave to those who know him best. Most people in the twenty-first century understand that this is simply the way it is; people often go by more than one name.

When reading the Bible, we need also to remember that people in ancient times frequently had more than one name as well. Keeping this in mind will help clarify various passages that may seem somewhat ambiguous. When studying the book of Genesis, it is helpful to bear in mind that Abram's name was changed to Abraham (Genesis 17:5), and Jacob's to Israel (Genesis 32:28). Later, while living in Egypt, "Pharaoh called Joseph's name Zaphnath-Paaneah" (Genesis 41:45). Numerous other individuals mentioned in the Bible also were known by more than one name.

- Moses' father-in-law was known both as Reuel and Jethro (Exodus 2:18; 3:1).

- Gideon acquired the name Jerubbaal because he destroyed the altar of Baal at Ophrah (Judges 6:32; 7:1; 8:29,35).

- Pharaoh Necho changed the name of King Josiah's oldest son, Eliakim, to Jehoiakim (2 Kings 23:34).

- The apostle Peter is sometimes called Peter, Simon Peter, Simon, and Cephas (Matthew 14:28; 16:16; 17:25; John 1:42; 1 Corinthians 1:12).
- And Saul is called Paul (Acts 13:9).

Attention needs to be given to how the Bible writers frequently used different names when referring to the same person, because recognition of such name usage may help clarify certain alleged contradictions. Take, for instance, Matthew 1:9. Someone might wonder why Matthew mentioned Uzziah as being the father of Jotham, while 2 Kings 15:1-7 and 1 Chronicles 3:12 call Jotham's father Azariah. The answer lies in the fact that both names apply to the same person. Within the same chapter (2 Kings 15), Jotham's father is called both Azariah (15:7) and Uzziah (15:32). The names are different, but they refer to the same person (cf. 2 Chronicles 26:1-23; Isaiah 1:1). Countless Bible questions can be answered logically just by acknowledging that the ancients often were just as flexible in their giving of names as people are in the twenty-first century.

GOOD WORKS–TO BE SEEN, OR HIDDEN?

Matthew 5:14-16; Matthew 6:1-4

When examining the various lists of alleged Bible contradictions that skeptics have compiled, a person likely will notice how some alleged contradictions seem to appear on almost every list. The question, "Has anyone seen God?" (cf. John 1:18; Genesis 3:30), appears quite frequently, as does the supposed difficulty of Joseph being the son of two different men (cf. Matthew 1:16; Luke 3:23). One question that also has made its way onto numerous skeptics' lists (somewhat to my surprise) is that of whether or not God wants His disciples to do good works to be seen of men. Purportedly, two statements that Jesus made within the Sermon on the Mount (Matthew 5-7) are incompatible. First, Jesus stated:

> You are the light of the world. A city that is set on a hill cannot be hidden. Nor do they light a lamp and put it under a basket, but on a lampstand, and it gives light to all who are in the house. **Let your light so shine before men, that they may see your good works** and glorify your Father in heaven (Matthew 5:14-16, emp. added).

Later, Matthew recorded a warning Jesus gave His audience, saying:

> Take heed that you **do not do your charitable deeds before men**, to be seen by them…. [W]hen you do a charitable deed, do not let your left hand know what your right hand is doing, that your charitable deed may be in secret; and your Father who sees in secret will Himself reward you openly (6:1,3-4, emp. added).

According to skeptics, these New Testament passages are contradictory. At one moment, Jesus supposedly said, "We should" let others see our good works, and in the next He said, "We shouldn't" let others see our good works (see Wells, 2001). Are the skeptics correct in their assertions? What is the truth of the matter?

The Bible student who carefully examines these passages (and others) will notice that Jesus never said that His followers must not do good deeds in the presence of others. On the contrary, He always has wanted good deeds to be done, but they are to be done for the purpose of giving **God** the glory, **not man**. Sadly, many Bible critics have twisted the true message of Jesus, in an effort to force a contradiction in His teachings (cf. 2 Peter 3:16). The Bible teaches that God **expects** His followers to be doing good deeds. To the churches of Galatia, the apostle Paul wrote: "As we have opportunity, let us do good to all, especially to those who are of the household of faith." During the last week of His life, Jesus taught that His disciples are responsible for doing such things as feeding the hungry, clothing the naked, and visiting the sick (Matthew 25:31-46). But these good works, and many others, are to be done in order to bring glory to **God**, not ourselves. When Jesus said, "Let your light so shine before men, that they may see your good works," He ended this sentence with the phrase, "and glorify your Father in heaven." A similar statement was written years later by the apostle Peter:

> Beloved, I beg you as sojourners and pilgrims, abstain from fleshly lusts which war against the soul, having your conduct honorable among the Gentiles, that when they speak against you as evildoers, **they may, by your good works which they observe, glorify God** in the day of visitation (1 Peter 2:11-12, emp. added).

Through the good works of mankind, **God** is to be exalted. ("To **Him** be the glory both now and forever"–1 Peter 3:18, emp. added). Man, on the other hand, must never perform godly works for the purpose of drawing attention to himself.

In their efforts to expose the Bible as a book of errors and Jesus as less than divine, skeptics frequently omit the part of Matthew 6:1-4 that gives the context of Jesus' statement concerning good deeds. Jesus was not forbidding all good deeds done in public. Rather, He was condemning the performance of "charitable deeds before men, **to be seen by them**" (6:1, emp. added). In the very next verse, Jesus elaborated on what He meant, saying, "Therefore, when you do a charitable deed, do not sound a trumpet before you as the hypocrites do in the synagogues and in the streets, that they may have glory from men." The hypocritical scribes and Pharisees, whom Jesus explicitly condemned earlier in this sermon (5:20), performed "all their works…to be seen by men" (Matthew 23:6). This was the attitude of which Jesus warned His listeners. Do not do charitable deeds in order to receive praise from men, but do them (whether private or public) to be seen of God.

Jesus taught that the proper motivation must lie behind every "good" action, in order for that action to be pleasing in God's sight. Some godly actions may be done in secret (e.g., giving monetarily to a good work, praying for the sick, fasting, etc.). Others can (and must) be done openly (e.g., preaching the Gospel–cf. Acts 2). In whatever actions we engage ourselves, in order for them to be pleasing to God, they must stem from a sincere heart whose motivation is to bring glory to God.

TO JUDGE, OR NOT TO JUDGE?
Matthew 7:1-5; John 8:24

One of the most oft'-quoted verses in the Bible is Matthew 7:1–"Judge not, that you be not judged." Those engaged in immoral behavior frequently quote this verse when attempting to defend their sinful lifestyle. Certain religionists quote it when being challenged to prove that their questionable practices are backed by biblical authority. A belligerent teenager might be heard reciting this phrase to his parents when they inquire about his occasional association with "the wrong crowd." And yes, skeptics even quote Matthew 7:1 in an attempt to show an inconsistency in Jesus' teachings. From church pews to barstools, from the "Bible belt" to Hollywood, Matthew 7:1 is ripped from its context and bellowed as some kind of scare tactic: "Do you dare judge me? Jesus said, 'Judge not, that you be not judged.'" Allegedly, Jesus meant that we cannot pass judgment on anyone at any time.

Sadly, Matthew 7:1 is not only among the most frequently quoted verses in the Bible, but also is one of the most abused verses in all of Scripture. Its exploitation becomes clear when the entire context of Matthew 7 is studied more carefully.

Throughout Matthew chapters 5-7 (often referred to as the Sermon on the Mount), Jesus publicly criticized the Jewish scribes and Pharisees for their self-righteousness and abuse of the Old Testament. Near the beginning of this sermon, Jesus stated: "For I say to you, that unless your righteousness exceeds the righteousness of the scribes and Pharisees, you will by no means enter the kingdom of heaven" (Matthew 5:20). The unrighteousness of the scribes and Pharisees was at the heart of the Sermon on the Mount. Jesus wanted His audience to understand that self-righteousness would not be permitted in the kingdom of heaven; rather, it would lead to "condemnation" in hell (5:20; cf. 23:14,33). A follower of God must be "poor in spirit" (5:3), not filled with pride. He must love his enemies, not hate them (5:44). He is to do good deeds, but only to please God, not men (6:1-4). The scribes and Pharisees were guilty of wearing "righteousness" on their sleeves, rather than in their hearts (6:1-8; cf. 23:1-36). It was in the midst of such strong public rebuke that Christ proclaimed:

> Judge not, that you be not judged. For with what judgment you judge, you will be judged; and with the measure you use, it will be measured back to you. And why do you look at the speck in your brother's eye, but do not consider the plank in your own eye? Or how can you say to your brother, "Let me remove the speck from your eye"; and look, a plank is in your own eye? Hypocrite! First remove the plank from your own eye, and then you will see clearly to remove the speck from your brother's eye (Matthew 7:1-5).

In Matthew 6:1-4, Jesus instructed us **not** to do charitable deeds…"as the hypocrites do" (to be seen of men). In 6:5-8, Jesus told us **not** to pray…"like the hypocrites" (to be heard of men). In 6:16-18, Jesus taught us **not** to fast…"like the hypocrites" (to be seen of men). Likewise, in Matthew 7:1-5, Jesus was teaching us that judging another is wrong…**when that judgment is hypocritical**.

But, what if we are doing charitable deeds **to be seen of God**? Then by all means, "do good to all men" (Galatians 6:10)! What if our prayers are led from a pure heart and with righteous intentions? Should we pray? Most certainly (cf. 1 Thessalonians 5:17). Can we fast today, if the purpose of our fasting is **to be seen of God** and not men? Yes. But what about passing judgment? In Matthew 7:1-5, did Jesus condemn **all** judging, or, similar to the above examples, did He condemn only **a certain kind** of judging? Matthew 7:5 provides the answer. After condemning unrighteous judgments (7:1-4), Jesus instructed a person to "first remove the plank from your own eye, and then you will see clearly to remove the speck from your brother's eye." He was saying, in essence, "Get your life right first. Then, in love, address your brother's problem." This is consistent with what Paul wrote to the church at Philippi: "Let each of you look out not only for his own interests, but also for the interests of others" (2:4). God never intended for Christians to be recluses who never interacted with those around them. Rather, He gave us the responsibility of helping others by lovingly correcting them when they sin. In Matthew 7, Jesus was not suggesting that a person can **never** judge. He was saying, **when** you judge, **judge righteously** (as when we pray, fast, and do good deeds–do it without hypocrisy–John 7:24). Incidentally, Jesus already had judged the Pharisees. Thus, He obviously was not teaching that we should never judge anyone.

Further proof that Jesus did not condemn all judging can be found throughout the rest of chapter 7. In fact, in the very next verse after His statements about judging, Jesus implicitly commanded that His followers make a judgment. He said: "Do not give what is holy to the dogs; nor cast your pearls before swine, lest they trample them under their feet, and turn and tear you in pieces" (7:6). Disciples of Christ must judge as to who are "dogs" and who are "hogs." Otherwise, how can we know when not to give that which is holy to "dogs"? Or how can we know when not to cast our pearls before "swine"? Jesus said we must judge between those who are "worthy," and those who are like dogs and pigs (cf. Matthew 10:12-15; Acts 13:42-46). A few verses later, Jesus again implied that His disciples must make a judgment.

> Beware of false prophets, who come to you in sheep's clothing, but inwardly they are ravenous wolves. You will know them by their fruits. Do men gather grapes from thornbushes or figs from thistles? Even so, every good tree bears good fruit, but a bad tree bears bad fruit. A good tree cannot bear bad fruit, nor can a bad tree bear good fruit. Every tree that does not bear good fruit is cut down and thrown into the fire. Therefore by their fruits you will know them (Matthew 7:15-20).

Question: How can we "watch out" for false prophets if we cannot make judgments as to who the false prophets are? According to Jesus, determining the identity of false teachers involves inspecting "their fruits" and making judgments—righteous judgments.

What does the rest of Scripture have to say to those who regard all judging as being wrong?

- In his letter to the churches of Galatia, Paul commanded those "who are spiritual" to restore those who have been "overtaken in any trespass...in a spirit of gentleness, considering yourself lest you also be tempted" (6:1). Certainly, determining who is spiritual and who has sinned involves making judgments.
- While addressing an issue in the church at Corinth where a man "had his father's wife" (1 Corinthians 5:1), Paul wrote through inspiration:

> In the name of our Lord Jesus Christ, when you are gathered together, along with my

> spirit, with the power of our Lord Jesus
> Christ, deliver such a one to Satan for the
> destruction of the flesh, that his spirit may
> be saved in the day of the Lord Jesus.... I
> have written to you not to keep company
> with anyone named a brother, who is sex-
> ually immoral, or covetous, or an idola-
> ter, or a reviler, or a drunkard, or an ex-
> tortioner—not even to eat with such a per-
> son.... Therefore "put away from your-
> selves the evil person" (1 Corinthians 5:
> 4-5,11,13b).

Paul commanded the church at Corinth to purge
a fornicator from its midst. This man's sin was even
to be addressed in a public manner. To follow Paul's
command, the church had to make a judgment (cf.
1 Corinthians 6:1-6). Paul also commanded the
congregation to "put away" others who were living in a state of sin. When we make such judgments
today, they are to be **righteous** judgments that
are based on facts and carried out in love. Such
judging should be performed in a merciful spirit
(Luke 6:36-37), and for the purpose of saving souls
("that his spirit may be saved in the day of the Lord
Jesus"—1 Corinthians 5:5). Judgments are to be
made from good (righteous) intentions. But judgments nevertheless **must** be made.

- Paul instructed the church at Ephesus to "have no fellowship with the unfruitful works of darkness, but
  rather expose them" (5:11). And to the Christians in
  Rome he wrote: "Now I urge you, brethren, note those
  who cause divisions and offenses, contrary to the doctrine which you learned, and avoid them" (16:17).
  Were churches going to have to make important judgments to comply with Paul's commands? Yes.

- Similarly, the apostle John indicated that "whoever transgresses and does not abide in the doctrine of Christ does not have God. He who abides in the doctrine of Christ has both the Father and the Son. If anyone comes to you and does not bring this doctrine, **do not receive him into your house nor greet him**; for he who greets him shares in his evil deeds" (2 John 9-11, emp. added). To determine whether or not we are going to allow someone into our homes, necessitates a judgment on our part.

- Finally, if all judgments concerning spiritual matters are wrong, then why would Jesus have commanded His disciples to go and teach the lost (Matthew 28:19-20; cf. Acts 8:4)? Before one ever teaches the Gospel to someone who is not a Christian, a judgment must be made. Is this person lost in sin, or saved "in Christ"? If we are to teach the lost today, then it is necessary to determine who is lost and who is not.

If we never can "judge people" in any sense, as many today suggest (through the misuse of Matthew 7:1), then the above commands never could be obeyed. But, they **must** be obeyed! Thus, (**righteous**) judgments can and must be made.

The popular and politically correct idea that "all judging is wrong" is anti-biblical. Those who teach that Jesus was condemning all judging in Matthew 7:1 are guilty of ignoring the context of the passage, as well as the numerous verses throughout the rest of the Bible which teach that judging the sinful lifestyles of others is necessary. One key ingredient that we need to incorporate in every judgment is "righteousness." Jesus commanded that His disciples first get their own lives right with God; then they can "see clearly" to be of help to others who are overcome in their faults (Matthew 7:5). As Jesus told the Jews in the temple on one occasion: "Judge not according to appearance, but judge righteous judgment" (John 7:24).

HATE YOUR PARENTS, OR LOVE THEM?
Luke 14:26; Exodus 20:12; Ephesians 6:2

From the pen of Moses and Paul, we read clear instructions that describe how children ought to treat their parents. Both the books of Exodus and Ephesians state that children should honor their fathers and mothers (Exodus 20:12; Ephesians 6:2). From the mouth of Jesus and a host of New Testament writers, we have been given the injunction to love others, which certainly would include our parents. Paul wrote: "Owe no one anything except to love one another, for he who loves another has fulfilled the law" (Romans 13:8). To illustrate how a person should love his neighbor, Jesus told the unforgettable story of the "Good Samaritan" (Luke 10:30-37). In light of these verses and the thoughts they contain, one easily can deduce that a person should love his or her parents. Not only is love for parents natural, but it also is commanded by God throughout the Scriptures...or is it? Luke, in his account of the life of Jesus, has the Messiah on record saying, "If anyone comes to Me and does not **hate** his father and mother, wife and children, brothers and sisters, yes, and his own life also, he cannot be My disciple" (Luke 14:26, emp. added). So which is it, should we **love** and honor our parents and family—or **hate** them?

Needless to say, this statement by Jesus has been seized by many skeptics and offered as "proof" that the Bible contradicts itself. Steve Wells, in his work *The Skeptic's Annotated Bible*, cites Luke 14:26 as a verse in contradiction to Exodus 20:12. He further attacks Luke 14:26 as a verse that goes against family values, and one that presents an unjust command (2001).

Admittedly, if the word "hate" in Luke 14:26 means what most twenty-first century Americans use the word to mean, then Jesus' statement is a contradiction, is unjust, and goes against decent family values. What anyone who studies the

verse should quickly discover, however, is that the word translated "hate" does not always mean "to despise, detest, loathe,
and abhor," which are synonymous with the general use of
the word "hate" in our modern culture. Instead, the word also
can include the meaning "to love less."

Atheist Dan Barker has disavowed such an explanation,
saying, "Most Christians feel obligated to soften the face meaning of the word 'hate' to something like 'love less than me,'
even though the Greek word *miseo* means 'hate' " (1992, p.
158). Barker failed to explore, however, the legitimate times
in the Bible (and in secular documents) where the word or its
Greek/Hebrew equivalent is given the meaning "to love less,"
and is not forced into a strict, uncompromising, literal usage
of detest, loathe, or abhor.

The story of Jacob, Rachel, and Leah perfectly illustrates
the biblical use of this term "hate" in its meaning of "to love
less." To briefly summarize the story, Jacob loved Rachel,
and agreed to work for her father Laban for seven years in order to marry her. At the end of the seven years, Laban tricked
Jacob, and gave Leah to him as a wife. When Jacob discovered the deception, he was given Rachel as a wife, but was
forced to work another seven years for her. In Genesis 29:30,
the Bible says that "Jacob also went in to Rachel, and he also
loved Rachel more than Leah." Yet, in the next verse the
Bible says, "And when the Lord saw that Leah was hated, He
opened her womb" (29:31, KJV). Jacob did not despise, detest, and treat Leah like an enemy, as in the modern use of the
word "hate." Instead, he simply loved Rachel more than he
loved Leah.

Numerous Greek scholars have added their combined
years of study to the discussion to testify that the word "hate"
(*miseo*) in Luke 14:26 does not mean "an active abhorrence,"
but means "to love less." E.W. Bullinger, in his monumental
work, *Figures of Speech Used in the Bible*, described the word
"hate" in Luke 14:26 as hyperbole. He rendered the word as

meaning "does not esteem them less than me" (1898, p. 426). W.E. Vine, the eminent Greek scholar, said the word *miseo* could carry the meaning of "a relative preference for one thing over another" (1940, p. 198). He listed Luke 14:26 under this particular definition. Lastly, A.B. Bruce, in *The Expositor's Greek Testament*, stated that "the practical meaning" of the word "hate" in this verse is "love less" (n.d., p. 575).

Add to all this the fact that, with His last few words, Jesus Christ showed honor to His mother, and made sure she had a provider (John 19:25-27). The simple meaning, then, of Jesus' statement in Luke 14:26 is that a person must be willing to sever ties with his or her family if those ties hinder the person from following and obeying Christ.

A DONKEY AND HER COLT
Matthew 21:1-9; Mark 11:1-7

Although most Christians would rather not concern themselves with some of the more minute details of Jesus' life reported in the New Testament, when challenged to defend the inerrancy of The Book that reports the beautiful story of Jesus, there are times when such details require our attention. Such is the case with Jesus' triumphal entry into Jerusalem during the final week of His life. People who wear the name of Christ enjoy reading of the crowd's cries of "Hosanna!," and meditating upon the fact that Jesus went to Jerusalem to bring salvation to the world. Skeptics, on the other hand, read of this event and cry, "Contradiction!" Allegedly, Matthew misunderstood Zechariah's prophecy, and thus contradicted what Mark, Luke, and John wrote regarding Jesus' final entry into Jerusalem (see van den Heuvel, 2003). Matthew recorded the following:

> Now when they drew near Jerusalem, and came to Bethphage, at the Mount of Olives, then Jesus sent two disciples, saying to them, "Go into the village

opposite you, and immediately you will find **a donkey tied, and a colt with her**. Loose them and bring them to Me. And if anyone says anything to you, you shall say, 'The Lord has need of them,' and immediately he will send them." All this was done that it might be fulfilled which was spoken by the prophet, saying: "Tell the daughter of Zion, 'Behold, your King is coming to you, lowly, and sitting on a donkey, a colt, the foal of a donkey.' " So the disciples went and did as Jesus commanded them. **They brought the donkey and the colt, laid their clothes on them, and set Him on them.** And a very great multitude spread their clothes on the road; others cut down branches from the trees and spread them on the road. Then the multitudes who went before and those who followed cried out, saying: "Hosanna to the Son of David! 'Blessed is He who comes in the name of the Lord!' Hosanna in the highest!" (Matthew 21:1-9, emp. added).

Skeptics are quick to point out that the other gospel writers mention only "one colt," which the disciples acquired, and upon which Jesus rode. Mark recorded that Jesus told the two disciples that they would find "**a colt** tied, on which no one has sat" (11:2). The disciples then "went their way, and found **the colt** tied by the door outside on the street, and they loosed **it**.... Then they brought **the colt** to Jesus and threw their clothes on **it**, and He sat on **it**" (Mark 11:4,7, emp. added; cf. Luke 19:29-38; John 12:12-16). Purportedly, "[t]he author of Matthew contradicts the author of Mark on the number of animals Jesus is riding into Jerusalem" ("Bible Contradictions," n.d.). Can these accounts be reconciled, or is this a legitimate contradiction?

First, notice that Mark, Luke, and John did not say that **only** one donkey was obtained for Jesus, or that **only** one donkey traveled up to Jerusalem with Jesus. The writers simply mentioned one donkey (the colt). They never denied that another donkey (the mother of the colt) was present. The fact that Mark, Luke, and John mention one young donkey does not mean there were not two. If you had two friends named Joe and Bob who came to your house on Thursday night, but the next day while at work you mention to a fellow employee that Joe was at your house Thursday night (and you excluded Bob from the conversation for whatever reason), would you be lying? Of course not. You simply stated the fact that Joe was at your house. Similarly, when Mark, Luke, and John stated that a donkey was present, Matthew merely supplemented what the other writers recorded.

Consider the other parts of the story that have been supplemented by one or more of the synoptic writers.

- Whereas Matthew mentioned how Jesus and His disciples went to Bethphage, Mark and Luke mentioned both Bethphage and Bethany.
- Mark and Luke indicated that the colt they acquired for Christ never had been ridden. Matthew omitted this piece of information.
- Matthew was the only gospel writer to include Zechariah's prophecy.
- Mark and Luke included the question that the owners of the colt asked the disciples when they went to get the donkey for Jesus. Matthew excluded this information in his account.

As one can see, throughout this story (and the rest of the gospel accounts for that matter), the writers consistently supplemented each others' accounts. Such supplementation should be expected only from independent sources—some of whom were eyewitnesses. It is very possible that Matthew was specific in his numbering of the donkeys, due to the likelihood that he was an eyewitness of Jesus' final entrance into Jerusalem.

Second, regarding the accusation that Matthew wrote of
two donkeys, instead of just one (because he allegedly misunderstood Zechariah's prophecy), it first must be noted that
Zechariah's prophecy actually mentions two donkeys (even
though only one is stated as transporting the King to Jerusalem). The prophet wrote: "Behold, your King is coming to
you...lowly and riding on a donkey [male], a colt, the foal of
a donkey [female]" (Zechariah 9:9). In this verse, Zechariah
used Hebrew poetic parallelism (the balancing of thought in
successive lines of poetry). The terms **male donkey**, **colt**,
and **foal** all designate the same animal—the young donkey
upon which the King (Jesus) would ride into Jerusalem (Mark
11:7). Interestingly, even though the colt was the animal of
primary importance, Zechariah also mentioned that this donkey was the foal of a female donkey. One might assume that
Zechariah merely was stating the obvious when mentioning
the mother's existence. However, when Matthew's gospel is
taken into account, the elusive female donkey of Zechariah
9:9 is brought to light. Both the foal and the female donkey
were brought to Christ at Mount Olivet, and both made the
trip to Jerusalem. Since the colt never had been ridden, or
even sat upon (as stated by Mark and Luke), its dependence
upon its mother is very understandable (as implied by Matthew). The journey to Jerusalem, with multitudes of people
in front of and behind Jesus and the donkeys (Matthew 21:8-
9), obviously would have been much easier for the colt if the
mother donkey were led nearby down the same road.

The focal point of the skeptic's proposed problem with Jesus' entry into Jerusalem is how He could have ridden on two
donkeys at once. Since Matthew 21:7 states: "They brought
the donkey and the colt, laid their clothes on them, and **set
Him on them**" (NKJV), some have concluded that Matthew
intended for his reader to understand Jesus as being some
kind of stunt rider—proceeding to Jerusalem as more of a clown
than a king. Such reasoning is preposterous. Matthew could

have meant that Jesus rode the colt while the other donkey walked along with them. Instead of saying, "He rode one donkey and brought the other with him," the writer simply wrote that He rode "them" into Jerusalem. If a horse-owner came home to his wife and informed her that he had just ridden the horses home a few minutes ago from a nearby town, no one would accuse him of literally riding both horses at once. He merely was indicating to his wife that he literally rode one horse home, while the other one trotted alongside or behind him.

A second possible solution to this "problem" is that Jesus **did** ride **both** donkeys, but He did so at **different** times. However unlikely this possibility might seem to some, nothing in Zechariah's prophecy or the gospel accounts forbids such. Perhaps the colt found the triumphant procession that began on the southeastern slope of the Mount of Olives near the towns of Bethphage and Bethany (about 1¾ miles from Jerusalem–Pfeiffer, 1979, p. 197) too strenuous. Zechariah prophesied that Jesus would ride upon a colt (9:9), which Jesus did. He also easily could have ridden on the colt's mother part of the way.

Perhaps a more likely answer to the question, "How could Jesus sit 'on them' (donkeys) during His march to Jerusalem?," is that the second "them" of Matthew 21:7 may not be referring to the donkeys at all. Greek scholar A.T. Robertson believed that the second "them" (Greek *auton*) refers to the **garments** that the disciples laid on the donkeys, and not to the donkeys themselves. In commenting on Matthew 21:7 he stated: "The garments thrown on the animals were the outer garments (*himatia*), Jesus 'took his seat' (*epekathisen,...*) upon the garments" (1930, 1:167). Skeptics do not want to allow for such an interpretation. When they read of "them" at the end of Matthew 21:7 (in the New King James Version), skeptics feel that the antecedent of this "them" must be the previous "them" (the donkeys). Critics like John Kesler (2003) also appeal to the other synoptic accounts (where Jesus is said to have sat upon "it"–the colt), and conclude that Matthew, like Mark and Luke, surely meant that Jesus sat upon the donkeys, and not just the disciples' clothes (which were **on** the donkeys). What critics like Kesler fail to acknowledge, however, is that in the Greek, Matthew's word order is different than that of Mark and Luke. Whereas Mark and Luke indicated that the disciples put their **clothes on the donkey**, Matthew's word order reads: they **put on the donkeys clothes**. The American Standard Version, among others (KJV, RSV, and NASV) is more literal in its translation of this verse than is the NKJV. It indicates that the disciples "brought the ass, and the colt, and **put on them their garments**; and he sat thereon" (Matthew 21:7, ASV; cf. RSV, KJV, NASV). When Matthew wrote that Jesus sat "on **them**," he easily could have intended for his readers to understand this "them" to refer to the clothes, and not to the donkeys. If the disciples' clothes were placed on both donkeys (as Matthew indicated), and then Jesus mounted the colt, one logically could conclude that Jesus sat on the clothes (which were placed upon the colt).

One of the fundamental principles of nearly any study or investigation is that of being "innocent until proven guilty." Any person or historical document is to be presumed internally consistent until it can be shown conclusively that it is contradictory. This approach has been accepted throughout literary history, and still is accepted today in most venues. The accepted way to critique any ancient writing is to assume innocence, not guilt. If we believe the Bible is innocent until proven guilty, then any **possible** answer should be good enough to nullify the charge of error. (This principle does not allow for just **any** answer, but any **possible** answer.) When a person studies the Bible and comes across passages that may seem contradictory at first glance, he does not necessarily have to pin down the exact solution in order to show their truthfulness. The Bible student need only show the **possi-**

bility of a harmonization among passages that appear to conflict, in order to negate the force of the charge that a Bible contradiction really exists. We act by this principle in the courtroom, in our treatment of various historical books, as well as in everyday-life situations. It is only fair, then, that we show the Bible the same courtesy by exhausting the search for possible harmony among passages before pronouncing one or more accounts false.

WHAT WAS THE INSCRIPTION ON THE CROSS?

Matthew 27:37; Mark 15:26; Luke 23:38; John 19:19

Controversy has surrounded the death of Christ on the cross for almost two millennia. In the days of the apostle Paul, it served as a "stumbling block" to the Jews and "foolishness" to the Greeks (1 Corinthians 1:23). Throughout the past 2,000 years, men and women of all ethnicities have rejected—for many objectionable reasons—the story of the crucified, resurrected Savior. Sadly, for some today, even the physical cross itself has become a stumbling block. Because of an alleged contradiction surrounding the actual words written on the cross of Christ, some believe that the message of the cross once preached by John, Paul, Peter, Philip, and others simply cannot be trusted. According to skeptics, the gospel writers disagreed regarding what the title read that appeared on the cross above Jesus' head.

Matthew: "This is Jesus the King of the Jews" (27:37).

Mark: "The King of the Jews" (15:26).

Luke: "This is the King of the Jews" (23:38).

John: "Jesus of Nazareth the King of the Jews" (19:19).

Question: Did Matthew, Mark, Luke, and John **disagree** on what was written on the cross, or did these four independent writers record trustworthy statements?

Before answering the above question, consider the following illustration. Tonight after getting home from work, I inform my wife (Jana) about an accusation I read on a billboard on the way home regarding one of our friends who is running for city council. I proceed to tell her that the accusation read: "John Doe is a thief." The following day, our niece (Shanon) comes by the house and mentions to Jana that she just saw a billboard (the same one that I had mentioned a day earlier) that read: "City council candidate John Doe is a thief." Finally, the next day, a friend (Rhonda) visits Jana and informs her about the same sign, saying it reads: "Montgomery City Council candidate John Doe is a thief." Question: Would anyone have justification for saying that Shanon, Rhonda, and I **disagreed** regarding what the billboard said? Certainly not! We all three reported the very same accusation ("John Doe is a thief"), except that Shanon mentioned the fact that he was a "city council candidate," and Rhonda added that he was a candidate from "Montgomery." All three of us reported truthfully the allegation we saw on the billboard. Similarly, the accusation above Jesus on the cross is the same in all four narratives—"the King of the Jews."

> Matthew: "This is Jesus **the King of the Jews**" (27:37, emp. added).
>
> Mark: "**The King of the Jews**" (15:26, emp. added).
>
> Luke: "This is **the King of the Jews**" (23:38, emp. added).
>
> John: "Jesus of Nazareth **the King of the Jews**" (19:19, emp. added).

The only variation in the inscription is in the personal name of Jesus. This alleged contradiction is easily explained by acknowledging that John recorded the full inscription, while the other writers assumed all to understand the personal name, and therefore simply focused on the accusation on which the crucifixion was based. The accusation was not that this man was Jesus of Nazareth, since there was no controversy regarding His name, nor His hometown. It was a known fact that the man crucified between the two thieves was indeed "Jesus of Nazareth." Somewhat like the controversial accusation mentioned above regarding John Doe, the key charge levied against Jesus was that He was "the King of the Jews," and this title was mentioned by all four gospel writers.

Also involved in this alleged problem regarding the accusation that appeared on the cross is the fact that the superscription was written in three different languages, and translation may have been involved in some instances. According to John, the title was "written in Hebrew, Greek, and Latin" (John 19:20; cf. Luke 23:38). Pilate is said to have written the inscription (John 19:19), and he (or whomever he ordered to write the inscription—cf. John 19:1) could have written a slightly different wording in each of the languages according to his proficiency in each language, or according to how much time he wanted to spend writing each one. Furthermore, as Bible commentator Albert Barnes noted: "One evangelist may have translated it from the Hebrew, another from the Greek, a third from the Latin, and a fourth may have translated one of the inscriptions a little differently from another" (1997).

The inscription on the cross of Christ mentioned by all four gospel writers proves yet again, not that the Bible contains discrepancies, but that the narrators wrote independently. They did not rely upon one another to ensure that their facts were exactly correct. Rather, their accurate accounts of Jesus' life stand solidly upon the "inspiration of God" (2 Timothy 3:16).

"MEET ME IN GALILEE"
Matthew 28:7,10

One question that skeptics frequently ask regarding various events in the Bible is "Why?" Why did God create the
Sun on day four after creating light on day one? Why did
God command the Israelites to walk around Jericho one time
a day for six days, and seven times on the seventh day before
the city was destroyed? Why did Jesus choose Judas as an
apostle if He knew that he would betray Him? And so on.
Since skeptics are unable to find legitimate internal contradictions about various occurrences in Scripture that seem pe-
culiar to them, they simply ask questions beginning with
"Why…?," in hopes that doubt will take hold of the Bible
reader—seeds of doubt that they hope eventually will grow
into full-fledged disbelief in the trustworthiness of the Bible.

One question I was asked by a skeptic is **why** an angel (and
later Jesus) informed Mary Magdalene and the other women
who came with her to the tomb of Jesus on the day of His resurrection, to tell the disciples to go meet Him in Galilee? If Jesus was going to meet the disciples in Jerusalem that very day
anyway, why did He instruct the women saying, "Go and tell
My brethren to go to Galilee, and there they will see Me" (28:
10)? Allegedly, "If Jesus was going to meet with the disciples
at Jerusalem first, then there was no need for Jesus to tell Mary
to remind the disciples about the scheduled meeting (cf. Matthew 26:32) in Galilee. Jesus Himself could have informed
them about the Galilean meeting when He appeared to them
later that evening in Jerusalem."

Although Christians are not obligated to answer knowl-
edgably every single question beginning with "Why…" (cf.
Isaiah 55:8-9; Romans 11:33), most of the time either the Scriptures or reason reveal logical answers. Such is the case with
the question concerning why Jesus commanded Mary Magdalene and the other women to tell the disciples to go meet
the Lord in Galilee when the Lord was going to appear to
them that evening in Jerusalem anyway.

Before consulting Scripture to answer this question, consider the following illustration. Your boss informs you at your house on a Thursday night that he has scheduled a meeting for you, your ten coworkers, and numerous others the following week beginning on Monday in Atlanta. However, on Friday morning, you awake to hear on the news that your boss was in a terrible accident on his way home from your house the previous night. He was run off of the road by a drunk driver, after which his car rolled down an embankment while he was thrown out of the front windshield. Reports are that he died in the ambulance on the way to the hospital. On Sunday afternoon, however, your son returns from visiting a friend in the hospital who just had knee surgery. He informs you that, to his surprise, he saw your boss checking out of the hospital—**alive!** Your son says: "He told me that he would meet you in Atlanta tomorrow." What would your reaction be? Although your son is a trustworthy teenager, how could your boss really be alive? And even if somehow he was resuscitated from an apparent death, surely he would not be checking out of the hospital already? Surely your son was just mistaken. And surely the meeting is not still going to occur?

If your boss got word about your unbelief in his well-being, do you think it would be appropriate for him either to contact you, or visit you, and show you firsthand that he is well? Of course it would. Even though he indicated to you on Thursday night, and to your son on Sunday, that he would meet you in Atlanta for a business meeting with dozens of others, it still would be appropriate for him to contact you (again) and assure you that the meeting is still on schedule. No one would see his "repetitious" testimony and presence in your home as something superfluous considering the ordeal he had just recently experienced.

If the skeptic can see the rationality of this illustration, one wonders why he cannot see the rationality of Jesus appearing to the disciples **in Jerusalem**, even after informing Mary Magdalene to remind them to meet Him **in Galilee**? The disciples had just seen their Lord arrested, tortured, and crucified. They were scared for their own lives. They even "forsook him" during His arrest in the garden (Mark 14:50; cf. 14:27). Peter denied knowing Him three times, just a short while later (Mark 14:66-72). And, on the day of Jesus' resurrection, John recorded how the disciples (except Thomas) met behind closed doors "for fear of the Jews" (John 20:19). These men obviously were traumatized by all of the events of the past couple of days. "They mourned and wept" for the loss of their leader (Mark 16:10). They were mentally and emotionally troubled.

Then entered Mary Magdalene and the other women who told the apostles (and those who are gathered together with them) that they had seen Jesus–**alive** (Luke 24:9-10)! Sadly, the disciples rejected the women's testimony. Luke recorded: "Their words seemed to them like idle tales, and they did not believe them" (24:11). The apostles doubted that Jesus was alive (cf. Luke 24:38). Later on that same day, Mark wrote that two other disciples informed them of Jesus' resurrection, but "they did not believe them either" (16:12-13). In fact, when Jesus appeared to the apostles (except Thomas) on the evening of His resurrection, He said: "Why are you troubled? And why do **doubts** arise in your hearts? Behold My hands and My feet, that it is I Myself. Handle Me and see, for a spirit does not have flesh and bones as you see I have" (Luke 24: 38-39, emp. added). The apostles later reported Jesus' appearance to their fellow apostle, Thomas, who had missed the opportunity to see, touch, and eat with Him. Like his fellow apostles, who previously had rejected the eyewitness testimony, Thomas responded, saying, "Unless **I see** in His hands the print of the nails, and put my finger into the print of the nails, and put my hand into His side, I will **not** believe" (John 20:25, emp. added).

Multiply many times the doubts you would have of seeing your employer for a meeting three days after he was ejected through the front windshield of his car and reported on the news to be dead. Only then might you come close to the frazzled mindset of the unbelieving apostles.

Why did Jesus appear to the apostles in Jerusalem before meeting with them (and many others—cf. 1 Corinthians 15:6) a three-days' journey away in Galilee? Both common sense and the Scriptures indicate that it was due to their unbelief in His resurrection. Jesus wanted to ensure that they believed He had risen!

SHOULD WE FEAR GOD?
2 Timothy 1:7; 1 John 4:18; Deuteronomy 6:13

The word "fear" appears in the New King James Version of the Bible 367 times. In some of these occurrences, the text is expounding upon "the fear of the Lord" and its relationship to wisdom (cf. Job 28:28; Psalm 111:10; Proverbs 1:7). In numerous other passages of Scripture, one can read where God commands that His creation fear Him (Leviticus 25:17; Deuteronomy 6:13; Matthew 10:28; et al.). It is widely known that one of the repeated truths in the Bible is that God's "mercy is on those who fear Him" (Luke 1:50). It also is well known, however, that in the New Testament Paul informed Timothy that "God has not given us a spirit of fear, but of power and of love and of a sound mind" (2 Timothy 1:7). The apostle John went even further, saying, "There is no fear in love, but perfect love casts out fear, because fear involves torment" (1 John 4:18).

Some time ago, Steve Wells, author of the *Skeptic's Annotated Bible*, highlighted 2 Timothy 1:7 and 1 John 4:18 (verses indicating Christians are **not** to fear), and placed alongside these verses twenty-six Bible references that specify **we are to fear God**. He then asked, "Should we fear God?" Obviously, it was Wells' intent to convince his readers that the Bible's discussion of fear is contradictory. How can a person fear God and not fear God at the same time? Although this is a question one might think that a skeptic never would raise due to its seemingly obvious answer, it nevertheless requires a response.

In most cases, when the Bible praises man's fearlessness and his need to move beyond fear, it is using the term in a different context than the way it is used when referring to "the fear of the Lord." The passage in 2 Timothy 1:7 is not teaching that we should not fear God; rather, Paul was instructing Timothy that we should not fear **for our lives** while doing the Lord's work. God wants His children to be fearless in their service to Him. Such courage will help His people "not be ashamed of the testimony of our Lord" (2 Timothy 1:8). Like the Israelites who were instructed by Joshua and Caleb not to fear the people of Canaan (Numbers 14:8-9), Christians must not fear their adversaries around them, nor the task before them. God expects His people to understand that "He who is in you is greater than he who is in the world" (1 John 4:4).

But what about 1 John 4:17? Is it not referring to fearing God? A person must keep in mind that the term "fear" is used in various senses in Scripture (and whenever different senses of the same word or thing are under discussion, the skeptics' allegations hold no value). Fear can mean terror, dread, and horror; but it also can mean awe, reverence, and respect. The "perfect love" about which John writes casts out the former, not the latter. As the late Guy N. Woods noted:

> "Fear," as here contemplated, is not that which the Psalmist declares is "the beginning of wisdom" (Psalm 111:10), a reverential, godly fear, which shrinks from any action which would displease God, the fear which an obedient child has for a loving father;...but **terror, dread, slavish fear**, such as is characteristic of a slave in the presence of a cruel and heartless master.... The fear that is absent from genuine love is the fear of

the whip in the hands of the master; the dread of the
chastisement which comes to the disobedient. Perfect (mature) love casts out such fear, because it cannot exist where genuine love is (1979, pp. 304-305,
emp. in orig.).

In Malachi 2:5, the prophet linked fear and reverence together in describing the attitude that Levi (whose name here
represents the entire priestly class) possessed at one point in
the past. Malachi stated: "So he feared Me, and was reverent
before My name." The Hebrew word transliterated *yare'*, frequently translated "fear," also means "religious awe." For
this reason, some modern versions (like the New American
Standard) have translated Malachi 2:5 thusly: "So he **re-
vered** Me, and **stood in awe** of My name."

Today, God expects His people to revere Him, not panic
at the thought of Him as a slave might fear his cruel master.
Furthermore, one way a Christian walks "in the fear of the
Lord" (Acts 9:31) is by boldly following in the steps of the
Savior, Who stood fearless in the face of His adversaries.

WAS ISAAC ABRAHAM'S "ONLY" SON?

Hebrews 11:17; Genesis 16:16; 25:1-2

Some verses in the Bible seem to stand in such glaring contradiction to other Bible passages that reconciliation appears
virtually impossible. But, after looking into the problem with
only a small amount of diligence, the solution generally becomes apparent, and the supposed contradiction vanishes
like a plate full of chocolate chip cookies in the midst of a
group of hungry teenage boys. Such is the case with Hebrews
11:17: "By faith Abraham, being tried, offered up Isaac: yea,
he that had gladly received the promises was offering up his
only begotten son." When this verse is compared to Abraham's history as recorded in the book of Genesis, we immediately notice that Isaac was not the "only begotten son" of

Abraham. In fact, we read that Abraham fathered Ishmael by Hagar (Genesis 16:16) more than a decade before the birth of Isaac. What's more, Genesis 25:1-2 indicates that Abraham had six more sons with a woman by the name of Keturah.

How is this seeming contradiction to be resolved? First, let us remember the general context of Hebrews 11:17. This verse comes near the end of a book whose writer has shown an intimate knowledge of the Old Testament. Even in the very chapter under discussion, we read a rather complete list of Old Testament heroes such as Abel, Enoch, Noah, Abraham, Isaac, Jacob, Moses, et al. Furthermore, much more obscure characters like Barak and Jephthah make their way into the discussion. Add to this the numerous allusions to Melchizedek and the priesthood in earlier chapters, and one soon realizes that the writer of Hebrews was a true Old Testament scholar. To assume that he thought, or accidentally wrote, that Abraham had **only one son** would be to attribute to the writer a most unlikely, grievous, careless mistake of colossal proportions.

In truth, the problem has nothing to do with the writer of the book of Hebrews, but everything to do with the translators of the Greek into English. In the Greek text of Hebrews 11:17, the word translated as "only begotten son" is *monogenes*. While this word could possibly be used to refer to an only child, that certainly was not its sole use. The Jewish historian Josephus used the word *monogenes* to refer to Izates, who had an older brother and several younger brothers *(Antiquities, 20.2.1)*. The well-respected *Greek-English Lexicon* by Arndt, Gingrich, and Danker explains that the word can be used to denote something that is "unique (in kind), of something that is the only example of its category" (1979, p. 527). This meaning fits perfectly the passage in Hebrews 11, where the writer was explaining that Abraham offered up his "only **promised** son." Abraham had no other children that fit in the category of being promised by God. Isaac was the only "example of a category"–that category being a son who was promised to Abraham and Sarah. Although Abraham had many other children by other women, he had no other child "of promise." Isaac was his unique son, the only one of promise: the "*monogenes.*"

Sometimes, clearing up a supposed contradiction in the Bible is as easy as looking up the possible meanings of a single word from the original language. Before we allow our faith to be shaken by superficial claims of contradiction, let us resolve to give the Bible the benefit of the doubt that even an ancient secular document would deserve. It borders on comical to imagine that the Hebrews writer, with his commanding knowledge of the Old Testament, accidentally "slipped" when referring to Isaac as Abraham's **only** son. Once again, we find that no contradiction exists; the honest Bible student has his or her question answered, the Bible skeptic has his or her allegation refuted, and the Bible remains the inspired Word of God.

Chapter 10

EVIDENCES FOR THE BIBLE'S INSPIRATION

After covering numerous alleged Bible discrepancies in over 500 pages of text in volumes one and two of *The Anvil Rings*, it seemed wise to dedicate the final chapter in this two-volume set to laying out a positive case for the Bible's inspiration. What is it that makes the Bible so different from all of the other books of the world? Why is it worthy of being considered a book "given by inspiration of God"?

THE CLAIM OF INSPIRATION

Do biblical claims of divine inspiration really mean anything? Should we stress the fact that thousands of times in the Bible a person can find sentences prefaced by the words "God said..." or "Thus said the Lord God..."? I once received a letter that read: "To say that 'all scripture is by inspiration of God' is pointless double-speak that proves **nothing**!" Is this an accurate statement?

Admittedly, the mere claim that a certain document is inspired of God does not mean He actually inspired it (e.g., *The Book of Mormon*). If a person attempts to defend the inspiration of the Bible solely on the premise that the Bible claims inspiration, likely his efforts to convince an unbeliever will fail (and rightly so). Simply because a particular book **claims** to be from God does not mean that it **is** from God. However, to say that the claim of inspiration "is pointless double-speak" greatly diminishes the importance of such a claim.

The fact is, the claim of inspiration at the hand of God is extremely rare. Many books assert special importance, while others claim to be a kind of "creed book." But, as Kenny Barfield noted in his book, *Why the Bible is Number 1*, it seems that less than ten documents exist in the whole world that openly claim divine inspiration (1997, p. 186). Sadly, misguided devotees of various religions clamor about defending books and various writings as allegedly being "inspired of God" when, in fact, the books themselves do not even make such a claim. Take for instance, the many Hindu writings. Of their six most notable "sacred" texts, including the Vedas, the Laws of Manu, and the Puranas, only the section of the Vedas known as the Rig Veda claims inspiration. Similarly, the Christian Science group has led many to believe that the writings of Mary Baker Eddy are inspired. Yet, even though her writings claim special importance, they never openly claim divine inspiration (Barfield, p. 186). Why would anyone want to follow a creed book and claim it is from God, when the book itself does not even make such a claim?

One of the best places to begin a study on the Bible's divine origin is with its claims of divine inspiration. In his second letter to his coworker, Timothy, Paul stated: "All Scripture is given by inspiration of God, and is profitable for doctrine, for reproof, for correction, for instruction in righteousness, that the man of God may be complete, thoroughly equipped for every good work" (2 Timothy 3:16-17). Peter wrote: "Knowing this first, that no prophecy of Scripture is of any private interpretation, for prophecy never came by the will of man, but holy men of God spoke as they were moved by the Holy

Spirit" (2 Peter 1:20-21). Furthermore, statements such as "God said…" or "these are the words of the Lord…" appear thousands of times in both the Old and New Testaments. Moses wrote in Exodus 20:1: "And God spoke all these words…." The psalmist wrote in 119:89: "Forever, O Lord, Your word is settled in heaven." In Matthew 22:31, the Lord asked: "have you not read what was spoken to you by God?" In fact, "[t]here are 2,700 such statements in the Old Testament alone, all of which make direct claim that the Bible is the Word of God" (Ridenour, 1967, p. 2). Such claims of inspiration are only "pointless double-speak" if we never continue to give the following evidence proving that the Bible truly is a book from Almighty God.

THE UNITY OF THE BIBLE

Imagine asking an actress from Hollywood, a farmer from Oklahoma, and a restaurant manager from Alabama to write independent essays about the intricacies of the Civil War, including its causes and effects. Even though they would all write at the same time about a war that occurred less than 200 years ago, numerous discrepancies would be apparent. The Hollywood actress might say the war was solely a result of slavery. The restaurant manager may assert the war was about states' rights, and states' rights alone. The farmer from Oklahoma might claim that the war was because of stubbornness on both sides–the North and South. The point is, these three individuals likely would have many contradictory things to say about the war. Their compositions would be recognized more for the disagreements and discrepancies they contained than for the agreements.

When we compare ordinary human authors to the writers of the Bible, we realize that the Bible truly is an amazing book written by individuals who were inspired by God. Considering that it was written by approximately 40 different writers over a period of about 1600 years (1500 B.C. to A.D. 100), and contains no contradictions in its original form, one has to admit that the Bible is no ordinary book. From Genesis through Revelation, the theme is Jesus Christ–His coming, His presence, and His return. Yet, the Bible writers were as different as the Hollywood actress and the Oklahoma farmer. Some were fishermen, some were farmers, some were military leaders, and some were kings. Some wrote in the Hebrew language, while others wrote in Aramaic or Greek. Some of the Bible writers penned letters while traveling, and others while in prison. And they covered topics as diverse as eschatology, soteriology, theology, psychology, geography, history, medicine, and many others. Yet when we look at the Bible, it shows amazing unity–unity that can be explained only by the fact that Bible writers were guided by a single Author–the Holy Spirit.

THE FACTUAL ACCURACY OF THE BIBLE

Repeatedly, history has shown itself to be an ally, rather than an enemy, to the sixty-six books that make up the English Bible. As a person reads through these books, he will find names of kings and queens, governors and priests. He will read of cities and villages, and sometimes even learn of the roads and passageways that connected them. The Bible was born among real historical people, places, and events, which allows twenty-first-century readers opportunities to inquire about its trustworthiness–inquiries that rabid infidels would rather you not take the time to consider, yet ones that, as you will see in the remainder of this chapter, should open your eyes to the truth of the matter: the Bible **is** factually accurate in **all** that it proclaims. The Bible's facts have withstood tests of reliability time and again. Examples abound.

Bible critics in the past once accused Isaiah of having made a historical mistake when he wrote of Sargon as king of Assyria (Isaiah 20:1). For years, this remained the sole historical reference–secular or biblical–to Sargon having been linked with the Assyrian nation. Thus, critics assumed Isaiah had erred. But in 1843, Paul Emile Botta, the French consular agent at Mosul, working with Austen Layard, unearthed historical evidence that established Sargon as having been exactly what Isaiah said he was—king of the Assyrians. At Khorsabad, Botta discovered Sargon's palace. Pictures of the find may be found in *Halley's Bible Handbook* (1962, p. 289). Apparently, from what scholars have been able to piece together from archaeological and historical records, Sargon made his capital successively at Ashur, Calah, Nineveh, and finally at Khorsabad, where his palace was constructed in the closing years of his reign (c. 706 B.C.). Isaiah had been correct all along. And the critics had been wrong—all along.

One of the most impressive pieces of evidence verifying the historical reliability of the Old Testament is known as the Moabite Stone (or the Mesha Inscription). The written inscription on the stone provides a piece of "rock-solid" evidence verifying part of the Bible's factual accuracy. Mesha, the king of Moab, had the stone cut in about 850 B.C. to tell of his many conquests and his reacquisition of certain territories that were controlled by Israel. In the over 30-line text composed of about 260 words, Mesha mentions that Omri was the king of Israel who had oppressed Moab, but then Mesha says he "saw his desire upon" Omri's son and upon "his house." The Mesha stele cites Omri as the king of Israel, just as 1 Kings 16:21-28 indicates. Furthermore, it mentions Omri's son (Ahab) in close connection with the Moabites, just as 2 Kings 3:4-6 does. In addition, both the stele and 2 Kings 3:4-6 list Mesha as the king of Moab. The stele further names the Israelite tribe of Gad, and the Israelite God, Yahweh. The Moabite Stone confirms facts that the Bible had reported for centuries. Sadly, such amazing confirmation frequently falls on deaf ears.

One of the most famous archaeologists of the 19th and 20th centuries was Sir William Ramsay, who disputed the accuracy of events recorded by Luke in the book of Acts. Ramsay believed those events to be little more than second-century, fictitious accounts. Yet after years of literally digging through the evidence in Asia Minor, Ramsay concluded that Luke was an exemplary historian. In the decades since Ramsay, other scholars have suggested that Luke's historical background of the New Testament is among the best ever produced. As Wayne Jackson has noted:

> In Acts, Luke mentions thirty-two countries, fifty-four cities, and nine Mediterranean islands. He also mentions ninety-five persons, sixty-two of which are not named elsewhere in the New Testament. And his references, where checkable, are always correct. This is truly remarkable, in view of the fact that the political/territorial situation of his day was in a state of almost constant change. Only inspiration can account for Luke's precision (1991b, 27[1]:2).

As a person reads through the New Testament book of Acts, and comes to the account where Herod addressed a group of people from Tyre and Sidon (Acts 12:21-23), he reads:

> So on a set day Herod, arrayed in royal apparel, sat on his throne and gave an oration to them. And the people kept shouting, "The voice of a god and not of a man!" Then immediately an angel of the Lord struck him, because he did not give glory to God. And he was eaten by worms and died.

Perhaps the person reading this account wonders whether or not "this whole Christian thing is for me," and whether there is any evidence that corroborates the information found in the New Testament. How much more open to the truth of God's Word might this skeptical gentleman be if he could come in contact with the vast amount of historical data that supports the facts found therein? In this particular case, he might find it very helpful to learn that a well-educated, first-century Jewish historian by the name of Josephus gave a detailed account of Herod's death in his work, *The Antiquities of the Jews* (18:8:2). Notice how the two accounts stand side by side.

- Where Luke wrote that Herod was "arrayed in royal apparel," Josephus wrote that "he put on a garment made wholly of silver, and of a contexture truly wonderful."

- Where Luke wrote that "the people kept shouting, 'The voice of a god and not of a man!,' " Josephus mentioned that "his flatterers cried out…that he was a god; and they added, 'Be thou merciful to us; for although we have hitherto reverenced thee only as a man, yet shall we henceforth own thee as superior to mortal nature.' Upon this the king did neither rebuke them, nor reject their impious flattery."

- And finally, where Luke recorded: "Immediately an angel of the Lord struck him, because he did not give glory to God. And he was eaten by worms and died," Josephus wrote: "A severe pain also arose in his belly, and began in a most violent manner. He therefore looked upon his friends, and said, 'I whom you call a god, am commanded presently to depart this life….' [H]is pain was become violent…. And when he had been quite worn out by the pain in his belly for five days, he departed this life."

Although the accounts of Luke and Josephus were written independently, regarding the death of Herod they agree in all of the essentials. Acts 12:20-23 represents only one of many examples in Scripture where secular history upholds its reliability. Over the past 1,900 years, the Bible has been examined more critically than any other book in the world, and yet it repeatedly is found to be historically accurate. Such accuracy surely gives the skeptic something important to consider in his examination of Scripture.

In his classic text, *Lands of the Bible*, J.W. McGarvey documented numerous instances in which the facts of the Bible can be checked, and in which it always passes the test. Are compass references accurate? Is Antioch of Syria "down" from Jerusalem, even though it lies to the north of the city (Acts 15:1)? Is the way from Jerusalem to Gaza "south" of Samaria (Acts 8:26)? Is Egypt "down" from Canaan (Genesis 12:10)? McGarvey noted that "in not a single instance of this kind has any of the Bible writers been found at fault" (1881, p. 378).

In their book, *A General Introduction to the Bible*, Geisler and Nix wrote: "Confirmation of the Bible's accuracy in factual matters lends credibility to its claims when speaking on other subjects" (1986, p. 195). Indeed it does! After previewing most of the above facts, and others of a similar nature, Wayne Jackson concluded:

> The Bible critic is likely to trivialize these examples as they are isolated from one another. When, however, literally hundreds and hundreds of these incidental details are observed to perfectly mesh, one begins to suspect that what have been called "undesigned coincidences" (from the human vantage point) become very obvious cases of divinely designed harmony—tiny footprints that lead only to the conclusion that God was the guiding Force behind the composition of the Sacred Scriptures (1991a, 11:3, parenthetical item in orig.).

Human history books have always required correcting and updating. Not so with the Bible. Truly, the Bible's facts have withstood the tests of time. And, the more time elapses, the more the evidence accumulates in the fact file of Scripture's reliability.

PREDICTIVE PROPHECY

One of the most impressive internal proofs of the Bible's inspiration is its prophetic utterances. Rex A. Turner Sr. has suggested:

> Predictive prophecy is the highest evidence of di-
> vine revelation. The one thing that mortal man can-
> not do is to know and report future events in the ab-
> sence of a train of circumstances that naturally sug-
> gest certain possibilities... (1989, p. 12).

If the Bible is inspired of God, it should contain valid, predictive prophecy. In fact, the Bible's prophecy–completely
foretold to the minutest detail, and painstakingly fulfilled
with the greatest precision–has confounded its critics for
generations. The Bible contains specific prophecies about
individuals, lands, nations, and even the predicted Messiah.

Thomas H. Horne defined predictive prophecy as "a miracle of knowledge, a declaration or representation of something future, beyond the power of human sagacity to discern
or to calculate" (1970, 1:272). The Bible confirms that definition:

> But the prophet who presumes to speak a word in
> My name, which I have not commanded him to speak,
> or who speaks in the name of other gods, that prophet
> shall die. And if you say in your heart, "How shall we
> know the word which the Lord has not spoken?"–when
> a prophet speaks in the name of the Lord, if the thing
> does not happen or come to pass, that is the thing
> which the Lord has not spoken; the prophet has spo-
> ken it presumptuously; you shall not be afraid of him
> (Deuteronomy 18:20-22).

The prophet Isaiah based the credibility of his message on
prophecy. To the promoters of idolatry in his day, he issued
the following challenge: "Let them bring forth and show us
what will happen; let them show the former things, what they
were, that we may consider them, and know the latter end of
them; or declare to us things to come" (Isaiah 41:22). His
point was this: It is one thing to make the prediction; it is entirely another to see that prediction actually come true and
be corroborated by subsequent history.

Two questions are in order: (1) does the Bible employ predictive prophecy; and (2) if it does, can the predictive prophecy be proven true? The answer to both questions is a resounding, "Yes!" Consider just a few brief examples.

Cyrus the Great

Imagine taking a trip to Philadelphia, Pennsylvania, and visiting the State House where the Constitutional Convention took place in 1787. During the tour, your guide points to a document dating back to just this side of the Convention—about the year 1820. The piece of parchment tells of a man named George W. Bush from Austin, Texas, who would be President of the United States within the next 200 years. But how could someone know that a man named George W. Bush would be born in the United States? And how could someone know more than a century before Mr. Bush was born that he would be President of the United States? Furthermore, how could someone in 1820 know that a man from Texas (named George W. Bush) would be President of the United States when Texas wasn't even part of the Union yet? Such a prophecy truly would be amazing! Yet, obviously, no such prediction was ever made. In fact, despite all of the publicity that "psychic hotlines" are getting these days, only God can foretell the future.

One of the reasons we can **know** the Bible is from God is because it contains **hundreds** of prophecies about individuals, lands, and nations similar to the example above. One such prophecy was about a man named Cyrus and two nations—Babylon and the Medo-Persian Empire. Isaiah vividly described how God would destroy the powerful kingdom of Babylon, "the glory of kingdoms" (13:19). Writing as if it had already occurred (commonly known as the "prophetic perfect," frequently employed in the Old Testament to stress the absolute certainty of fulfillment, e.g., Isaiah 53), Isaiah declared Babylon would fall (21:9). He then prophesied that

Babylon would fall to the Medes and Persians (Isaiah 13; 21: 1-10). Later, he proclaimed that the "golden city" (Babylon) would be conquered by a man named Cyrus (44:28; 45:1-7). This is a remarkable prophecy, especially since Cyrus was not even born until almost 150 years after Isaiah penned these words.

Not only did Isaiah predict that Cyrus would overthrow Babylon, but he also wrote that Cyrus, serving as Jehovah's "anointed" and "shepherd," would release the Jews from captivity and assist them in their return to Jerusalem for the purpose of rebuilding the temple. All of this was written almost two hundred years before Cyrus conquered Babylon (in 539 B.C.). Amazing! Secular history verifies that all of these events came true. There really was a man named Cyrus who ruled the Medo-Persian Empire. He did conquer Babylon. And just as Isaiah prophesied, he assisted the Jews in their return to Jerusalem and in the rebuilding of the temple.

The Fall of Tyre

The Bible foretells the destruction of the city of Tyre with miraculous precision. The prophet Ezekiel predicted that Nebuchadnezzar, king of Babylon, would destroy the city (Ezekiel 26:7-8). Many nations were to come up against Tyre (26:3). The city would be leveled and scraped clean like a bare rock (26:4). The city's stones, timbers, and soil would be cast into the sea (26:12). The surrounding area would become a place for the spreading of fishermen's nets (26:5). And, finally, the city never would be rebuilt to its former glory (26:14).

History records that each of these predictions came true. Tyre, a coastal city from ancient times, had a somewhat unusual arrangement. In addition to the inland city, there was an island about three-fourths of a mile offshore. Nebuchadnezzar besieged the mainland city in 586 B.C., but when he finally was able to inhabit the city in about 573 B.C., his victory was hollow. Unbeknownst to him, the inhabitants had vacated the city and moved to the island—a situation that remained virtually unchanged for the next 241 years. Then, in 332 B.C., Alexander the Great conquered the city—but not with ease. To get to the island, he literally had his army "scrape clean" the inland city of its debris, and he then used those materials (stones, timbers, and soil) to build a causeway to the island.

The city never regained its once-famous position of wealth and power. The prophet Ezekiel looked 1,900 years into the future and predicted that Tyre would be a bald rock where fishermen gathered to open their nets. And that is exactly what history records as having happened (see Major, 1996, pp. 93-95).

Time and again biblical prophecies are presented, and fulfilled, with exacting detail. Jeremiah wrote: "...when the word of the prophet comes to pass, the prophet will be known as one whom the Lord has truly sent" (28:9).

The Coming of the Messiah

In addition to its prophecies concerning people, places, and events, the Old Testament contains more than three hundred messianic prophecies. A messianic prophecy is one that tells about a coming "Messiah" or Savior. These prophecies were written to tell the world about the One Who would come to save humankind from sin. The prophecies about the Messiah said that He would be rejected and know grief (Isaiah 53:3), and be betrayed by a friend (Psalm 41:9) for thirty pieces of silver (Zechariah 11:12). In fact, He was rejected and betrayed (John 13:18; Matthew 26:15). He would be spit upon and beaten (Isaiah 50:6; 53:5), and in death His hands and His feet were to be pierced (Psalm 22:16). This is exactly what happened (Matthew 27:30; Luke 24:39). Although He would die and be placed in a rich man's tomb (Isaiah 53:9; Matthew 27:57), His bones would not be broken (Psalm 34:20; John 19:33), nor would His flesh see corruption, because He would be raised from the dead (Psalm 16:10; Acts 2:22ff.) and eventually ascend into heaven (Psalm 110:1-3; 45:6; Acts 1:9-10). These prophecies were written hundreds of years before they were fulfilled. But Jesus Christ fulfilled each of them in every detail.

Although the stories of men's lives generally are written **after** they die, the history of Christ's life was written **before He was even born!** How? Because God inspired the prophets who wrote the accounts. No book but the Bible contains such prophetic accuracy. Truly, "no prophecy of Scripture is of any private interpretation, for prophecy never came by the will of man, but holy men of God spoke as they were moved by the Holy Spirit" (2 Peter 1:20-21).

SCIENTIFIC FOREKNOWLEDGE

The unity of the Bible, as well as the predictive prophecy contained therein, are indeed remarkable, but there are many other areas that show the Bible to be beyond the capabilities of human authors. From anthropology to zoology, the Bible presents astonishingly accurate scientific information that the writers, on their own, simply could not have known. Space limitations prohibit an in-depth examination of the Bible's scientific foreknowledge, but a few of the more prominent examples are mentioned here. (For additional information, see Thompson, 1999a, pp. 44-57.)

From the Field of Astronomy

How did Moses (Genesis 15:5) and Jeremiah (33:22) know that the stars literally are innumerable–like the grains of sand on the seashore? For most of the world's history, astronomers came up with figures ranging from the hundreds to about a thousand (Hipparchus–150 B.C.–1,026 stars; Ptolemy–A.D. 150–1,056 stars; Kepler–A.D. 1600–1,005 stars). All of these men lived prior to the invention of the telescope and so relied upon human eyesight. Astronomers now know that there are billions of stars, and the counting continues. How could the writers of the Bible have known the number of stars to be innumerable long before anyone else? Just a lucky guess?

From the Field of Biology

In his sermon on Mars' Hill, Paul stated to the Athenians that it is God who gives all life (Acts 17:25). Until scientists in the last few centuries (such as Franscesco Redi and Louis Pasteur) proved through the scientific method that life only arises from life, men were of the mindset that life arose spontaneously. Even in the twenty-first century, many evolutionists are still trying to create life. But, to date, no one ever has "created" life. They do well, in fact, even to get one of the simplest "building blocks"–amino acids. Paul knew long ago that it was God who gives life. How did Paul, an itinerant preacher of the first century A.D., know this?

From the Field of Medicine

1. In Genesis 17:12, God commanded Abraham to circumcise all newborn males on the eighth day after they were born. Have you ever considered what was so important about the eighth day? Wouldn't the second, ninth, or twenty-fifth have been just as good as the eighth? Actually, the eighth day is extremely important because in humans, blood clotting depends upon three key factors: (a) platelets; (b) vitamin K; and (c) prothrombin. Only in the twentieth century did doctors learn that vitamin K is responsible for the production (by the liver) of prothrombin. If the quantity of vitamin K is deficient, there will be a prothrombin deficiency, and hemorrhaging may occur.

Interestingly, it is only on the fifth to seventh days of a newborn's life that vitamin K is present in adequate quantities. Vitamin K–coupled with prothrombin–causes blood coagulation, which is important in any surgical procedure. A classic medical text, *Holt Pediatrics*, corroborates that a newborn infant has

> ...peculiar susceptibility to bleeding between the second and fifth days of life.... Hemorrhages at this time, though often inconsequential, are sometimes extensive; they may produce serious damage to internal organs, especially to the brain, and cause death from shock and exsanguination (Holt and McIntosh, 1953, pp. 125-126).

Obviously, then, if vitamin K is not produced in sufficient quantities until days five through seven, it would be wise to postpone any surgery until sometime after that. But why did God specify day **eight**?

On the eighth day, the amount of prothrombin present actually is **elevated above 100 percent of normal**. In fact, day eight is the only day in the male's life in which this will be the case under normal conditions. If surgery is to be performed, day eight is the perfect day to do it. We know these facts today because we have been able to study millions of babies over many years, but Abraham had no such research methods. The medical information employed by Abraham, and confirmed by Moses, was accurate scientifically then, and still remains so to this very day. No culture around the Israelites possessed such scientific acumen, which, by the way, was light-years ahead of its time. How, then, did Abraham and Moses come to know the best time for circumcision, unless, of course, this particular fact was revealed to them by God, and recorded in His Word through inspiration?

2. Moses told the Israelites (Leviticus 17:11-14) that "the life of the flesh is in the blood." He was correct. Because the red blood cells can carry oxygen (due to hemoglobin in the cells) life is made possible. In fact, the human red blood cells carry, for example, approximately 270,000,000 molecules of hemoglobin per cell (see Perutz, 1964, pp. 64-65). If there were any less, there would not be enough residual oxygen to sustain life after, say, a hard sneeze or a hefty pat on the back.

We know today that the "life of the flesh is in the blood." But we did not know that in George Washington's day. How did the "father of our country" die? We bled him to death (see Havron, 1981, p. 62). People felt that the blood was where evil "vapors" were found, and that getting rid of the blood would make a person well again. Today, of course, we know that is not true. Think of how often blood transfusions have made life possible for those who otherwise would have died. Today we know the truth of the matter. How did the biblical writer know it?

3. A final example from the field of medicine of the Bible writers' scientific foreknowledge is found in Deuteronomy 23:12-14, where Moses instructed the Israelites always to bury human waste products. Today, of course, with centuries of experience behind us, we know that this is an excellent sanitary hygienic practice. But the common course of action in Moses' day, and for centuries to follow, was to dump waste products in any convenient place. History has recorded the folly of this kind of action.

In Europe during the Middle Ages, "Black Plague" swept over the continent on two different occasions, slaughtering more than 13 million people in the process. Europeans routinely dumped waste of all kinds out their windows and into the public streets where decomposition took place and microorganisms flourished.

One of those microorganisms—the one we know today as *Yersinia pestis*—grew in the waste products and contaminated the fleas associated with those waste products. The fleas, using rats as their hosts, subsequently traveled into the people's houses. Once inside a dwelling, the fleas then jumped from the rats onto the humans, biting them and infecting them with the plague organism. As this cycle was repeated over and over, millions perished. Yet if the people simply had obeyed God's injunction, as given by Moses to the Israelites, all of the death and horror of two separate epidemics could have been avoided. How did Moses know to instruct the Israelites regarding such public health hygiene laws, when none of the nations surrounding God's people enlisted such practices–and would not for centuries? He wrote "by inspiration of God."

CONCLUSION

The Bible claims to be inspired by God. Literally thousands of times, the writers who penned this book let their readers know that their writings were different from those of ordinary men. Are there other books in the world that claim inspiration? Yes, but they are few and far between. And none of them exhibits such amazing qualities as the predictive prophecy and scientific foreknowledge that can be found in the Bible. Furthermore, the unity of the Bible and its accurate historical documentation of biblical people, places, and events is unparalleled in human history, and bears testimony to the fact that the very existence of the Holy Scriptures cannot be explained in any other way except to acknowledge that they are the result of an overriding, superintending, guiding Mind. Every human being should welcome the Bible "not as the word of men, but as it is in truth, the word of God" (1 Thessalonians 2:13).

REFERENCES

Acharya, S. (1999), *The Christ Conspiracy: The Greatest Story Ever Sold* (Kempton, IL: Adventures Unlimited Press).

Andrews, Michelle (2004), "Author, Author*?*" *U.S. News & World Report*–Special Collector's Edition, released in the Fall of 2004, pp. 28-29.

Archer, Gleason L. (1982), *An Encyclopedia of Bible Difficulties* (Grand Rapids: Zondervan).

Arndt, William, F.W. Gingrich, and Frederick Danker (1979), *A Greek-English Lexicon of the New Testament and Other Early Christian Literature* (Chicago, IL: University of Chicago Press).

Austin, Steven A. and D. Russell Humphreys (1990), "The Sea's Missing Salt: A Dilemma for Evolutionists," *Proceedings of the Second International Conference on Creationism–1990,* ed. R.E. Walsh and C.L. Brooks (Pittsburgh, PA: Creation Science Fellowship).

Bales, James (1960), *The Hub of the Bible–Or–Acts Two Analyzed* (Shreveport, LA: Lambert Book House).

Bancroft, H.H. (1883), *Works: The Native Races of the Pacific Slope –Mythology* (San Francisco, CA: A.L. Bancroft).

Barfield, Kenny (1997), *Why the Bible is Number 1* (Eugene, OR: Wipf and Stock Publishers).

Barker, Dan (1992), *Losing Faith in Faith* (Madison, WI: Freedom From Religion Foundation, Inc.).

Barnes, Albert (1956a), *Notes on the New Testament–Luke-John* (Grand Rapids, MI: Baker).

Barnes, Albert (1956b), *Notes on the Old and New Testaments: Acts* (Grand Rapids, MI: Baker).

Barnes, Albert (1997), *Barnes' Notes* (Electronic Database: Biblesoft).

Bates, Bobby (1979), "Whosoever Shall Call Upon the Name of the Lord Shall be Saved," *Firm Foundation*, 96:5, March 20.

Batten, Don and Jonathan Sarfati (2000), "How Did Fish and Plants Survive the Genesis Flood?," [Online], (Answers in Genesis), URL: http://www.answersingenesis.org/docs/444. asp.

Bauer, Walter, William Arndt, and F.W. Gingrich (1957), *A Greek-English Lexicon of the New Testament and Other Early Christian Literature* (Chicago, IL: University of Chicago Press).

"Bible Contradictions" (no date), *Capella's Guide to Atheism*, [Online], URL: http://web2.iadfw.net/capella/aguide/co ntrad. htm#num%20animals%20Jesus%20rode.

Botterweck, G. Johannes, Helmer Ringgren, and Heinz-Josef Fabry (1998), *Theological Dictionary of the Old Testament* (Grand Rapids, MI: Eerdmans).

Brand, Leonard (1997), *Faith, Reason, & Earth History: A Paradigm of Earth and Biological Origins by Intelligent Design* (Berrien Springs, MI: Andrews University Press).

"Brother" (1998), *Fausset's Bible Dictionary* (Electronic Database: Biblesoft).

Brown, F., S.R. Driver, and C.A. Briggs (1979), *The New Brown-Driver-Briggs-Gesenius Hebrew and English Lexicon* (Peabody, MA: Hendrickson).

Brown, T. Pierce (1976), "Calling on His Name," *Firm Foundation*, 93:5, July 20.

Bruce, A.B. (no date), *The Expositor's Greek Testament*, ed. W. Robertson Nicoll (Grand Rapids, MI: Eerdmans).

Bruce, F.F. (1953), *The New Testament Documents–Are They Reliable?* (Grand Rapids, MI: Eerdmans), fourth edition.

Bryant, Buddy (no date), "What Saves? Baptism or Jesus Christ?" *Tabernacle Baptist Church*, [On-line], URL: http://www.llano.net/baptist/whatsaves.htm.

Bullinger, E.W. (1898), *Figures of Speech Used in the Bible* (Grand Rapids, MI: Baker, 1968 reprint).

Butler, Bill (2002), "Creationism = Willful Ignorance," [On-line], URL: http://www.durangobill.com/Creationism.html.

Butt, Kyle (2004), "The Skeptic's Faulty Assumption," [On-line], URL: http://www.apologeticspress.org/modules.php?name=Read&cat=7&itemid=2230.

Butt, Kyle and Dave Miller (2003), "Who Hardened Pharaoh's Heart?" [On-line], URL: http://www.apologeticspress.org/modules.php?name=Read&cat=7&itemid=2259.

Cassuto, Umberto (1929), *Biblical and Oriental Studies* (Jerusalem: Magnes Press, 1973 reprint).

Chapman, Colin (1981), *The Case for Christianity* (Grand Rapids, MI: Eerdmans).

Clark, Harold W. (1968), *Fossils, Flood and Fire* (Escondido, CA: Outdoor Pictures).

Clarke, Adam (no date), *A Commentary and Critical Notes* (Nashville, TN: Abingdon).

Clarke, Adam (1996), *Adam Clarke's Commentary* (Electronic Database: Biblesoft).

Coffman, James Burton (1984), *Commentary on the Gospel of Matthew* (Abilene, TX: ACU Press).

Coffman, James Burton (1986), *Commentary on 1 & 2 Thessalonians, 1 & 2 Timothy, Titus, & Philemon* (Abilene, TX: ACU Press).

Coffman, James Burton (1992), *Commentary on Second Samuel* (Abilene, TX: ACU Press).

"Contradictions in the New Testament," (no date), [On-line], URL: http://www.islam4all.com/chapter6.htm.

Cook, F.C., ed. (1981 reprint), *The Bible Commentary* (Grand Rapids, MI: Baker).

Cook, J.M. (1983), *The Persians* (London: The Orion Publishing Group).

Cukrowski, Kenneth L., Mark W. Hamilton, and James W. Thompson (2002), *God's Holy Fire* (Abilene, TX: ACU Press).

Davidson, Benjamin (1970), *The Analytical Hebrew and Chaldee Lexicon* (Grand Rapids, MI: Zondervan).

Dawson, John William (1895), *The Historical Deluge in Relation to Scientific Discovery* (Chicago, IL: Revell).

"Does Water Baptism Save? A Biblical Refutation of Baptismal Regeneration" (no date), [On-line], URL: http://www. mid dletownbiblechurch.org/salvatio/baptsave.htm.

Drange, Theodore M. (1996), "The Argument from the Bible," [On-line], URL: http://www.infidels.org/library/modern/ theodore_drange/bible.html.

Dummelow, J.R. (1937), *One Volume Commentary* (New York: MacMillan).

Dungan, D.R. (1888), *Hermeneutics* (Delight, AR: Gospel Light, reprint).

Fausset, A.R. (1998), *Fausset's Bible Dictionary* (Electronic Database: Biblesoft).

Feinberg, Charles (1942), "Exegetical Studies in Zechariah: Part 10," *Bibliotheca Sacra*, 99:428-439, October.

Feinberg, Charles (1945), "Exegetical Studies in Zechariah," *Bibliotheca Sacra*, 102:55-73, January.

"Fool," (1986), *Nelson's Illustrated Bible Dictionary* (Electronic Database: Biblesoft), orig. published by Thomas Nelson Publishers of Nashville, Tennessee.

Forrester, E.J. (1996), "Jealousy," *International Standard Bible Encyclopaedia* (Electronic Database Biblesoft).

Foster, R.C. (1971), *Studies in the Life of Christ* (Grand Rapids, MI: Baker).

Gallup, George Jr. and D. Michael Lindsay (1999), *Surveying the Religious Landscape: Trends in U.S. Beliefs* (Harrisburg, PA: Morehouse Publishing).

Geisler, Norman and Thomas Howe (1992), *When Critics Ask* (Wheaton, IL: Victor Books).

Geisler, Norman and William E. Nix (1986), *A General Introduction to the Bible* (Chicago, IL: Moody).

Gesenius, William (1847), *Hebrew and Chaldee Lexicon* (Grand Rapids, MI: Baker, 1979 reprint).

"The Godhead" (no date), [On-line], URL: http://www.geocities.com/Athens/Atlantis/3074/GE13_trinity.htm.

Greenleaf, Simon (1995), *The Testimony of the Evangelists* (Grand Rapids, MI: Kregel Classics).

Grizzell, Gary L. (1986), "Rahab the Harlot and Situation Ethics," *The Defender*, 15[9]:66-67,70,72, September.

Habermas, Gary R. (1996), *The Historical Jesus* (Joplin, MO: College Press).

Halley, H.H. (1962 reprint), *Halley's Bible Handbook* (Grand Rapids, MI: Zondervan).

Hamilton, Victor P. (1990), *The Book of Genesis: Chapters 1-17* (Grand Rapids, MI: Eerdmans).

Harris, R.L., G.L. Archer, and B.K. Waltke (1980), *Theological Wordbook of the Old Testament* (Chicago, IL: Moody).

Havron, Dean (1981), "Curious Cure-Alls" *Science Digest*, 89[8]:62, September.

Henry, Matthew (no date), *Genesis to Deuteronomy* (MacLean, VA: MacDonald).

Hobbs, Herschel (1964), *What Baptists Believe* (Nashville, TN: Broadman).

Holt, L.E. and R. McIntosh (1953), *Holt Pediatrics* (New York: Appleton-Century-Crofts), twelfth edition.

Horne, Thomas H. (1970 edition), *An Introduction to the Critical Study and Knowledge of the Holy Scriptures* (Grand Rapids, MI: Baker).

"How to Become a Christian" (no date), *The Billy Graham Evangelistic Association*, [On-line], URL: http://www.billygra ham. org/believe/howtobecomeachristian.asp.

"Inerrancy: Where Conservative Christianity Stands or Falls," (no date), [On-line], URL: http://users.vei.net/smijer/ch ristianity/bunk.html.

Jackson, Wayne (1986), "From Our Mail," *Christian Courier*, 22:23, October.

Jackson, Wayne (1987), "Questions and Answers," *Reason & Revelation*, 13:14, April.

Jackson, Wayne (1988), "Principles of Bible Prophecy," *Reason & Revelation*, 8:27-30, July.

Jackson, Wayne (1991a), "Bible Unity—An Argument for Inspiration," *Reason & Revelation*, 11:1, January.

Jackson, Wayne (1991b), "The Holy Bible—Inspired of God," *Christian Courier*, 27[1]:1-3, May.

Jackson, Wayne (1997), "The Role of 'Works' in the Plan of Salvation," *Christian Courier*, 32:47, April.

Jamieson, Robert (1948 reprint), *Critical & Experimental Commentary* (Grand Rapids, MI: Eerdmans).

Jamieson, Robert, A.R. Fausset, and David Brown (1997), *Jamieson, Fausset, Brown Bible Commentary* (Electronic Database: Biblesoft).

Jenni, Ernst and Claus Westerman (1997), *Theological Lexicon of the Old Testament* (Peabody, MA: Hendrickson).

Jevons, W. Stanley (1928), *Elementary Lessons in Logic* (London: Macmillan).

Josephus, Flavius (1987 edition), "Antiquities of the Jews," *The Works of Josephus*, transl. William Whiston (Peabody, MA: Hendrickson).

Kaiser, Walter (1983), *Toward Old Testament Ethics* (Grand Rapids, MI: Zondervan).

Kaiser, Walter (1988), *Hard Sayings of the Old Testament* (Downers Grove, IL: InterVarsity).

Kaiser, Walter C. Jr., Peter H. Davids, F.F. Bruce, and Manfred T. Brauch (1996), *Hard Sayings of the Bible* (Downers Grove, IL: InterVarsity Press).

Kearley, F. Furman (1979), "The Significance of the Genesis Flood," *Sound Doctrine*, March/April.

Keil, C.F. and F. Delitzsch (1996), *Keil and Delitzsch Commentary on the Old Testament* (Electronic Database: Biblesoft), new updated edition.

Kesler, John (2003), "Jesus Had Two Asses," [On-line], URL: http://exposed.faithweb.com/kesler2.html.

Kistemaker, Simon J. (1993), *Exposition of the First Epistle to the Corinthians* (Grand Rapids, MI: Baker).

Lenski, R.C.H. (1961a), *The Interpretation of St. Matthew's Gospel* (Minneapolis, MN: Augsburg).

Lenski, R.C.H. (1961b), *The Interpretation of St. John's Gospel* (Minneapolis, MN: Augsburg).

Lenski, R.C.H. (1961c), *The Interpretation of the Acts of the Apostles* (Minneapolis, MN: Augsburg).

Leupold, H.C. (1942), *Exposition of Genesis* (Columbus, OH: Wartburg Press).

Lewis, Jack P. (1991), *Questions You've Asked About Bible Translations* (Searcy, AR: Resource Publications).

Lloyd, Steven M. (1990), "Answering False Doctrines Relating to James," *Studies in James*, ed. Dub McClish (Denton, TX: Valid Publications).

Luther, Martin (1530), *Luther's Large Catechism*, (Saint Louis, MO: Concordia), 1978 reprint.

MacPhail, Bryn (no date), "Does James Contradict Paul Regarding Justification?" *The Reformed Theology Source*, [On-line], URL: http://www.reformedtheology.ca/faithworks. html.

Major, Trevor (1996), "The Fall of Tyre," *Reason & Revelation*, 16: 93-95, December.

Marks, J.H. (1962), "Flood," *The Interpreter's Dictionary of the Bible* (Nashville, TN: Abingdon).

Marsden, George (1987), *Reforming Fundamentalism: Fuller Seminary and the New Evangelicalism* (Grand Rapids, MI: Eerdmans).

Massey, Gerald (1985), *Gnostic and Historic Christianity* (Edmond, WA: Holmes Publishing Group).

Mathewson, Steven D. (1989), "An Exegetical Study of Genesis 38," *Bibliotheca Sacra*, 146:373-392, October.

McDowell, Josh (1999), *The New Evidence that Demands a Verdict* (Nashville, TN: Nelson).

McGarvey, J.W. (no date), *The Fourfold Gospel* (Cincinnati, OH: Standard).

McGarvey, J.W. (1875), *Commentary on Matthew and Mark* (Delight, AR: Gospel Light).

McGarvey, J.W. (1881), *Lands of the Bible* (Philadelphia, PA: Lippincott).

McKinsey, C. Dennis (no date), "Jesus, Imperfect Beacon," *Biblical Errancy* [On-line], URL: http://members.aol.com/ckb loomfld/bepart11.html#issref113.

McKinsey, C. Dennis (no date), "Problems with the Credentials and Character of Jesus," *Biblical Errancy* [On-line], URL: http://mywebpages.comcast.net/errancy/issues/iss190.htm.

McKinsey, C. Dennis (1983a), "Commentary," *Biblical Errancy*, pp. 1-4, February.

McKinsey, C. Dennis (1983b), "Commentary," *Biblical Errancy*, pp. 1-2, November.

McKinsey, C. Dennis (1983c), "Commentary," *Biblical Errancy*, p. 1, December.

McKinsey, C. Dennis (1983d), "Contradictions," [On-line], URL: http://members.aol.com/ckbloomfld/bepart12.html.

McKinsey, C. Dennis (1985), "Commentary," *Biblical Errancy*, pp. 1-2, January.

McKinsey, C. Dennis (1988a), "Editor's Note," *Biblical Errancy*, p. 6, March.

McKinsey, C. Dennis (1988b), "Letter 263," *Biblical Errancy*, p. 6, May.

McKinsey, C. Dennis (1992), [On-line], URL: http://members.aol.com/chas1222/bepart56.html.

McKinsey, C. Dennis (1995), *The Encyclopedia of Biblical Errancy* (Amherst, NY: Prometheus).

McKinsey, C. Dennis (1998), "Commentary," *Biblical Errancy*, November.

McKinsey, C. Dennis (2000), *Biblical Errancy* (Amherst, NY: Prometheus).

Miller, Dave (2003a), "Modern-day Miracles, Tongue-Speaking, and Holy Spirit Baptism: A Refutation," *Reason & Revelation*, 23:17-24, March.

Miller, Dave (2003b), "The Thief on the Cross," [On-line], URL: http://www.apologeticspress.org/modules.php?name=Read&cat=9&itemid=2321.

Mitchell, T.C. (1974), *The New Bible Dictionary*, ed. J.D. Douglas (Grand Rapids, MI: Eerdmans).

Mohler, R. Albert Jr. (2001), "Being Baptist Means Conviction," *Why I Am a Baptist*, ed. Tom Nettles and Russell Moore (Nashville, TN: Broadman & Holman).

Morgan, Donald (2003a), "Biblical Inconsistencies," [On-line], URL: http://www.infidels.org/library/modern/dona ld_morgan/inconsistencies.shtml.

Morgan, Donald (2003b), "Was Jesus a Hypocrite?" [On-line], URL: http://www.infidels.org/library/modern/donald_m organ/hypocrite.shtml.

Morris, Henry M. (1976), *The Genesis Record* (Grand Rapids, MI: Baker).

Morris, Henry M. and John C. Whitcomb (1961), *The Genesis Flood* (Grand Rapids, MI: Baker).

Morris, Leon (1995), *The Gospel According to John* (Grand Rapids, MI: Eerdmans), revised edition.

Morton, Jean S. (1978), *Science in the Bible* (Chicago, IL: Moody).

NIV Study Bible (1985), (Grand Rapids, MI: Zondervan).

Packer, J.I. (1958), *"Fundamentalism" and the Word of God* (Grand Rapids, MI: Eerdmans).

Packer, J.I. (1973), *Knowing God* (London: Hodder and Stoughton).

Paine, Thomas (1795), *Age of Reason* (New York: Knickerbocker Press, 1924 reprint).

Patterson, R.D., and Hermann J. Austel (1988), *The Expositor's Bible Commentary: 1 & 2 Kings*, ed. Frank E. Gaebelein (Grand Rapids, MI: Zondervan).

Perloff, James (1999), *Tornado in a Junkyard: The Relentless Myth of Darwinism* (Arlington, MA: Refuge Books).

Perutz, H.F. (1964), *Scientific American*, pp. 64-65, November.

Pfeiffer, Charles (1979), *Baker's Bible Atlas* (Grand Rapids, MI: Baker Book House), revised edition.

Pollard, Edward Bagby (1996), "Daughter," *International Standard Bible Encyclopaedia* (Electronic Database Biblesoft).

"Prayer of Salvation" (no date), [On-line], URL: http://www.j esussaves.cc/prayer_of_salvation.html.

Preus, Robert (1984), "Notes on the Inerrancy of Scripture," *Evangelicals and Inerrancy*, ed. Ronald Youngblood (Nashville, TN: Thomas Nelson Publishers).

Rabin, Chaim (1974), "The Origin of the Hebrew Word *Pilegeš*," *Journal of Jewish Studies*, 25:362.

Ramm, Bernard (1954), *The Christian View of Science and Scripture* (Grand Rapids, MI: Eerdmans).

Rehwinkel, Alfred M. (1951), *The Flood* (St. Louis, MO: Concordia).

Richards, Larry (1993), *735 Baffling Bible Questions Answered* (Grand Rapids, MI: Revell).

Ridenour, Fritz (1967), *Who Says God Created?* (Glendale, CA: Gospel Light).

Robertson, A.T. (1930), *Word Pictures in the New Testament–Volume 1* (Nashville, TN: Broadman).

Robertson, A.T. (1931), *Word Pictures in the New Testament–Volume 4* (Nashville, TN: Broadman).

Robertson, A.T. (1932), *Word Pictures in the New Testament–Volume 5* (Nashville, TN: Broadman).

Robertson, A.T. (1997), *Robertson's Word Pictures in the New Testament* (Electronic Database: Biblesoft).

Roth, Ariel (1988), *Origins: Linking Science and Scripture* (Hagerstown, MD: Review and Herald Publishing).

Schlemper, David (1998), "Two Heresies–Regarding Damnation and Salvation," [On-line], URL: http://www.patrio tist.com/miscarch/ds20030317.htm.

Schoch, Robert M. (2003), *Voyages of the Pyramid Builders* (New York: Jeremy P. Parcher/Putnam).

"Shâbath" (1995), *Enhanced Strong's Lexicon* (Electronic Database: Logos).

Shelly, Rubel (1990), *Prepare to Answer* (Grand Rapids, MI: Baker Book House).

Smith, Mark A. (1995), "Gospel Wars: Galilee -vs-Jerusalem," [On-line], URL: http://www.jcnot4me.com/Items/contradictions/GALILEE-vs-JERUSALEM.htm.

Staten, Steven F. (2001), "The Sinner's Prayer," [On-line], URL: http://www.chicagochurch.org/spirituallibrary/thesinners prayer.htm.

Strong, A.H. (1907), *Systematic Theology* (Old Tappan, NJ: Fleming H. Revell).

Strong, James (1996 reprint), *The New Strong's Exhaustive Concordance of the Bible* (Nashville, TN: Nelson).

Tacitus, Cornelius P. (1952 reprint), *The Annals and the Histories*, trans. Michael Grant (Chicago, IL: William Benton), Great Books of the Western World Series.

Tanner, J. Paul (1997), "The Message of the Song of Songs," *Bibliotheca Sacra*, 154:142-161, April.

Tasker, R.V.G. (1967), *The Epistle of James* (London: Tyndale Press).

Thayer, J.H. (1958 reprint), *A Greek-English Lexicon of the New Testament* (Edinburgh: T. & T. Clark).

Thayer, J.H. (1977 reprint), *A Greek-English Lexicon of the New Testament* (Grand Rapids, MI: Baker).

Thompson, Bert (1999a), *In Defense of the Bible's Inspiration* (Montgomery, AL: Apologetics Press).

Thompson, Bert (1999b), *The Global Flood of Noah* (Montgomery, AL: Apologetics Press).

Thompson, Bert (2001), *The Origin, Nature, and Destiny of the Soul* (Montgomery, AL: Apologetics Press).

Thomson, William M. (1859), *The Land and the Book* (New York: Harper and Brothers).

Tobin, Paul N. (2000), "Internal Contradictions in the Bible," *The Rejection of Pascal's Wager*, [On-line], URL: http://www.geocities.com/paulntobin/internal.html.

Turner, Rex A. Sr. (1989), *Systematic Theology* (Montgomery, AL: Alabama Christian School of Religion).

van den Heuvel, Curt (2003), "Matthew Misunderstood an Old Testament Prophecy," *New Testament Problems*, [On-line], URL: http://www.2think.org/hundredsheep/bible/ntprob.shtml.

van Praag, Herman M. (1986), "The Downfall of King Saul: The Neurobiological Consequences of Losing Hope," *Judaism*, 35:421.

Vincent, Marvin R. (1997), *Word Studies in the New Testament* (Electronic Database: Biblesoft).

Vine, W.E. (1940), *An Expository Dictionary of New Testament Words* (Old Tappan, NJ: Revell).

Ward, Ronald A. (1974), *Commentary on 1 and 2 Timothy and Titus* (Waco, TX: Word Books).

Warfield, Benjamin (1970), *The Inspiration and Authority of the Bible* (Philadelphia, PA: Presbyterian Reformed Publishing Company).

Warren, Thomas B. (1972), *Have Atheists Proved There Is No God?* (Jonesboro, AR: National Christian Press).

Warren, Thomas B. and L.S. Ballard (1965), *Warren/Ballard Debate on the Plan of Salvation* (Jonesboro, AR: National Christian Press).

"Water Baptism is not for Salvation," (no date), Southwest Baptist Church, Wichita Falls, TX, [On-line], URL: http://www.southwest-baptist.org/baptism.htm.

Webster, Allen (1993), "Did God Approve of Rahab's Lie?," *Words of Truth*, 29[25]:2,4, June 18.

Wells, Steve (2001), *Skeptic's Annotated Bible*, [On-line], URL: http://www.Skepticsannotatedbible.com.

Whitcomb, John C. (1973), *The World That Perished* (Grand Rapids, MI: Baker).

Whitcomb, John C. and Henry M. Morris (1961 reprint), *The Genesis Flood* (Grand Rapids, MI: Baker).

Willis, John T. (1984), *Genesis* (Abilene, TX: ACU Press), orig. published in 1979 by Sweet Publishing Company, Austin, Texas.

Wilson, R. Dick (1996), "Artaxerxes," *International Standard Bible Encyclopaedia* (Electronic Database: Biblesoft).

Woodmorappe, John (1996), *Noah's Ark: A Feasibility Study* (Santee, CA: Institute for Creation Research).

Woods, Guy N. (1979), *A Commentary on the New Testament Epistles of Peter, John, and Jude* (Nashville, TN: Gospel Advocate).

Wundt, William (1916), *Elements of Folk Psychology*, trans. Edward L. Schaub (New York: Macmillan).

Wycliffe Bible Commentary (1985), Electronic Database: Biblesoft.

Yeager, Darrin (2003), "Baptism: Part 3 in the FUD Series," [On-line], URL: http://www.dyeager.org/articles/baptism.php.

Young, Robert (1974 reprint), *Analytical Concordance to the Bible* (Grand Rapids, MI: Eerdmans).

Youngblood, Ronald F. (1992), *The Expositor's Bible Commentary–1 & 2 Samuel* (Grand Rapids, MI: Zondervan).

Zerr, E.M. (1952), *Bible Commentary* (Raytown, MO: Reprint Publications).

SUBJECT INDEX

A

'ach (Hebrew word meaning "brother")–218
adelphos (Greek word meaning "brother")–219
Anno Domini–51
Antioch of Syria–272
Arabia–137-138
Astronomy–277
Aztecs–105

B

Babel–29,112-113
Babylon–274-275
Babylonian Mythology–107
baptidzo (Greek word meaning "to immerse")–194
Baptism–175,177,179,182-183, 193-194,196-198
behemah (Hebrew word)–93
Bethany–249,251
Bethlehem–204,227
Bethphage–249,251
Biology–278
Black Plague–280
Book of Mormon, The–265

C

Cana–121-122
Canaanites–157-158,228-230
Ceremonial laws–201
challôwn (Hebrew word meaning "window")–97,99
Chronology–111-138
Circumcision–279
Concubine–220-222
Cubit–81,96

D

Damascus–136-137,166,173, 175

E

`elem (Hebrew word)–117
Egypt–222-229,272
epikaloumai (Greek word)–163

F

Fear–259,260-261
Flood Legends–103
Flood, Noahic–79-109,158

SCRIPTURE INDEX

6:9-11–139
6:16–20
10:1-4–14
10:8–12-13
10:11–200
10:13–34
11:3–52-53
12:31–41
13:4–40,43
14:1,39–41
14:21–16
14:37–13
15:12-19–71
15:45–14
15:47–52
15:57–168
2 Corinthians
3:2-11–202
5:21–22,69,78
11:2–43
11:2-4–41
11:3–14
12:20–40
Galatians
1:12–5,13
1:16–136-137
1:16-18–144
1:17-18–137
2:11ff.–15
2:16–177
3:8–21
3:16–19
3:27–176,178
4:4–22

4:21–16
5:6–186
5:19-21–177
5:21–68
6:1–242
6:10–241
Ephesians
1:4–172
1:7–176
2:8-9–167,172,176-177,180,
 187-188
2:10–188
2:12–176
2:14-17–200
2:15–188
3:5–13
3:11–172
4:4–197
4:25–146
4:26–71
4:28–139
5:11–243
6:2–56,245
Philippians
2:4–241
2:6-8–52
4:6–30
Colossians
2:12–175,179
2:13-17–203
2:14–213
2:16–199-200
3:1–52
3:9–146

NAME INDEX

A

Alexander the Great–276
Arndt, William–262

B

Baker, Mary–266
Bales, James–163
Ballard, L.S.–181
Bancroft, H.H.–109
Barfield, Kenny–266
Barker, Dan–141,199-200, 246
Barnes, Albert–197,215,225, 227,255
Botta, Paul Emile–269
Brand, Leonard–95
Brauch, Manfred–11
Brown, David–30,228
Brown, T. Pierce–163
Bruce, A.B.–247
Bruce, F.F.–11
Bryant, Buddy–177
Bullinger, E.W.–185,246
Butler, Bill–100,102

C

Cassuto, Umberto–227
Clark, Harold W.–108
Clarke, Adam–57,92,152,214
Coffman, Burton–39,61,215
Cukrowski, Kenneth–10
Cyrus–274

D

Danker, Frederick–262
Davids, Peter–11-12
Dawson, William–104
Delitzsch, F.–228
Dungan, D.R.–185

F

Fausset, A.R.–30,228
Feinberg, Charles–207
Flemming, Brian–49
Frazer, James G.–109

G

Gallup Jr., George–9
Geisler, Norman–272
Gingrich, F.W.–262